Dear Sarojini

Love

Indu Kulkarni
Mumbai
Feb. 2016.

THE NOVELS OF
WILLIAM GOLDING

THE NOVELS OF
WILLIAM GOLDING

INDU KULKARNI

ATLANTIC
PUBLISHERS & DISTRIBUTORS

Published by
ATLANTIC PUBLISHERS AND DISTRIBUTORS
B-2, Vishal Enclave, Opp. Rajouri Garden, New Delhi-27
Phones : 25413460, 25429987, 25466842

Sales Office
7/22, Ansari Road, Darya Ganj, New Delhi-02
Phones : 23273880, 23285873, 23280451
Fax : 91-11-23285873
web : www.atlanticbooks.com
e-mail : info@atlanticbooks.com

© Atlantic Publishers and Distributors, 2003

ISBN 81-269-0288-4

Typeset at
APD Computer Graphics, Delhi
Printed in India at
Nice Printing Press, Delhi

PREFACE

William Golding had always fascinated me as a problematic writer and I wished to work on him in depth. I have referred to all the critical works on Golding available in Bombay, in the British Museum Library, London and the National Library, Edinburgh. I have also consulted relevant journals and periodicals for this book.

I would like to dedicate this book to my late father, R.S. Mani, a headmaster and lover of literature. I express my deep gratitude to Late Dr. M.C. Jussawalla, my guide for her fine critical comments and valuable suggestions regarding technique and form. Our sessions were illuminating and memorable.

I would like to thank Sir William and Ann Golding for their kind hospitality at their home in Cornwall and Sir William for an enlightening interview.

I would also like to thank: The British Council for offering me a Visitorship to the U.K. in June 1990; Professors M. Kinkead-Weekes and I. Gregor, University of Kent, Canterbury; Professor John Carey, Merton College, Oxford; Dr. Avril Henry, University of Exeter, Exeter; Professor David Skilton, University of Cardiff, Wales; Professor S.J. Boyd, University of St. Andrews, Scotland. They were all most cordial and friendly. Dr. S. Kandaswamy, Department of English, University of Bombay and the Library Staff for their help. Mr. Easwaran supervised typing of the book.

I could not have finished the book if it were not for the moral support and criticism of my husband, Anil Kulkarni and my family for cheerfully bearing with me.

I hope Golding's lovers would enjoy reading this book as much as I enjoyed writing it.

INDU KULKARNI

CONTENTS

1

INTRODUCTION

◆

The world turns and the world changes
But one thing does not change
The perpetual struggle of Good and Evil—*T.S. Eliot*

William Golding has achieved the unique distinction of being both a fabulist and a realist. His charm lies in the complex blend of seemingly irreconcilable polarities like spirit and flesh, good and evil, pleasure and pain, joy and grief, in his novels. He is at once orthodox like Melville and unorthodox like Forster, an iconoclast like Ibsen and Shaw, religious like T.S. Eliot, Greene and Conrad and bitterly critical like Swift, Orwell and Dickens. In daring to diagnose the sickness that afflicts the modern world, he probes the heart of darkness in man over whom 'Looms the Horror of the Shade.'[1] M. Kinkead-Weekes finely observes that 'he is neither modern like Blake and Wordsworth, nor romantic like Joyce and Conrad; he is both intensely 'sceptical' and intensely 'religious;' he uses the visionary against the visual and the visual against the visionary.'[2]

His protagonists remind us of Henley, 'Whose head is bloody, but unbowed in the fell clutch of circumstance,'[3] whose soul cannot be profaned in darkness however terrible the ordeal. Dean Jocelin smitten with the mortal sin of the pride of Lucifer, the fallen angel, aspires to erect a spire on Stilbury cathedral. He subjects his master-builder, Roger, his clerical subordinates, the workmen and the red-haired Goody he secretly lusts after, to hellish tortures, even death. He himself dies in the agony and the ecstasy of spinal tuberculosis, for such is the dreaded price of the fulfilment of an artistic vision.

The spire still stands—a miracle in faith and stone for *vita brevis, ars longa*, 'Life is short art is long.'

Golding's novels are in a paradoxical sense, set in time pre-lapsarian, *The Inheritors*, medieval, *The Spire*, eighteenth century, *Rites of Passage*, *Close Quarters*, and *Fire Down Below*, twentieth century, *Darkness Visible*, *The Pyramid*, *Pincher Martin*, *Free Fall*, and *Lord of the Flies*, yet timeless as the mortal context of man, in a moral landscape, remain fixed. The advance of science cannot drive out of man's soul his 'terrors of darkness,'[4] irrational desires and immortal longings which belong to the world of his spirit. C.T. Thomas comments that Golding revealed himself as 'an intrepid and inveterate navigator through the dark regions of the human heart. His oeuvre to date has been the evocation of a vision almost Hobbesian in its unrelieved gloom and pessimism: '"The life of man, solitary, poor, nasty, brutish, and short."'[5]

This study aims at examining Golding's preoccupation with contemporary evils challenging the soul of man. Firstly, the upsurge of violence, terrorism, war mania that has unleashed the beast in man to stalk innocent prey. Next, the evil of sexual perversions, man's libido liberated from shame, guilt and fear. Thirdly, the predominant disease of modern society— class-conflict or the evils of social stratification that oppress man's sense of equality and joy. Finally, religion, a personal matter between Man and his Maker, perverted in the twentieth century by fanaticism, nihilism and various evil practices.

Golding tries to salvage the ravaged soul of man from the wreckage of twentieth century godlessness, entropy and the malaise of whoring after false gods, principally ideologies. Delving into man's psyche, Golding discovers the roots of primitive fear, faith, and love in the collective unconscious[6] of mankind that binds all men together.

A product of wartime disillusionment, a rebel against Wellsian rationalism, with a scientific and enquiring mind, Golding adopts an ambivalent attitude towards the problem of evil, that is neither ancient nor modern, but a curious mix of both. The crux of Golding's credo is the necessity of evil for the regeneration of the human spirit. Sin and salvation are welded into one in the *felix culpa* of Adam.[7]

The scope of the thesis requires a selection of salient characteristics of contemporary evils. While the factors determining evil in the world are myriad, the criteria for their selection is guided by the fact of their being widely prevalent in modern society. Golding's novels mirror these evils through the travails of his protagonists and the intricate plot structure. The characters are a means to the development of the central idea. They are often mere cogs in the machine. In *Lord of the Flies* for example, the evil of regression, the grim truth of the beast lurking within man erupting when the restraints imposed by civilization are withdrawn, is powerfully demonstrated by the amoral vicious and barbaric bloodlust of Jack, Roger and others.

Golding himself admits that the idea and the plot of the novel is more important to him than any other consideration as a writer.[8] The complex crafting of his novels around a dominant idea evokes admiration. In reflecting the deep anguish of his age, Golding is particularly sensitive to the problem of evil in human existence today. Steeped in Egyptian, Hellenic and Christian lore, he became obsessed with the issue of man's moral freedom, his fall and its consequences.

This pessimism was due partly to his searing war experiences. As he told Jack Biles, 'We all saw a hell of a lot in the war that can't be accounted for except on the basis of original evil. Man is born to sin. Set him free, and he will be a sinner, not Rousseau's "noble savage."'[9] His conviction of two decades ago has not changed now, though a note of the need for amelioration creeps into his nautical trilogy.[10] Yet his basic stand remains: '"Before the war I paid lip service to a progressive view of humanity and I got despoliated by what I saw in the war...Human beings have a strand or element of real malignancy. We can't refuse to recognise that there is active human evil."'[11] But Albert Camus shows in *The Plague* ('La Peste') that wars must recur because the plague germ, a symbol of evil in man's soul can never be eradicated. It can be temporarily controlled, even destroyed as the efforts of Dr. Rieux indicate. But it will reappear and create havoc once more. This is the author's message through the central character. Recent history in the devastating Gulf War has borne out the truth of this.

In his epigraph to *Darkness Visible*, Golding appeals through Aeneas's prayer: "SIT MIHI FAS AUDITA LOQUI (Allow me to retell what I was told).

> 'Ye realms, yet unreveal'd to human sight,
> Ye gods who rule the regions of the night,
> Ye gliding ghosts, permit me to relate
> The mystic wonders of your silent state!'[12]

Like Aeneas, he has traversed the Stygian darkness and experienced the horrors of hell. Pincher's bloated ego lives in a self-contained world of Self ruled by overmastering Greed for money, glory, power and sex seen in the callous, unscrupulous use of friends, associates—a veritable hell. Pincher Martin's being which is Greed incarnate resists destruction at death. So, as Golding himself explains, 'he rejects salvation for the "persona" must be destroyed, and Pincher's thirst for individual life invents a rock which is only the memory of an aching tooth. To a man greedy for life, tooth-ache is preferable to extinction, and that is the terrible secret of purgatory, it is all the world that the God-resisting soul cannot give up.'[13]

We see Pincher's parallel in Graham Greene's Pinkie with his satanical pride in *Brighton Rock*. His demands on life are so bizarre that they go beyond the laws of man and God. He is a pathological killer like Martin and has no sense of mortal sin. A belief in good and evil, and fear of retribution do not belong to the war-torn thirties. Greene feels that they can only be abandoned to God's law. The 'absolute blackness of God's lightning' finally pervades Pincher's center 'timeless and without mercy.'[14]

Frederick Karl comments on another novel, Gerald Hanley's *Without Love*, (1957), that combines Greene's paradoxical belief with Conrad's nihilism. Hanley argues that it is better to fight God, and to sin in doing so, than to feel nothing, '"for the love of God is alive in that resentment of the struggler and we do not know the size of the hunger in the secret heart."' Hanley's Mike Brennan is (like Pincher), 'a Pinkie grown up, the "adolescent" of our times who will destroy and be destroyed.'[15]

Golding believes in the taint of the Original Sin[16] on man's soul that longs nostalgically for the paradisal innocence of

Adam in *Lord of the Flies*,[17] to be again the pre-lapsarian innocent Neanderthalers Lok and Fa in *The Inheritors*. Samuel Mountjoy in *Free Fall* tries to pinpoint exactly when he lost this innocence—for Paradise Hill is a child's Eden where he 'floats through life like a bubble, empty of guilt, empty of anything but immediate conscienceless emotions generous, greedy, cruel, innocent,'[18] or with Johnny trespassing in the general's estate— 'To me, then, we remain these two points of perception, wandering in paradise.'[19] He realises that he has sacrificed everything—joy and innocence for sex, for Beatrice in his mad lust of youth. '"If I want something enough I can always get it provided I am willing to make the appropriate sacrifice."'[20]

Golding reinforces the argument that evil is associated with knowledge and experience. Eden is where we all begin in life till we are expelled in adolescence by our sense of guilt and shame born of the thirst for knowledge of evil. That is why Golding's ideal age is that of a youngster poised on the brink of adolescence—like Ralph—uninhibited, happy...'not yet old enough for adolescence to have made him awkward... a mildness about his mouth and eyes that proclaimed no devil.'[21]

Evil is embraced by man for the awesome power it gives him over others—in sexual abuse, martial outrages, exploitation of inferior classes by superior ones or vice-versa, in religious persecution. The Devil in Shaw's *Man and Superman* tells Ana of the gulf between the angelic and the diabolic temperament. 'What more impassable gulf could you have? (the earth is full of Devil's Bridges); but the gulf of dislike is impassable and eternal.'[22]

Samuel Mountjoy, poised between the worlds of the flesh and the spirit, the rational and the imaginative, represented by Nick Shales, his science master and Rowena Pringle, his catechism teacher, chooses the exact one and so abjures his spirit and the miraculous world of Jehovah and Moses. 'I was not to knock on that door again, until in a Nazi prison camp I lay huddled against it half-crazed with terror and despair.'[23]

It is self-awareness in the vale of hate and despair that shows him the light. Sammy admits silently to the mad Beatrice—'The innocent and the wicked live in one world—But we are neither the innocent nor the wicked. We are the guilty. We fall down. We crawl on hands and knees. We weep and tear each other.'[24]

Having fallen into the impassable gulf of hate, only some beacon of love can redeem man. When Sammy bitterly observes that 'there is no bridge,'[25] between the worlds of innocence and experience, between the worlds of Shales and Pringle, he has felt but not accepted the fire of selfless love that forges all links.

This bridge hinted at in *Free Fall*, is built by Golding in *The Spire* when Jocelin, the corrupt Dean of Stilbury erects a four hundred foot spire, which is not only 'an apocalypse in stone,'[26] but a sublimation of his phallic lust for Goody. He is deluded by an overweening presumption in his great work. Leighton Hodson remarks 'He has not understood his own humanity.'[27] In wrecking the lives of Roger, Goody, Pangall and others, he realises he has been breeding hate, his sanctity is a mask of hypocrisy and he admits to Roger that he is 'a building with a vast cellarage where the rats live.... I injure everyone I touch, particularly those I love. Now I've come in pain and shame, to ask you to forgive me.'[28]

His perception of the spire on his deathbed is as two eyes that slide together in one vision. 'Terror and joy split the darkness.'[29] Dr. Tiger observes that 'Jocelin's divine exultation of the apple tree completes his spiritual regeneration. The spire connects heaven and earth.'[30]

To view Good and Evil as irreconcilable Absolutes is a narrow view. Somerset Maugham observes succinctly, 'There is no explanation for evil. It must be looked upon as a necessary part of the order of the universe. To ignore it is childish; to bewail it senseless.'[31] Shakespeare in *Henry V* says:

'There is some soul of goodness in things evil,
Would men observingly distil it out
....
Thus may we gather honey from the weed,
And make a moral of the devil himself.'[32]

Mahatma Gandhi asks: 'Must I do all the evil I can before I learn to shun it? Is it not enough to know the evil to shun it? If not we should not be sincere enough to admit that we love evil too well to give it up.'[33] The point that emerges is that man cannot wish evil away, or fly from it as the cowardly Barclay does in *The Paper Men*. He has to face it and conquer it.

Golding's fascination for evil springs from two points—a reaction to his father's Wellsian rationalism and a compulsive lure to wrest the truth about the dichotomy of existence evinced in hell/heaven; Good/Evil; Spirit/Flesh. Peter Moss wonders at his black pessimism and conjectures that in this way, inspite of a happy childhood 'one can explore the darker sides of human nature with more objectivity.'[34]

This infinite curiosity Golding felt about the other side of the known, good, male—this need to explore, this urge to know what it is like to be other people. Sammy asks Beatrice '"What is it like to be you?"'[35] He wishes to fathom her feminine mystery of sweetness, vulnerability, her mind and body. He seeks fusion and identity with her. John Carey observed that 'Very few writers make me see this violent contradiction in states of characters. It is a very attractive facet.'[36] Pincher Martin experiences the same mad desire to divine the prim Mary's secret. 'Obsession. Not love. Or if love, insanely compounded of this jealousy of her very being. Odi et amo.'[37] When Sophy in *Darkness Visible* realizes the truth that *The way towards simplicity is through outrage*,[38] we marvel at Golding's skill in projecting us into the mind of a terrorist! Similarly Sophy's polar twin is Matty, the Christ-like burnt child—a victory over entropy and hate. Stephen Medcalf, in appreciating Golding's Ka, his genius, says, 'The grief, terror and wrath of *Lord of the Flies* and all Golding's novels coexist with an enjoyment of the process of things and an ecstatic apprehension of beauty.'[39]

In Golding's novels, as in Ibsen's plays, the tragedy stems from an outrage, a breach in the right order of things. To Ibsen the signal outrage in modern life is the falsification of the essential self—the blinding of the personal vision, the perversion of passion leading to hate. The individual is thwarted in his drive towards achieving supreme good. In *Ghosts* Mrs. Alving battles against rigid social convention to win an integrity of mind, in *The Master Builder* Solness is corrupted in his noble art; going from church building to home building, in

Rosmersholm the issue of paganism versus Christianity, egoism versus altruism, and assertion of self is fought out in the soul of the modern Rebecca West. Golding's Samuel Mountjoy realizes that only through selflessness can 'people move without killing each other.'[40]

A close contemporary is Iris Murdoch, who is equally obsessed with the problem of evil. Randall Stevenson quotes from her novel, *A Fairly Honourable Defeat*, (1970), how humans are fascinated by evil. Julius claims '...good is dull. What novelist ever succeeded in making a good man interesting? It is the characteristic of this planet that the path of virtue is so unutterably depressing. Evil, on the contrary is exciting and fascinating and alive. It is also very much more mysterious than good. Good can be seen through. Evil is opaque.'[41]

The key to Golding's grappling with the question of evil lies in Jung's interpretation of Good and Evil in man. Jung revalues religion as a reaction to an excess of rationalism, true in the case of Golding, whose father was a staunch Wellsian rationalist. To Jung, Evil is a debilitating psychic force, which does not originate from any ontological duality. It is relative in its origin, arising from a negative, false, idea and it disappears when corrected, leading to a greater good. So, in all human development, evil is the way to good.[42]

Jung shifts the idea of evil to God, thus resolving the dualism by bringing the Creator down to the level of the common man. Into the Western Christian dogma of the Trinity, in the form of Father, Son and Holy Spirit, Jung infused the idea of an imperfect perfection or *Volkommenheit*. As a quaternary structure expresses a state of *Vollstandigkeit* or perfection,[43] it requires the complementarity of opposites that is Good and Evil reconciled, to achieve it.

Golding's heroes become aware of the evil in the human condition as a psychic reality and try to integrate it, instead of dismissing it. Wilfred Barclay, the depraved porno-novelist is violently jolted into an acceptance of this evil within him in a psychic seizure he has in confronting a pagan or Christ-like idol, an archaic Greek statue, 'I knew in one destroying instant that all my adult life I had believed in God and this knowledge was a vision of God.'[44] This terrible experience awakens his conscience to realise that evil is a part of him, '"Not sin. I, am sin."'[45] Or again Pincher Martin declares, '"I am poisoned I am in servitude to a coiled tube the length of a cricket pitch. All the terrors of hell can come to nothing more than a stoppage. Why drag in good and evil when the serpent lies coiled in my own body?"'[46]

L.L. Dickson viewed Golding as a consistent moralist who used 'techniques of allegory to explore the nature of evil in man. Integral to all novels is the motif of the quest into the nature of good and evil. Among the themes he identifies as central to the novels, are the importance of human compassion and conflict between the humanistic and the scientific, between the spiritual and the rational.'[47] Golding is compelling because of his uncompromising treatment of evil, which is close to the heart of twentieth century man. A.T. Broes observes that 'the world in which the myth of progress has failed but the rival myth of necessary evil and universal guilt has come back without bringing God with it.'[48]

Herman Melville's fondness for allegory, his profound interest in man's ambiguous position in the universe, the inscrutability of God and other moral-metaphysical issues of Good and Evil are reflected in Golding's novels. As M. Kinkead-Weekes and I. Gregor remark, *Rites of Passage* 'echoes with the sound of other men's art—Melville, Conrad, Richardson, Coleridge. The cumulative effect is...dazzling.'[49]

Billy Budd's tale is a metaphoric one, the pagan handsome viking is perverted to Great Evil in a moment of irrational impulse. He assaults Claggart for falsely accusing him of fostering a mutiny aboard *The Indomitable*. The irreligious Billy knows only the religion of honour, humanity, peace and love. He cannot comprehend the secret lust and malignity of Claggart. Melville's irony is implicit in '"struck dead by an angel of God! Yet the angel must hang!"'[50] Billy is hanged and faces death fearlessly for 'fear is more prevalent in highly civilized communities than so-called barbarous ones' as Melville satirically observes!'[51] The vulgar subversion of Colley's manhood, his humiliation and death is an assault by Evil on his innate simplicity and goodness. E.M. Forster speaks of *Billy*

Budd as a remote unearthly episode in which Melville reaches back into blackness. Melville says 'in certain moods no man can weigh this world without throwing in a something somehow like Original Sin to strike the uneven balance.... He threw it in. The balance righted itself, and he gave us harmony and temporary salvation.'[52] Billy Budd is like the pre-lapsarian innocent Lok of *The Inheritors*, doomed to sin and death like Adam.[53]

When John Wain pointed out that Golding was more of an allegorist than a novelist, he was right, for his novels focus on the problem of evil and man's depravity. Golding has 'certain perceptions about the human condition which he...goes ahead and—creates an allegory to represent.'[54] Golding presents the conflict between good and evil with the intention of reforming human nature like most other allegorists. Melville's allegorical vision in *Moby Dick* plays on the dichotomy of life-death, Good-Evil and love-hate in the universe. To Ishmael, the white whale symbolises immortality and the immensity of God and Nature, to Ahab, it is an Evil to be outraged and defeated.

For Ahab the whale is a symbol of his 'intellectual and spiritual exasperations'—'a monomaniac incarnation of all those malicious agencies,' so he piled on its hump 'the sum of all the general rage and hate felt by his whole race from Adam down;....'[55] As Alfred Kazin points out, 'the book is at once primitive, fatalistic and merciless,...like so many twentieth century novels, in its significant emphasis on the subjective individual consciousness.'[56] Ishmael and Ahab are polar ends of the human psyche like Colley and Talbot or Nathaniel and Pincher. While Ahab and Pincher seek to dominate Nature, conquer Infinity, Nathaniel and Ishmael symbolize acceptance not revenge. The powerful interplay of opposing principles in the thrill of blackness and the joy of moral enlightenment—this relationship of paradox is seen in *Moby Dick* and in *Darkness Visible* and *Pincher Martin*.

Ishmael is lured towards the midnight fires in the try-works, a vision of Hell very much like Jocelin and his men watching the creeping earth in *The Spire*. The balance lies in accepting the blackness and admitting that 'there is a wisdom that is woe, but there is a woe that is madness.'[57] Jocelin's and

Ishmael's souls can dive like 'Catskill eagles into the blackest gorges'[58] and fly out again. To forge through darkness to find a greater light, darkness and light must be known together. As Melville wrote in his *Battle-Pieces*:

> 'No utter surprise can come to him
> Who reaches Shakespeare's core:
> That which we seek and shun is there—
> Man's final lore.'[59]

Golding shows us how contemporary man embraces darkness as it holds the promise and danger of wholeness. Like Ahab, Samuel Mountjoy longs 'for that swan-white seal of ultimate knowing.'[60] Human experience of evil, darkness and terror can be felt, but inadequately described. 'Our loneliness is the loneliness of that dark thing that sees as at the atom furnace by reflection, feels by remote control and hears only words .... To communicate is our passion and our despair.'[61]

Both Conrad and Greene, two eminent novelists are skilled surgeons in the dissection of contemporary man's tendency to veer towards darkness in quest of light. Golding's credo is Conradian in two respects—Firstly, the worth of a man is judged by his behaviour in a crisis. As Golding says, his themes are concerned with 'man at an extremity, man obsessed, man drowning in a literal sea or in the sea of his own ignorance.'[62] Secondly, the belief in the presence of a treacherous streak, some malice or malignity in nature that threatens man's fate or honour. The tragic vanity of a will that is valiant but whose conduct is cowardly is seen in Jim and Sammy. Conrad is as involved as Golding with the weakness in man's moral fibre.

Golding's optimistic conviction is that 'We must produce *homo moralis*, the human being who cannot kill his own kind, nor exploit them nor rob them.'[63] Stein says in *Lord Jim*, 'There is no cure for your humanity short of death. One thing alone can save us from being ourselves cured!...Yes...the question is not how to get cured, but how to live? How to be!'[64]

In his pessimism and fondness for the fall and descent of man, Conrad is close to Golding. Jim longs to be a hero, an idealist, but is too weak to evade reality like Sammy. Tony Tanner remarks, 'He is both a martyr and a betrayer—a Christ who acts like Judas, a Judas who dies like Christ.'[65] Conrad constantly uses chiaroscuro effects, like the forces of darkness threaten to engulf the principle of light—Jim. Conrad's central metaphor is of the butterfly and the beetle—the spiritual and the earthy mark, the frail idealist versus the cynical self-preserving empiricist. Jim aspires to be a butterfly but can only fly like a beetle!

Proud, sensual Sammy's fall from grace is a consequence of his amoral pursuit of Beatrice, pursuing dreams and ideals regardless of the cost. As Frederick R. Karl points out, 'the archetype for this kind of self-destructive anti-hero is Conrad's Jim, the man of pretentious claims who is unable to fulfill the role he has envisaged for himself and who is hounded by his own insufficiency until he destroys himself.'[66] Jim tries to exorcise his guilt by committing suicide, while Sammy tries to make reparation by visiting his lunatic beloved, Beatrice. It is an acceptance of one's evil transgression that marks the beginning of regeneration of man's depraved spirit.

Sammy can also be compared to Conrad's Kurtz in *Heart of Darkness*. The godlike Kurtz becomes a rapacious ogre in the jungle exploiting the natives unscrupulously. The sombre darkness in the heart of Africa brings the brute out in Kurtz. Lionel Trilling pertinently asks, 'Is this not the essence of the modern belief regarding the nature of the artist, the man who goes down into that hell which is the historical beginning of the human soul, a beginning not outgrown but established in humanity, as we know it now, preferring the reality of its hell to the bland lies of the civilisation that has overlaid it?'[67]

It is this pit of blackness that Jocelin, Sammy and Barclay venture into to wrest from a knowledge of evil, the worth of themselves, to forge a new identity of the interrelatedness of man. If Kurtz were wholly evil, he would not finally judge himself as 'The Horror!'[68] a recognition of his own evil helps to redeem him. Conrad is more secular and Golding more religious in his depiction of codes of honour. Golding studies moral failure while Conrad concentrates on heroism and disgrace.

S.J. Boyd compares Colley's beastly blunder to the rash betrayal of the youth in Conrad's *The Shadow Line*.[69] In surrendering to the dark pagan powers of the unknown, Colley commits fellatio in a drunken orgy with a sailor and dies of shame. The world of conventional morality cannot comprehend Colley's joy, his discovery of the equatorial paradise of innocence.

Graham Greene's novels are religious in the sense that Golding's are. Greene finds that evil has a spiritual glamour and spiritual goodness is often linked to moral weakness in his novels. Querry, the rakish French Catholic architect in *A Burnt-Out Case* is as morally crippled as his leprosy mutilated servant. Deo Gratias is physically crippled-a burnt-out case. Wilfred Barclay, the porno-novelist in *The Paper Men*, is as devoid of moral scruples as Querry. He suffers an awareness of his moral depravity and is shot like Querry, while ruminating on the absurdity of life—and hoping for 'an uncovenanted mercy' like the one that drives him to give Rick his life papers.[70] One feels unsure whether the sinfully depraved Querry and Barclay achieve salvation or not. Predominant evils of money, power, sexual permissiveness, the modern artist's notoriety, hyper violence in an 'angst'—ridden society give a true portrait of this nightmarish twentieth century world of ours in both the novels.

Greene's theme is the paradox of potential salvation in earthly failure. Instead of describing the good soul's journey to the heavenly City of God—as in Bunyan's *Pilgrim's Progress*, Golding and Greene portray the proverbial sinner, the whiskey priest, Scobie; Jocelin, Barclay and Sammy stumbling along almost forsaking God and embracing the devil. While the church demands dogmas and conformity, God works in mysterious ways to save the sinner. As Father Rank in *The Heart of the Matter* says, '"The Church knows all the rules. But it doesn't know what goes on in a single human heart;"'[71] or Jocelin in *The Spire* says 'How proud their hope of hell is. There is no innocent work. God knows where God may be.'[72]

Greene explores the dilemma of sinful humanity, his sanctified sinner, Scobie, commits the mortal sin of suicide to secure the happiness of the two women he loves. He tries to implicate Christ in his betrayal by arguing that since God cannot be murdered, Christ had killed himself for love. Greene's God, like Golding's is a merciful compassionate one radiating

Love. When Parson Colley commits suicide in *Rites of Passage* he offers up his life to make reparation for his crime. *Pedigree* finds Love as Matty's heavenly spirit comes to claim him in *Darkness Visible*. The miracle of love can transform the commonplaces of flesh and blood into the lyric of human relationships.

The motif of pursuit and struggle can be traced in Greene and Golding. In Greene it is the pursuit of a man's soul, his inner self, by God. Caught between pain and pain, the characters are tormented by pity, and are afraid of damnation. They become victims of their own unforgettable love for God. Pincher Martin's ruthlessly resilient ego clings to his selfhood till the Greater Being's merciless compassion absorbs his being. The Lieutenant in *The Power and the Glory* is described as 'a little dapper figure of hate carrying his secret of love.'[73] The failure of man to keep faith in his ideals is focused on; but this depressive view of folly and evil is balanced by the mystery of love and faith as seen in the predicament of the fugitive whiskey priest.

The anguish of the priest, afraid of pain and suffering, full of a tender love for his natural daughter portrays an unusual martyr.[74] He believes in God, and Greene demonstrates the undying power and glory that shine through his weaknesses. Golding evokes our admiration for the weak fallible priest, Jocelin in *The Spire*. He is earthy, corrupt but full of love with an indomitable faith in God.

Greene's novels form one of the most impressive surveys of modern social violence, intermingling good and evil in the contradictory traits of his protagonists—honesty and corruption, spiritual and sexual. This pattern of evil involves various forms of betrayal—sexual, political, social and spiritual linked to guilt, sin and expiation as seen in Golding's novels too. Oliver in *The Pyramid* realises the enormity of his cruel lust and callousness only when he recognises Evie as a human being with feelings like himself. 'I stood, in shame and confusion, seeing this object of frustration and desire as...a person rather than a thing.'[75]

As in Golding's *Darkness Visible*, so in Greene's *Brighton Rock*, nowhere is the link between Good and Evil and their interdependence more evident than here. Pinkie, the ruthless killer in *Brighton Rock* has his counterpart in Sophy, the avenging sadist—terrorist of *Darkness Visible*. Greene states the integration of this paradox: 'Good or evil lived in the same country, spoke the same language, came together like old friends, feeling the same completion, touching hands.'[76] When the scarred saint Matty apprehends the evil lure of Sophy, the whore of the Apocalypse, he perceives the great truth that 'What good is not directly breathed into the world by the holy spirit must come down by and through the nature of men.'[77] In the godless underworld of vice and corruption, Pinkie's soul is driven to choose damnation in gambling and perverted sex. Rose, the epitome of love, goodness and Matty's counterpart sacrifices herself to be a complement to Pinkie's evil.

Golding's characters parallel Greene's in the ironic moral dilemmas they experience in realising how far the actual world betrays the ideal, and how essential evil is to the recognition of good and wholeness. Brian Davies quotes John Hicks' argument that 'the existence of evil is necessary for the perfect development of human beings. Man is prone to sin. Evil is indulged in as God does not coerce man to accept him.'[78] It is the challenge of free will that allows man to choose his destiny, to fall freely like Samuel and then rise to greater heights of moral grandeur in remorse and love, which is the agent of grace and redemption. A world without perils, trials would be morally static, a paradise without any challenges to man's spirit. Evil is inevitable if there is to be a world of free human agents.

Golding's credo is neither wholly secular like Conrad's nor religious in Greene's sense of the word. As V.S. Pritchett observes, 'He is the most original of our contemporaries in his intense visual gift...torn between a primitive inheritance and the glimmer of an evolving mind.'[79] In our present day world of anarchy, futility, depravity and soullessness, Golding underlines a profound modern need for humanism and love. A need to break down barriers between classes, sexes, races as is achieved by Matty in the transcendental experience with Sim and Edwin. '"We broke a barrier, broke down a partition. Didn't we now?"'[80] For, as the benevolent enlightened Edwin reminds Sim, '"Remember we're multi-racial and all religions are one, anyway."'[81]

His novels are a powerful indictment of the real evils in the world—social evils of intolerance, exploitation, victims of social wrong like Evie, Piggy, Sammy and Colley who revolt ineffectually against the inexorable hierarchy. The conflict between the church and the State is seen in *Rites of Passage*, the nautical trilogy. Cardinal Newman's description of sinful, fallen humanity defeated with its 'dreary hopeless irreligion'[82] is terrifyingly true of the contemporary scene. Science and rationalism have led to a loss of faith today. Materialism has driven man to lose his reverence for life; permissiveness and over indulgence in sex has aggravated perversions and crimes in a fragmented society. Lost in a whirl of ephemeral pleasures, man's soul is starved of spiritual sustenance. It is this shocking depravity of man in his defeat of innocence, knowledge and progress earned at the dread cost of Joy and Love that Golding bemoans.

The main thrust of this study has been to analyse in Golding's novels certain factors which have created the problem of evil in the twentieth century. These are War and violence, sex and sexuality, class conflict and religion. To examine Golding's unique stand on the question of modern man's rapid regression, one has to review his age. The themes of the moderns center on terror and violence, rootlessness in an unstable irrational universe.

Two world wars have resulted in unbelievable deterioration in matters of public and personal morality. A sense of desolation, futility, vanity of aspirations besieges man's soul. The cataclysmic experience of war fosters negative emotions like hate, alienation, nihilism and despair, for war is a tragic cleavage between nations blinded by hatred. Golding examines the tenuous link between civilisation and savagery in *Lord of the Flies* and *Pincher Martin*. War subverts humanity, giving man the license to kill his own kind. War hysteria provokes sadism and fear of death, pain arouses man to barbaric acts. The transformation of Sammy in *Free Fall* is a pointer, as is the ruthless conduct of Lord Talbot in *Close Quarters*. '"I am coming to. A weapon for the love of God! A meat axe—sledge hammer—anything. I will engage to carve and eat the first

Frenchman I come across."'[83] Man's appetite for evil is whetted
by the attendant power that violence gives him, he indulges in
acts of aggression. Time and again Golding poses the query
whether man's progress at the dread price of destruction,
terrorism, violence, 'unwinding into nothingness'[84] as Sophy
envisages it, is worth it.

Elemental violence also plays a pivotal role in novels like
Pincher Martin, where the merciless Atlantic ravages the
shipwrecked sailor, elemental fury of the deep and the Leviathan
in the nautical trilogy, the fall of the torrent—a violent metaphor
for the fall of man in *The Inheritors*. Golding's love for the
grotesque and macabre in Nature is seen reflected in the
barbaric instincts it arouses in man-nature's natural! While
violence cannot be divorced from human life, Golding
illuminates the truth of the violence in human endeavour, the
creative fire seen in tortured artists like Sammy, Jocelin and
Tuami. The universal pessimist in Golding decries man's
savagery but the cosmic optimist believes that it can be
channelised into creative ventures not destructive ones. The
price of art is pain, suffering, and sacrifice.

Golding's peculiar preoccupation with Original Sin and
man's fall from grace can be traced in the depraved deeds of
Pincher Martin, Jocelin's lust, Sophy's sexual sadism, Sammy's
frailty of the flesh, Colley's bestiality and Jack's incipient
libido rearing its ugly head in the orgy of the hunters. Sex
becomes evil when used to molest, exploit or hurt others.
Twentieth century sexual licentiousness, promiscuity and
freedom leads to crime, victimisation of innocent beings and
evil perversions of child abuse by pederasts seen in *Free Fall*
and *Darkness Visible*. A penetrating psychological insight into
the subconscious of the characters is evident. Freud's views
of the evils of repressed sexuality in the portrait of the sinful
child is revealed in the portraits of Samuel Mountjoy, Jack,
Oliver, and Barclay.

The Pyramid, in particular, is a veritable museum piece of
sexual perversions—pederasty, flagellation, masochism, sadism,
masturbation and various other pathological states. Golding
deplores the abuse of children, for he equates innocence with
goodness and knowledge with evil. Samuel's symbolic baptism—

a subverted sacrament in *Free Fall* ironically underlies man's
willingness to sacrifice everything blindly to the pleasures of
the senses. So Sammy's retribution of guilt in the imprisoned
dark of the German prison is his hallucination of a severed
penis 'this fragment of human flesh...to shatter all the taboos
of humanity, to crash through with an exhibition so brutal...'[85]
that it shatters his spirit.

Modern psychologists accept the fact that though regression
opposes progress, it serves through conflict of a tension the
forward-going trait of a personality. Only through a degree of
control and sublimation can man achieve a higher goal and
evolve into a homo moralist. The author's attitude is firm
and compassionate towards man's foibles. But his keen insight
into man's primeval beastliness is comparable only to the
zoomorphic harshly realistic animal poetry of Ted Hughes.[86]

The ferocity of his predatory pikes, thrushes and hawks is
echoed in Golding's Tuami, Pincher, Jack, Jocelin and Sammy
whose civilization is a mere mask beneath which lies a
seething cauldron of repressed predatory tendencies. Other
contemporaries like Iris Murdoch in *A Severed Head* and Graham
Greene in *Brighton Rock* and *The Heart of the Matter* examine
the problem of sexual perversions.

Even in today's world, the evil of social stratification cannot
be ignored. A major social evil of the twentieth century, namely
class-war appears in *Sons and Lovers* of D.H. Lawrence and
Pygmalion by Bernard Shaw. Although the problem is not as
horrifying as Golding's portrayal of it, yet the tension created
by class-conflict in the marital relationship of Gertrude and
Morel, its unhappy effects on their children, especially Paul,
subtly victimised by his own mother, and the differences in
values and outlook are sensitively delineated. The novel is a
major contribution towards creating an awareness of the evil
nature of class-distinction in society.

In *Pygmalion*, a comedy, the question of class-conflict is
treated with meaningful humour. Basically it is reprehensible
as it deals a blow to human dignity, especially, when a
substantial bank balance and highly educated speech are
taken to be the measure of not only social success but individual
worth. Shaw's exposure of the hypocrisy of the upper class is

a thought-provoking criticism ridiculing pretentious English values, social demands and status.

Class barriers promote evils like revenge, exploitation, humiliation and the pathology of class-war can crush humans. In *The Pyramid*, the members of the mummified society of Stilbourne are doomed to be entombed in their petty prejudices, complexes, hates and jealousies. Golding feels very deeply about this endemic disease in English society. Even humble clergymen like Colley are not spared. Issues of class are perennial evils in society resulting in the injustice and persecution of innocent individuals like Evis of inferior status. Sammy regrets and resents his promotion from a slum child to charity child, from Rotten Row in Paradise Hill to Father Watts-Watt's home. "'I boasted in compensation...for the shape of our social pyramid that I was rector's son, sort of—and became unpopular. It was in the shadows of this unpopularity that I moved slowly into adolescence, when the skin is flayed off and a feather weighs like lead and pricks like a pin. I was at home nowhere."'[87] Class evils of snobbery, hypocrisy, cruelty have survived the onslaughts of time, of socialism and continue to disrupt human relationships. Social maladjustments of individuals trapped in the hierarchical pyramid of class-war can be fatal.

Golding examines the phenomena of social rebels, deviant behaviour, terrorism and chaos symptomatic of a diseased society, unloving, inhuman and intolerant. George Orwell had always decried totalitarianism—the collective control of the state over the individual. In *Animal Farm* he shows it to be little else save the tyranny of crafty minds. So the pigs, Snowball and Napoleon become suitable embodiments of human baseness and ruthless cunning. It is a political set-up where the animosity of man undoes nobler natures like Boxer whose goodness and efficient toil are rewarded by the knackers. The credo of the nasty pigs is 'ALL ANIMALS ARE EQUAL. BUT SOME ANIMALS ARE MORE EQUAL THAN OTHERS.'[88]

In *The Castle*, Kafka portrays a different type of social tyranny in the personification of Klamm, the owner of the castle. He is never seen but his presence is felt—an invisible force, autocratic, with a despotic hold over the villagers who are his subjects. It is an aloof mind who exercises authority and who is feared by all the villagers. With tyranny of this kind, goes the presentation of evil in the form of *alienation* and consequent *isolation* of the individual from the community. It is the unfortunate experience of K, the land surveyor, who is neither welcomed nor allowed to become part of the village community. The villagers being unfriendly and aloof in their behaviour, K remains an outsider till the end. A flexible stance is vital to progress as the myth of a Utopian society of any kind is foolish to entertain. Golding follows in the footsteps of satirists like Fielding, Swift and Orwell and is an ironist *par excellence*.

Deeply religious, but unconventional and unorthodox, Golding, voices a fear that Christianity has failed man in the West, for he is faced with a wild fundamentalism, anomie and rootlessness in the twentieth century. Brushing aside the role of dogma as fringe religion and kitchen theology for which he has little sympathy, Golding feelingly expresses the hope of a world religion of man in the future.[89] As Walter Sullivan has rightly observed, 'One of Golding's remarkable qualities is his compound of traditional and modern, his curious mix of existentialism and Freudianism with the old heritage of Christian mystery now passing out of vogue.'[90] He has succeeded in assimilating in his vision of experience diverse doctrines of anthropology, theology, and psychoanalysis with a poetic vigour and immediacy that is impressive. The conflicting portrait of Fallen Angel versus Fallen Man shows us Golding as a religious realist. While he retains his belief in the point of Original Sin, he rejects dogma and studies the loss of ethical values in the second half of the twentieth century.

Golding reviews the evil perversions of faith which are unleashing divisive not cohesive forces, sowing hate, superstition, fear, erecting barriers between peoples. This decay of true religion is attributed to profane ideologies that lead man's soul astray from his Maker. Golding stresses the need for 'a religious fear'[91] as T.S. Eliot puts it in *The Idea of a Christian Society*. In the irrational excesses and sacrileges of his protagonists, we see the truth of Lucretius: *Tantum religio potuit suadere malorum* (Such evil deeds could religion provoke).[92] In the portraits of Dean Jocelin and Reverend Colley we see how religious people are prone to vanity, self-interest and impudence. We see the ego of the server.

Jocelin's calling the spire 'God's Folly,'[93] and Colley's righteous anger at Captain Anderson's irreverence shown to his cloth—'MY MASTER HIMSELF has been insulted and though HE may—forgive it; I have a duty to deliver a rebuke rather than suffer that in silence! Not for ourselves, O LORD but for THEE!'[94]

As Russell opines, 'Religion is an evil if made public, for it prevents us from removing the fundamental causes of war, from teaching ethical precepts to our children in scientific rational co-operation in place of the old fierce doctrines of sin and punishment.'[95] Evils like prejudice and intolerance must be stamped out. Golding condemns the moral vices of Greed, sexual aberration or lust, fanaticism and pride.

He respects the Jungian view that Vollstandigkeit or perfection is impossible without the complementary of opposites *viz.*, the dichotomy of Good and Evil is a terrible one yet it needs to be harmonised in the nature of man. It thus follows as T.S. Eliot has shown in *Four Quartets* that:

'Sin is Behovely, but
All shall be well and
All manner of thing shall be well.'[96]

For Golding's protagonists their sin is a 'felix culpa' or like Greene's Pinkie in *Brighton Rock* a special damnation which merits a special salvation—'betwixt the stirrup and the ground'[97] Pinkie seeks mercy and finds it. In Golding the greater the sinner the greater the saint, as the old adage says. Spiritual stagnation is the greatest evil and must not be endured as the *Gita* tells us.[98] Golding would also agree with Baudelaire.[99]

Golding fervently believes in the glory of gradual spiritual evolution in man. Though it carry within it the seeds of progression and regression the Jungian view of the 'rhythm of destruction and construction, of error, and truth, of loss and gain, of depth and height'[100] is right. Golding wants man to find himself in every sense of the word and T.S. Eliot's invocation in *Ash Wednesday* is eloquent:

'Suffer us not to mock ourselves with falsehood
Teach us to care and not to care
Teach us to sit still.'[101]

NOTES

1. W.E. Henley: 'Invictus,' st. 10.1-10, *The Golden Treasury*, Selected by F.T. Palgrave, London, O.U.P., 1943, 476.

2. M. Kinkead-Weekes: 'The Visual and the Visionary in Golding,' *William Golding, The Man and his Books*, (ed.) John Carey, London, Faber and Faber, 1986, 65.

3. W.E. Henley: 'Invictus,' 11.1-3,
    'Out of the night that covers me
    Black as the pit from pole to pole
    I thank whatever Gods may be
    For my unconquerable soul.' from *The Golden Treasury*, 476.

4. W. Golding: 'The Ladder and the Tree,' *The Hot Gates*, London, Faber and Faber, 1965, 172.

5. C.T. Thomas: 'Jocelin's Folly or a Bible in Stone?: A Perspective on Golding's *The Spire*,' in *Aspects of William Golding*, (ed.) Dr. S. Kandaswami, Kerala, Department of English, University of Calicut, 1986, 1.

6. C. Jung explains how the extraverted intuitive is concerned with the world of reality, while the introverted intuitive is concerned with the collective unconscious, the dark world of experience, in Frieda Fordham's *An Introduction to Jung's Psychology*. Harmondsworth, Penguin, 1954, 43-53.

7. The ancients call Adam's fall *felix culpa* a 'happy sin' because it had been retrieved with immense advantage by the incarnation of the Son of God. So God has permitted evil to bring about a greater good.

8. W. Golding: A Personal Interview in Cornwall on June 26, 1990.

9. Quoted from *Talk: Conversations with William Golding*, Jack Biles, New York, Harcourt Brace, Jovanovich, 1970, 105.

10. W. Golding: *Fire Down Below*, London, Faber and Faber, 1989, ch. 16, 206.
    Mr. Prettiman says, '"We don't pray to God, he gives us what we need, we are eternally grateful—we do not need priests, we are all priests!"' His faith in a benevolent Being conquers his fears of death.

11. W. Golding: Quoted from *The Guardian*. Friday, June 22, 1990, 21.

12. Virgil: *Aeneid*, Bk. VI, 11. 374-377, trans. John Dryden, New York, Airmont, 1968, 151.

13. Quoted in Archie Campbell's 'William Golding': *Pincher Martin, From the Fifties*, (B.B.C Radio Drama Series), (eds.) Michael Bakewell and Eric Evans, London, 1961, 34.

14. W. Golding: *Pincher Martin*, London, Faber and Faber, 1956, Ch. 13, 201.

15. Frederick R. Karl: 'Graham Greene's Demonical Heroes,' *A Reader's Guide to the Contemporary English Novel*, London, Thames and Hudson, 1968, 94.

16. 'I am convinced of Orignal Sin,' said W. Golding in *William Golding. The Man and his Books*, (ed.) John Carey, 174.

17. The boys crash onto a paradisal tropical island where fruit, flower and pig abound. The joy in this Eden is soured by their evil jealousies and petty hates climaxing in brutal murders committed by Jack and his hunters.

18. W. Golding: *Free Fall*, London, Faber and Faber, 1959, Ch. 1, 19.

19. *Ibid.*, Ch. 2, 45.

20. *Ibid.*, Ch. 12, 236.

21. W. Golding: *Lord of the Flies*, London, Faber and Faber, 1954, Ch. l, 10-11.

22. G.B. Shaw: 'Man and Superman,' Act III. *The Complete Plays of G.B. Shaw*, London, Odham's Press, 1934, 374.

The devil boasts that he has the largest following in England where people are free to choose between classical concerts and racecourses.

23. W. Golding: *Free Fall*, Ch. 11, 217.

24. *Ibid.*, Ch. 14, 251.

25. *Ibid.*, 253.

Sammy feels torn between the worlds of science and spirituality that may find a point of intersection in his repentance—'The moral order. Sin and remorse. They are all true. Both worlds exist side by side. They meet in me.'—*Ibid.*, Ch. l3, 244.

26. W. Golding: *The Spire*, London, Faber and Faber, 1964, Ch. 5, l08.

27. Leighton Hodson: *William Golding*, Edinburgh, Oliver and Boyd, 1969, 93.

28. W. Golding: *The Spire*, London, Faber and Faber, 1964, Ch. 11, 210.

29. *Ibid.*, Ch. 12, 223.

30. Dr. V. Tiger: *The Dark Fields of Discovery*, London, Marion Boyars, 1974, 198.

31. W.S. Maugham: *The Summing Up*, London, William Heinemann, 1938, 73.

32. W. Shakespeare: 'Henry the Fifth,' Act IV, Sc. l, 11. 4-5, 11-12, London, ELBS and Collins, 1964, 571.

33. M.K. Gandhi: *Non-Violence in Peace and War*, Vol. II, Ahmedabad, Navjivan Publishing House, 1948, 74.

34. Peter Moss: 'Alec Albert Golding,' William Golding. *The Man and his Books*, 26.

35. W. Golding: *Free Fall*, Ch. 4, 103.

36. Professor John Carey: A Personal Interview at Oxford on June 20, 1990.

37. W. Golding: *Pincher Martin*, Ch. 7, 103-104.

   Pincher sees her as 'a treasure of demoniac and musky attractiveness that was all the more terrible because she was almost unconscious of it.' Ch. 10, 148.

38. W. Golding: *Darkness Visible*, London, Faber and Faber, 1979, Ch. 11, 167.

39. Stephen Medcalf: 'Bill and Mr. Golding's Daimon,' *William Golding. The Man and his Books*, 34-35.

40. W. Golding: *Free Fall*, Ch. 13, 248.

41. Randall Stevenson: *The British Novel Since the Thirties*, London, B.T. Batsford, 1987, 173-174.

42. R. Hostie: *Religion and the Psychology of Jung*, New Haven, Yale University Press, 1935, 190-205.

   Tennyson in 'In Memoriam' voices the same view:
   'Oh yet we trust that somehow good
   Will be the final goal of ill,
   To pangs of nature, sins of will,
   Defects of doubt, and taints of blood.'—A.L. Tennyson: *Selected Poems*, (ed.) Michael Millgate, London, O.U.P., 1963, LIV, 11. 1-4.

43. R. Hostie: *Op. cit.*, 200-208.

   Matty's character in *Darkness Visible* shows how Goodness in the face of evil must suffer, for when love meets sin, it will be crucified.

44. W. Golding: *The Paper Men*, London, Faber and Faber, 1984, Ch. 11, 123.

45. *Ibid.*, 127.

46. W. Golding: *Pincher Martin*, Ch. 11, 163.

47. L.L. Dickson: *The Modern Allegories of William Golding*, Tampa, University of S. Florida Press, 1990, 1-3.

48. A.T. Broes: *Lectures on Modern Novelists*, Pittsburg, Carnegie Series, No. 7. 1963, 330.

49. M. Kinkead-Weekes and I. Gregor: *William Golding: A Critical Study*, London, Faber and Faber, 1985, 278.

50. Herman Melville: 'Billy Budd,' *Six Great Modern Short Novels*, Bombay, Pearl Publications, 1969, 121.

51. *Ibid.*, 141.

52. E.M. Forster: *Aspects of the Novel*, Harmondsworth, Penguin, 1963, 146.

53. Melville must have been thinking of Milton's depiction of the state of Innocence and the Fall of Man in *Paradise Lost* when he wrote the tragedy of *Billy Budd*.

54. Interview with Frank Kermode, 'The House of Fiction,' in *The Novel Today*, (ed.) Malcolm Bradbury, London, Fontana, 1977, 130.

55. Herman Melville: *Moby Dick*, New York, Random House, 1926, Ch. 61, 183.

56. Alfred Kazin: 'Introduction to Moby Dick' in *Melville. A Collection of Critical Essays*, (ed.) R. Chase, New Jersey, Prentice-Hall, 1962, 41.

57. H. Melville: *Moby Dick*, Ch. 116, 423.

   In creating *Lear* or *Macbeth*, Shakespeare did not seek good and shun evil. He sought and shunned one and the same thing, the double-faced image of life.

58. *Ibid.*, 423.

59. F.O. Matthiessen: Billy Budd, Foretopman in *Melville. A Collection of Critical Essays*, (ed.) R. Chase, New Jersey, Prentice-Hall, 1962, 167.

60. W. Golding: *Free Fall*, Ch. 1, 29.

61. *Ibid.*, Ch. 11, 8.

62. W. Golding: 'Belief and Creativity,' *A Moving Target*, London, Faber and Faber, 1982, 199.

63. W. Golding: 'Utopias and Antiutopias,' *A Moving Target*, 184.

64. J. Conrad: *Lord Jim*, New York, Doubleday, Page and Company, 1925, 212.

65. Tony Tanner: '*Conrad: Lord Jim*,' Studies in English Literature, London, Edward Arnold, 1963, 7.

66. Frederick R. Karl: *Op. cit.*, 256.

67. L. Trilling: 'Kurtz: Hero of the Spirit,' *Conrad: Heart of Darkness*, Casebook, (eds.) A.E. Dyson and C.B. Cox, London, Macmillan, 1982, 64.

68. J. Conrad: 'Heart of Darkness,' *The World's Classics*, Oxford, O.U.P., 1984, 149.

69. S.J. Boyd: *The Novels of William Golding*, Sussex, The Harvester Press, 1988, 160.

70. W. Golding: *The Paper Men*, Ch. 16, 190.

71. G. Greene: *The Heart of the Matter*, London, William Heinemann, 1948, 297.

72. W. Golding: *The Spire*, Ch. 12, 222.

73. G. Greene: *The Power and the Glory*, Harmondsworth, Penguin, 1971, Ch. 4, 58.

74. *Ibid.*, Part 2, Ch. 1, 82.

   He prayed silently, 'O God, give me any kind of death—without contrition, in a state of sin—only save this child.'

75. W. Golding: *The Pyramid*, London, Faber and Faber, 1967, 111.

76. G. Greene: *Brighton Rock*, Harmondsworth, Penguin, 1976, 127.

77. W. Golding: *Darkness Visible*, Ch. 14, 237-238.

78. Brian Davies: *An Introduction to the Philosophy of Religion*, Oxford, O.U.P., 1982, 18-19.

79. V.S. Pritchett: 'Pain and William Golding' in *New Statesman*, August 2, 1958, 146-147.

80. W. Golding: *Darkness Visible*, Ch. 13, 234.

81. *Ibid.*, Ch. 12, 203.

82. Quoted in G. Greene's *The Lawless Roads*, London, Penguin, 1938, Epigraph.

83. W. Golding: *Close Quarters*, London, Faber and Faber, 1987, Ch. 4, 44.

84. W. Golding: *Darkness Visible*, Ch. 11, 167.

85. W. Golding: *Free Fall*, Ch. 9, 182.

86. 'Dark deadly eye, those delicate legs
    Triggered to stirrings beyond sense—
    With a start, a bounce, a stab'—*Thrushes*, 11.3-4.
    'Killers from the egg: the malevolent aged grin.
    They dance on the surface among the flies.
    ……………...
    And indeed they spare nobody.'—*Pike* 11, 3-4; 22. Quoted from *The Faber Book of Modern Verse*, (ed.) M. Roberts, London, Faber and Faber, 1965, 398-400.

87. W. Golding: *Free Fall*, Ch. 11, 193.

88. G. Orwell: *Animal Farm*, The E.L.B.S., London, Penguin, 1971, 114.

89. W. Golding: A Personal Interview in Cornwall on June 26, 1990.

90. Wailer Sullivan: 'Long Chronicle of Guilt: William Golding's *The Spire*,' *Hollin's Critic*, June 1964, 1-12.

91. T.S. Eliot: 'The Idea of a Christian Society,' *Selected Prose of T.S. Eliot*, (ed.) Frank Kermode, London, Faber and Faber, 1975, 291.

92. Quoted in Brian Davies: *Op. cit.*, 95.

93. W. Golding: *The Spire*, Ch. 6, 121.

94. W. Golding: *Rites of Passage*, London, Faber and Faber, 1980, 240-241.

95. Betrand Russell: *Why I am not a Christian*, London, O.U.P., 1957, 37.

96. T.S. Eliot: 'Little Gidding,' Part III, 11.17-19, *Four Quartets*, London, Faber and Faber, 1955, 41.

97. G. Greene: *Brighton Rock*, Part 7, London, William Heinemann & The Bodley Head, 1970, 284.

98. The *Gita* tells us 'Action is greater than inaction. Perform therefore thy task in life. Even the life of body could not be if there were no action.'—Ch. 3, 1.8. Quoted from *The Bhagavad Gita*, trans. Juan Mascaro, Harmondsworth, Penguin classics, 1962, 56.

99. Elizabeth Drew explains Eliot's argument in *The Hollow Men*, how self-destruction by deeds even if evil, is preferable to passive non-entity. She quotes Baudelaire, 'So far as we are human, what we do must be evil or good; so far as we do evil or good, we are human; and

it is better, in a paradoxical way, to do evil than to do nothing: at least, we exist.' From Elizabeth Drew's *T.S. Eliot. The Design of his Poetry*, London, Eyre & Spottiswoode, 1950, 121.

100. C. Jung: *The Integration of Personality*, trans S.M. Dell, London, Kegan Paul, 1940, 89.

101. T.S. Eliot: 'Ash Wednesday,' Part VI, St. 6, *The Penguin Book of Contemporary Verse*, (ed.) Kenneth Allott, Harmondsworth, Penguin, 1980, 103-104.

2

WAR AND VIOLENCE

◆

It is a fact that no civilization has been wholly unaffected by the primitive traits in human nature. Bertrand Russell succinctly observed that at present time 'The fiercest and most dangerous animal with which human beings have to contend is man.'[1] History bears out the unpalatable truth that both primitive and civilized people can be barbaric, violent and unjust. C.E.M. Joad rightly notes that the past of man has been a 'pretty beastly business.'[2] Spain, England and Germany who have been in the forefront of European civilization for centuries stand indicted. In the sixteenth century, Spaniards tortured the Aztecs of America; Englishmen oppressed the Irish and Welsh peasants in the twelfth and thirteenth centuries respectively, and the Germans indulged in mass murder of six million Jews in World War II.[3] Undue violence has kept pace with the growth of European civilizations. 'Therein lies the tragedy of civilized man, his advance has been accompanied by belligerence and cruelty, and the improvement in material benefits has been more than matched by the decline in moral standards.'[4]

Among the post-war group of poets, Ted Hughes has a positive taste for emotional violence. The ugly and grotesque traits in animals are reflected also in similar human traits in Golding's men. This fondness for violence is a natural reaction to the horrors of Auschwitz and Belsen, the aftermath of World War II. Ted's predatory world of *Pike*, *Thrushes* takes us back to the brutality of the primeval world of creatures startlingly close to the masked civilized world of man in Golding's novels. Golding denounces the evil of racial prejudice and the violence that it provokes. In contemplating the wrinkles on the aged face of Europe, he admits, 'I have fallen into something like despair.'[5] He endorses the truth of George Orwell's comment on the destructive force of international contests. 'Anyone who has watched a television programme of a game between two European nations must agree with him. There is savagery for you. There is bloodlust. There is ugly nationalism raising its gorgon head.'[6]

Six of Golding's novels are set in present times, *Lord of the Flies, Pincher Martin, Free Fall, Darkness Visible, The Pyramid* and *The Paper Men*. They have grim relevance to the war-torn nuclear age of ours. He probes behind the so-called civilized code of conduct. He delves into the latent primitive, uninhibited savagery of man's evil nature.

Samuel Mountjoy's declaration that 'There are no morals that can be deduced from natural science, there are only immorals.... Mine was an amoral, a savage place in which man was trapped without hope, to enjoy what he could while it was going.'[7]

In extremis, man's rationality is flouted and he falls back on his natural self-preservative instinct, and thereby becomes an irrational animal, a savage automaton. Ralph, the leader of the boys is deposed and isolated by the despotic Jack and his hunters. Fugitive Ralph yields to fear, loneliness and despair. 'Darkness and the horrors of death'[8] transform the dreamer into a savage aroused by the threats of Roger's sadism, the falling boulders and the nerve wracking ululation. He wounds one of the boys in self-defence. Terrorised, 'Ralph launched himself like a cat, stabbed, snarling with the spear, and the savage doubled up.'[9] To survive, Ralph must himself become a beast!

Wilfred Barclay experiences 'blind terror'[10] when he drops into space while walking with Tucker in the foggy Weiswald. His paralysing fear makes him an instinctive beast. 'Terror was as much an element as space. Here was no dalliance of the mind with the worthlessness or worth of life. The animal knew beyond all question what was precious beyond everything. All that was conscious was a wish that wished itself, for the terror like the bombing, the shooting, the soughing of shells- to stop.'[11]

Golding's fondness for animal imagery for depicting the sufferings of his characters in the throes of purgatorial fire is noteworthy. Samuel Mountjoy's craven fear at the sluggish loathsome object in the centre of his cramped cell is a nightmarish strain. The scene is gothic.[12] His guilt and fear make him think the damp rag is a mutilated penis. He recoils in hate. He is no longer human. 'Here the thing that cried came up against an absolute of helplessness. It struck with the frantic writhing and viciousness of a captive snake against glass and bars.'[13] Man's rapid descent from man to beast, and from beast to an inanimate object is powerfully projected.

S.J. Boyd compares *Lord of the Flies* with Swift's *Gulliver's Travels*. 'Swift thus gives us a painfully simple sketch of the human condition, We aspire to reasonableness, to live in rational societies, but the nature of the beast within us, the innate propensity towards violence, cruelty and self-destructive wickedness, makes such optimistic schemes incapable of realization. Swift rubs our noses mercilessly in our own filth.'[14] Golding demonstrates that the concomitants of civilization can check the tide of savagery only temporarily. Violence is a baser instinct in man's psyche. It is a part of the primitive, barbaric self that seeks power, gratification and comfort at any cost. It stems from the negative emotions of anger, hate, jealousy, revenge and pride. Jack Merridew, Oliver, Pincher Martin, Barclay, Lok and Samuel Mountjoy are trapped in a web of violence like Edward Albee's beastly humans.[15]

The twentieth century has been popularly diagnosed as 'The Age of Depression' with its cult of violence, terrorism, fanaticism, sexism, spiritual malaise and agnosticism. If Mammon-worship began in the nineteenth century, violence is now deified as the Omnipotent Force. It has authority and power, this monster manifests itself in racist riots, communalism and war hysteria. As Goldsmith proved in *The Deserted Village*, 'Where wealth accumulates men decay,' so Golding shows conclusively that where violence predominates men have decayed.

The vogue of violence is an expression of the martial tendency of man to fight for the exhibition of power, and to conquer his weaker fellow beings. In the modern world there is an increasing tendency to resort to violence in any form. In response to a question posed about violence.[16] Golding asserted that it was the decline of spiritual values in society that had resulted in the escalation of the cult of violence.

C.S. Lewis remarks that 'Civilization by which I here mean barbarism made strong and luxurious by mechanical power hates civility from below; Sanctity rebukes it from above.'[17] Golding's theme in *Lord of the Flies* is that civilisation is a moral paradox, a mere facade of talk and refinement. His world is pre-social and atavistic in its features. He studies the constant battle between primitive levels of response and deceptive consciousness viz., the beast and the human. 'In short, Golding rejects the idea of progress through history, and history figures in his work as a paradox [...] there is a deeply modernistic and post-Freudian element in Golding's fictive universe.'[18]

The contemporary novel views the landscape of a chaotic universe which woos destruction. Throughout a good deal of modern literature, the image of the world as hell is evoked likewise with a degree of violence and intensity unprecedented. The unrelieved terror and depravity of William Borroughs' novel. *The Naked Lunch* can be compared to the persistent rejection of death and negation of life in Golding's *Pincher Martin*. The grim terror and humourless despair of T.S. Eliot, Ernest Hemingway, Samuel Beckett and William Golding are traceable to the historical disintegration of society from a relative stability to anarchy. 'All Golding's books are violent; as I say, his basic figure for terror, violence, and bloody creation is childbirth.'[19] Violence also has its genesis in war, which can be defined as a collective mania to destroy mankind. Golding has seen and experienced the ravages of two World Wars and we cannot wonder at his deep pessimism about the nature of man. 'For we are in the age of the fragment and wreckage, those timbers, it may be, washed up on some wild seashore.'[20] War cauterizes a man's emotions and deadens his sensitivity to pain or hurt. Hardened criminals like Pincher Martin can hardly feel the pangs of remorse:

'Their senses in some scorching cautery of battle
Now long since ironed
Can laugh among the dying, unconcerned.'[21]

Golding explained how H.G. Wells and even his father, who was an optimist, believed in the perfectibility of man. '"The war-torn twentieth century gave the lie to it. It became a cry of despair." All prevailing beliefs were swept away and man changed disastrously.'[22] The disillusioned individual is forced to change with such cataclysmic events. Samuel Mountjoy speaks of the whirlwind, 'The world around us was sliding on and down through an arch into a stormy welter where morals and families and private obligations had no place. There was a Norse Sense of no future in the air.'[23] The prime evil of war is found in the sanction it gives man to kill, mutilate and injure his fellow men. Samuel takes vicarious delight in torture. 'I welcomed the destruction war entails, the deaths and terror. Let the world fall. There was anarchy in the mind where I lived and anarchy in the world at large, two states so similar that the one might have produced the other. The shattered houses, the refugees, the death and torture—accept them as a pattern of the world and one's own behaviour is little enough disease. Why bother about one savaged girl when girls are blown to pieces by the thousand? There is no peace for the wicked but war with its waste and lust and irresponsibility is a very good substitute.'[24] His rhetoric is terrifying but convincing. The rage and frustration of the young with their enormous vitality and drive find a natural outlet in the ventilation of violence in war.

The Stanhope twins, Sophy and Toni in *Darkness Visible* woo violence and war with professional pride and skill; to win freedom, power and Money. So Sophy perceives her black truth, in a flash of dark intuition that 'the way towards simplicity is through outrage.'[25] Toni is involved in terrorist activities abroad and covers herself with shameful glory and achieves notoriety. Golding, the philosopher and war veteran, has rightly observed that, '"All wars are a form of terrorism."'[26] As long as man is a victim of megalomania, he will subdue and dominate other men, and worship violence and war.

Ironically, man is the only creature in creation who indulges in violence and evil for its own sake. Faith is implicit in the animal world—the instinct to protect and survive. The human species alone tries to break the primal faith by proving that the gun is mightier than motherhood.[27] We agree with John

Ray that when war begins, the devil makes hell bigger. War engenders nihilistic attitudes to life.

Golding detests reductionists and finds that human nature is potent in its bestiality, despite the 'sweetness and light' of Arnold's belief and the gloss of civilised refinements. If anything, man is more barbaric and brutal than his ancestors. This is seen in *The Inheritors* where the new people attack and overrun the gentle Neanderthalers. Golding asserted in his Nobel Prize lecture that just as bad money drives out good, so inferior culture drives out superior.

Golding was irate that the western world was deeply influenced by the theories of Marx, Darwin and Freud. In quest of his own belief, he did eventually reject their dogmas. He confesses to have been a rope holder in their procession once upon a time. 'The simplistic popularization of their ideas has thrust our world into a mental straitjacket from which we can only escape by the most anarchic violence. These men were reductionist.... I do indeed believe that at bottom the violence of the last thirty years and it may be the hyperviolence of the century has been less a revolt against the exploitation of man by man, less a sexual frustration, or an adventure in the footsteps of Oedipus, certainly less a process of natural selection operating in human society, than a revolt against reductionism, even when the revolutionary, or it may be the terrorist, does not know it.'[28]

If Darwin's theory of natural selection were true, we should have perfect humans today, both biologically and culturally! Instead, we have specimens hag—ridden by time, neurotic, violent, unhealthy and unhappy—'driven like ghosts from an enchanter fleeing.'[29] Darwin remarked that 'as natural selection works solely by and for the good of each being, all corporeal and mental endowments will progress towards perfection...with all these exalted powers—Man still bears in his bodily frame the indelible stamp of his lowly origin.'[30]

And Herbert Spencer had argued that 'the ultimate development of the ideal man is logically certain. But extinct species-extinct cultures testify to the possibility of miscarriage.'[31] Can we blame Golding for his harsh realism and pessimism regarding the real disease of man? In his abhorrence of war, he is like the soldiers of F.T. Prince. His hatred of the war, its terrible pressure that begets:

'A machinery of death and slavery
....
He plays with death and animality.'[32]

In castigating the evils of violence, greed, ambition and revenge in man, Golding is like Butler, Swift, Huxley, Shaw and Orwell. He had particular admiration for Huxley, who suffered '—a contempt for *l' homme moyen sensual*, for most of us in fact... Huxley seems always to have had an equation in his mind between evil and dirt as if morality were at bottom a kind of asepsis.'[33] Human nature is a constant, it encompasses the vices of lust, sloth, pride, avarice and seems totally unaffected by the march of time. Each novel of Golding's proves this beyond the shadow of a doubt.

Golding's portrayal of violence is seen when the characters are driven to extremes. They are dramatically buttressed by the violence of the elements: the boiling sea in *Lord of the Flies* and *Pincher Martin*; the Leviathan—like sea in the nautical trilogy; blitz fire in *Darkness Visible, Lord of the Flies* and *Free Fall. The Inheritors* with its metaphorical significance of light and darkness; overwhelming earth as in *The Spire, The Inheritors, The Pyramid,* and *The Paper Men* and, finally, the thunder-cloud of violence hangs grimly over all the novels. The display of violence in man is a mere echo of the reverberating violence in Nature. In desiring to unravel the riddle of man's irrationality and unpredictability, Golding is preoccupied with various forms of sadism. 'They have been themes of man at an extremity, man tested like building material, taken into the laboratory and used to destruction; man isolated, man obsessed, man drowning in a literal sea of his own ignorance.'[34]

The survival instinct is so strong in man that it precludes all other feelings, when under siege. The aristocratic dandy, Edmund Talbot experiences a thrill of horror at the prospect of death as a possible French ship is sighted on their voyage. '"...Deverel, give me a weapon—anything! ...A weapon for the love of God! A meat axe—sledge-hammer—anything. I will engage to carve and eat the first Frenchman I come across!"'[35] The genteel Lord has turned savage and bloody in true

Anglo-Saxon fashion. In the anti-climax the ship turns out to be an English vessel, the *Alcyone*! But for a brief spell, Edmund had regressed into a Hagar-like caveman willing to kill to save his skin. The gap between civilization and savagery is very small, the atavistic instinct is so potent that under the terrible force of circumstances man can become a beast.

Lord of the Flies deals with the case of human regression in a group of British schoolboys. And here Golding is like the Spanish novelist, Camilo Jose Cela. Both see violence as a ritual, as a way of life and also as a natural expression of hapless beings trapped in a terrible universe.[36] From being one homogeneous group, slow stirrings of resentment at the failure of the signal fire, the jealousy of Jack on the election of Ralph as leader of the group causes a rift between them. The two factions: Jack's hunters and the remaining rational ones consisting of Piggy, Ralph, Sam and Eric and the littleuns are at war with each other.[37] Jack is a natural savage whose killer instinct lies dormant till his cunning brain devises a way to give it full rein. Behind the mask, 'Jack hid, liberated from shame and self-consciousness,' 'his laughter became a bloodthirsty snarling.'[38] Violence is hinted at when Jack hesitates to slaughter the piglet in the jungle, 'They knew very well why he hadn't: because of the enormity of the knife descending and cutting into living flesh; because of the unbearable blood.'[39] Freed from the restraints of civilization, he becomes a 'furtive thing, ape-like,'[40] stalking his prey. His bloodthirsty assault on Piggy, that smashes Piggy's spectacles, is the culmination of a series of minor clashes among the boys and the fanning of negative emotions like thwarted pride, humiliation, frustration, hunger and anger. Ralph and Piggy accuse the hunters of letting the signal fire go out just when a passing ship might have rescued them.[41] Primitive joy at bloodshed is experienced in killing the pig '...Knowledge that they had outwitted a living thing, imposed their will upon it, taken its life like a long satisfying drink.'[42] This appetite for violence is evil. Jack's power and arrogance as food procurer, his compulsive hate of Ralph and his rationality is Hitlerian in its potency.[43] Now they have no compunction to kill. From pighunt to man-hunt, the mob fury of the boys is vented on the boy-beast, Simon. '"Kill the beast! Cut his throat! Spill his blood!"'[44] The

stick sharpened at both ends is a totemic symbol of evil
depravity to cripple and wound both man and beast.[45] The
unchannellised energies of the sadistic boys burgeon in violence
and bloodlust. Roger regresses from a bully, chucking stones
at Henry and scattering Percival's sandcastle,[46] to battering
Simon and executing Piggy. 'The Hangman's horror clung
round him.'[47]

P. Redpath quotes widely from Mary Midgley's *Beast and
Man: The Roots of Human Nature* to explain how primitive
man became a dangerous beast on inventing weapons to
defend himself. 'Deep within all these noble races there lurks
the beast of prey, bent on spoil and conquest. This hidden
urge has to be satisfied from time to time, the beast let loose
in the wilderness.'[48]

Children are known to break out into sporadic eruptions
of violence as they lack the diabolic machinations of the
adult. 'Golding equates the *Lord of the Flies* with the demonic
force latent in man; this is generally kept in check by the
rational part of human nature, but in the absence of reason
or social pressure, breaks out in an act of barbaric bloodletting.'[49]
Other philosophers like U.G. Krishnamurthy have stated that
the 'body is not concerned about values. Any attempt on the
part of man to bring about a change in himself or in others
is against the way nature is operating. I can't even definitely
say there is such a thing as evolution.'[50]

In *The Inheritors* Golding's powerful rhetoric is, '—Are
violence, destruction and death the price of progress?' The
new people fear the Neanderthalers as strange animals... 'It
was a strange creature, smallish, and bowed. The legs and
thighs were bent and there was a whole thatch of curls on the
outside of the legs and arms.... There was no bridge to the
nose.... The shadows lay most darkly in the caverns above its
cheeks and the eyes were invisible in them.'[51] This irrational
fear is mutually echoed in the mistrust and hate of the
Neanderthalers. To Lok they appear 'menacing and wasplike.'[52]

A brilliant analysis of the new men is given by S.J. Boyd.
He writes, 'They are predators, conquistadors, their life feeds
on death. They gain the world by disinheriting the meek... their
attitude to nature is belligerent. Their personal lives are violent

and fraught with trauma—Tuami and Vivani's illicit love-making is an example. Their ultimate recourse is a quasi-cannibal orgy in which Liku is eaten.'[53] Fa associates evil wreckage and death with the new people. She observes that the new people took the log and Mal died. He was on the cliff and so was killed. '"They killed Nil and threw her into the water. And the old woman. They have taken Liku and the new one."'[54] Their violent rituals of chopping Pine tree's finger[55] to make propitious their stag hunt, horrifies Lok. He pictures the hunters as '...a famished wolf in the hollow of a tree.'[56] Lok and Fa drink the new honey that smells of dead things and fire and become as depraved and violent as the new people. Fa observes that the dread of the water is less terrible than the new people. 'The water is better than the new people.'[57] Golding connects evil with bloodshed and physical violence, a desecration of living things in nature. 'Indulging in senseless slaughter only means that we are violating our pact with Oa, our Great Earth Mother.'[58] Golding establishes the fallacy of linking civilisation with peace, refinement and gentility. He mocks Darwin and Wells in *The Inheritors*, for their complacency in linking civilization with the development of culture in man. The image of the hulking dim-witted Neanderthal brute has been radically revised by modern anthropologists. Despite his brutish body he had a bigger brain than that of modern man. He was indeed a hominid. In the light of twentieth century human behaviour, we should be cautious of whom we call brutish.

The entire action of *Pincher Martin* is one long snarl of violence, from the 'writhing and kicking knot of his own body'[59] in the burning churning seas to the 'quacking mouth' and the 'crumbled serration of the rock and claws'[60] in the end.

While the immediate present is fraught with dread violence, the flashbacks of the past of Pincher's life are one interminable saga of violence. His egotism and arrogance make him a prey to cruelty, self-aggrandisement and revenge. He glories in inflicting pain on others. Like Jack, he oppresses others. His tenacity in clinging to the rock of his imagination springs from his overriding arrogance. We marvel at his sadistic skill in theft, brutality, attempted rape and murder. His magnificent resistance to death is heroic...'he was convulsed and struggling....

He spat and snarled.'[61] The negative emotion of hate keeps him alive. Pincher has deliberately cultivated a life free from emotions so as to escape the crisis of conscience in maiming others to achieve his own ends.[62] The pain and endurance of Martin in the rock crevice remind him of the trench tortures in the battlefield.[63]

The metaphor of maggots symbolises the devouring greed of Pincher, who would according to Pete's insinuation eat all the other maggots, and finally be himself dug up[64] and devoured. Pincher is the epitome of violence and greed. His memories are full of outrages.... 'Waiting for the police by the smashed car. Waiting, for the shell after the flash of the gun.'[65] If death can be visualised as a violation of life then the novel *Pincher Martin* portrays this in his self-administered enema in the hope of expelling the serpent in his intestines.[66]

In reducing him to a pair of red claws, Golding emphasizes man's violent attachment to his corporeal existence, that fiercely shuns death and oblivion. Civilized man often experiences a nostalgia to return to his primitive state. 'Pincher's claws seem an echo of Eliot's horror of reductive irrationalism in *The Love Song, of J. Alfred Prufrock*:

> I should have been a pair of ragged claws
> Scuttling across the floors of silent seas.

This nostalgia for a simpler existence is attributed only to the timorous Prufrock and the image itself is one of inverted Darwinism, a pure and horrifying regression to one of the lowest forms of animal life.[67] M. Kinkead-Weekes and I. Gregor, comment on the gruesome pathos of dereliction in the end. '"Broken, defiled. Returning to the earth, the rafters rotted, the roof fallen in—a wreck. Would you believe that anything ever lived there?"'[68]

In *Free Fall* we see that the evil of violence can take the form of mental torture. Dr. Halde, the cold calculating psychologist in the Nazi concentration camp admits to Sammy that '"It is the karma of our two nations that we should torture each other."'[69] Sammy is grilled for information in the prison-room and Dr. Halde 'precipitates him into the pit of his own being so that its nature is fully and horribly revealed to him. He is not tortured, but allowed to torture himself....'[70]

The ugly reality of Sammy's consuming ego is summed up by Halde. '"What embryo if it could choose, would go through the sufferings of birth to achieve your daily consciousness? There is no health in you, Mr. Mountjoy. You do not believe in anything enough to suffer for it or be glad. There is no point at which something has knocked on your door and taken possession of you. You possess yourself."'[71]

Violence and gang warfare in his schooldays are succeeded by his violation of Beatrice's virginity. His timid friend, Phillip, '...liked to inflict pain and a catastrophe was his orgasm.'[72] This boy becomes his Machiavelli in the fagcard fights. Sammy confesses that 'Once a human being has lost freedom there is no end to the coils of cruelty. I must.... They said the damned in hell were forced to torture the innocent live people with disease. But I know now that life is perhaps more terrible than that innocent medieval conception. We are forced here and now to torture each other.'[73]

Golding's artists experience moments of the egotistical sublime which renders them immune to the pain of others. Blake tells us how the man of genius is preoccupied with the question of solipsism.[74] Artists achieve their ends without the slightest scruple or consideration for others. A thread of violence and suffering binds the covetous actor, Pincher Martin.[75] Samuel Mountjoy, the painter who hangs in the Tate gallery is accused by Dr. Kenneth Enticott, the psychiatrist, when he visits the incontinent lunatic Beatrice '"You and your bloody pictures. You use everyone. You used that woman. You used Taffy. And now you've used me."'[76]

Jocelin, the religious artist envisions the bible in stone, a diagram of prayer, to fulfill an ambition to build a four hundred foot spire.[77] A chastened, crippled Jocelin admits to the dying Roger, '"Once you said I was the devil himself. It isn't true. I'm a fool. Also I think—I'm a building with a vast cellarage where rats live; and there's some kind of blight on my hands. I injure everyone I touch, particularly those I love. Now I've come in pain and shame, to ask you to forgive me."'[78] The lascivious Barclay is dogged by his filthy past.... "You booze and wench and lie and cheat and exploit and posture like a—I've put you to bed, lied for you, covered up for you—."' Elizabeth, his wife, condemns him for his depravity.[79]

The tribal artist Tuami carries on a adulterous affair with Marlano's wife, Vivani. 'Their fierce and wolf like battle ended. They had fought it seemed, against each other, consumed each other rather than lain together so that there was blood on the woman's face and the man's shoulder. They hunted down pleasure as the wolves will follow and run down horses;....'[80] In his jealous lust, he sharpens his ivory dagger to murder Marian,[81] but changes his mind.

In a critical overview, one can posit the statement that the price of art or any creative endeavour is paid with violence and suffering. One critic gives the harsh verdict that Golding finds 'meaningless fulfilment in thrills and horrors.'[82] While V.S. Pritchett states clearly that 'Pain is the essence' of Mr. Golding's subject. Mr. Golding's sensibility to pain is the spring of his imagination, and if, in all three stories, the heroes are smashed up, he is by no means a morbid or sadistic writer.... 'Pain is simply the whole condition of man; it is a sign that he is awake and struggling with his nature, and, especially with the terror which so suddenly scatters the mind.'[83] The artist cannot evade violence, his will is a blazing passion (like Jocelin's). Great art is rooted in the turbulent sea of seething emotions. There are the tortured lives of artists like Mozart, Vincent Van Gogh, Theodore Dostoevsky, R.L. Stevenson, D.H. Lawrence, Aldous Huxley and Sylvia Plath, who have often mirrored the violence and chaos in the world of their own lives too.

Violence in *The Pyramid* is superficially camouflaged or concealed by the trappings of civilization. Here the overwhelming pressures of society warp people's emotions, judgments, and behaviour, triggering off a chain of violent events. Oliver and Bobby have a boxing bout over their claim for Evil, the local tart.[84] Oliver gloats over his deceitful triumph, 'I had felt an instant of black malice, cruel joy, and *sheer* intention before I hit him with my fist.'[85] Evie's father, Sergeant Babbacombe belts her for walking abroad and losing her chain. Bobby's motorbike accident puts Olly's rival out of circulation. Olly's perspicacious mother remarks acidly, '"Nobody else was hurt—more's the pity!"'[86] Callous Oliver's casual affair with Evie brings to light her incestuous relationship with her father and Captain Wilmot.[87] It is no wonder that Oliver is both repelled and attracted by Evie. In contrast to Imogen, his dream love, Evie is '...this object, on an earth that smelt of decay, with picked bones and natural cruelty—life's lavatory.'[88] 'Not that Evie is a lower-class angel in disguise, for she exhibits both malice and perversity; but Oliver is so conditioned by his world that he can hardly conceive of Evie as a person in her own right.'[89]

Oliver's childhood memories revive the traumatic episode of the failed artist, Mr. Dawlish 'cawing like a furious rook and smashing with his cane a poor man's phonograph.'[90] The grown-up Oliver understands that Mr. Dawlish is 'a thwarted man, violently acting out his prejudices and the drama of his fruitless ambitions.'[91] His ruthless education of his daughter Bounce, (Oliver's music teacher), makes her severe and harsh with her pupils. A repressed life, a thwarted romance, Henry exploits her generosity, a consuming hate climaxes in her self-immolation in her own house.

David Skilton observes, 'The three story-segments are punctuated by such traumatic moments, most of them involving the nakedness and exposure of Oliver or those around him. In these moments, the harshness of life is laid bare, and the surface of social comedy is ripped open to reveal the alarming disorder that reigns underneath.'[92] The rather slow to discern Oliver is horrified at this hell beneath the stagnant Stilbourne!

M. Kinkead-Weekes and I. Gregor maintain that *Darkness Visible* is Golding's 'most risk taking book,'[93] for he plunges into a vortex of violence in the modern world. A horribly scorched child walks out of 'a burning bush' in blitzed London. The Captain who rescues Matty, just misses an explosion. 'He turned back to his own smashed machine and saw that the tow was coming. He came, silent and filled in an extraordinary way with grief, not for the maimed child but for himself, a maimed creature whose mind had touched for once on the nature of things.'[94] The scarred, ugly Matthew, gift of the Lord is cast into our world of global crime, terrorism, religious perversions and the evils of modern technology. 'That twentieth-century man has perpetrated "darkness visible," in hells unimaginable to Milton, is a fact—London, Dresden, Hiroshima— but in the astonishing overture to the novel, Golding not only makes his readers realise inferno, but also what he means by seeing.'[95] The evil of violence is projected in two ways: firstly, by the wanton cruelty of a blind world that sees the ugliness of Matty as evil; secondly, through the deliberate indulgence in violence by the deceptively beautiful Sophy, Toni and Gerry. Outwardly charming they mislead Goodchild, Bell and Pedigree.

Matty suffers the 'white-hot anguish' of a violent rejection of the world of men. Mr. Pedigree, the homosexual, falsely implicates him in the suicide of Henderson. '"That horrible ugly boy! I wouldn't touch him if he were the last one left on earth!" On being arrested, he screams at Matty. "You horrible, horrible boy! It's all your fault!"'[96] This ghastly looking gentle child—the fruit of war is violently shunned by all. At Frankley's shop, 'he was perpetually employed and never knew that people gave him jobs to get him out of their sight.'[97]

While the grotesque horror of Matty's struggle continues in Australia, Sophy, the queen of violence and evil, takes centre stage in the novel. In Goodchild's words, '"Sophy had everything in the world—youth, beauty, intelligence."'[98] She finds that she has a natural propensity for violence and evil. She experiences a heady power in killing the dabchick.[99]

She woos violence and stumbles on the truth that the rapture felt in a sado-masochistic act like stabbing Roland gives her an orgasm.[100] Sophy embarks on a career of crime and violent outrage when she finds an ideal partner in Gerry, the mafia man. She has adopted violence as a religion to worship and practise as a fanatic devotee. 'The pebble or the knife to the hand. To act simply. Or to extend simplicity into the absolute of being weird whether being weird meant anything or not—as it must when magic efforts *fester* with dirt.'[101] She has a morbid fascination for murdering and asks Bill about the sickly details. In her lust to kill, she resembles Jack and Roger of *Lord of the Flies*. Her appetite for violence has to be sated, and she conspires to kidnap and sexually outrage a child. She worships entropy, 'Everything's running down. Unwinding. We're just tangles. Everything is just a tangle, and it slides out of itself bit by bit toward something that's simpler and simpler, and we can help it. Be a part.'[102] Sophy aspires to be a catalyst in aiding the masses to slide into the abyss of nothingness. As

Abraham Maslow pointed out, Valuelessness is 'variously described as anomie, amorality, as hedonia, rootlessness, emptiness, hopelessness, the lack of something to believe in and to be devoted to.'[103] People with violent attitudes to life have no values. Our civilization will soon be a lost one, if we do not root out violence.

Some human beings are caught in a hurricane of violence. But to indulge consciously in it is a form of depravity. At times, it is a form of penance imposed on oneself. Matty inflicts the torture of the chains and wheels to punish himself for desiring women.[104] Jocelin scourges himself to subdue the travails of the flesh—his carnal desire for Goody Pangall.[105] And Reverend Colley suffers remorse and guilt for his sexual sin, so he starves himself to death.[106] Guilt works invisibly, corroding the minds and souls of men. Colley's rash suicide is understandable in the given circumstances.

According to common Christian belief, Colley's suicide would be a moral outrage. The prevalent belief is that man has no right to take his own life. But post-war twentieth-century nihilists would be supremely indifferent to this form of death. It is not the man's death, but his motive of guilt or shame behind it that shocks one. It is incredible that 'Men can die of shame.'[107] Talbot colours our judgment. He blames Colley's own nature, 'which, manifesting its darkness in an act of bestiality, was unable to cope with the discovery.'[108]

The issue here is not one of violence alone. The complex plot of the novel unfolds with the gradual arousal of Colley's primitive sensibility by the anti-clerical Captain Anderson, who arrogantly walks through Colley on the quarterdeck knocking him down. This violent display of anger is unpardonable. 'There was I thought, and indeed was freighted by the thought, a kind of stare in his eyes, a suffusion of blood in all his countenance that made me believe he might well assault me physically.'[109]

Colley's charitable effort to intervene in the violent brawl between Deverel and Cumbershum is angrily spurned.[110] Puzzled, hurt, and terrorized, Colley is abducted from his hutch by the devils, Deverel and Cumbershum, and subjected to the obscene rites of eating muck and being doused in dirty water. 'Yet now, as I struggled each time to get out of the wallowing, slippery paunch, I heard what the poor victims of the French Terror must have heard in their last moments and oh!—it is crueler than death, it must be—it must be so, nothing; *nothing* that men can do to each other can be compared with that snarling, lustful storming appetite.'[111] Outraged and shunned by the officers and the Captain, Colley ventures below deck to drink and make merry with the jolly tars,[112] as a violent reaction to his rejection and humiliation on deck. Colley's daring act of defying the decorum of the upper deck by micturating in public is understandable.[113] It is obvious that Captain Anderson, Deverel, Cumbershum and Talbot are involved in a web of deceit to cover up the real facts about his death. They stand indicted in the crime of complicity as they made no efforts to save him. Captain Anderson would like to reject 'our general indifference from the log, while Summers's outburst shows that he feels deeply about it, '"...Sir, I tell you. It is likely enough that the man, helplessly drunk, suffered a criminal assault by one, or God knows how many men and the absolute humiliation of it killed him."'[114] Edmund realises with a start that summers had known this all along, '"Mr. Colley is willing himself to death. Come! I have known it happen among savage peoples. They are able to lie down and die."'[115]

The experience of reading Golding's *The Spire* is like visiting a Chamber of Horrors. The peculiar mix of the superstition, faith, and fear of the Middle Ages is evident in the violent action. Dean Jocelin's eccentric plan of erecting a four hundred foot spire on Stilbury cathedral is fraught with terrible mishaps. Golding explains that 'the book is about the human cost of building the spire...the protagonist forces through the building of the spire against all odds, not counting the cost to himself or anyone else because he thinks he does God's will. He does not think of beauty-might never have heard of it. He only sees it part by part, and when it is finished cannot bear to look at it because of the folly and wickedness the job forced on him.'[116]

The metaphors of violence have a savage raw realism that reinforce the sexual and eschatological import of the novel. If the church is the model of a man lying down, then the spire, 'springing, projecting, erupting from the heart of the building'[117] is a distinctly phallic symbol, linked to his suppressed lust for Goody. He likens his work to a surgeon's, 'Now I lay a hand on the very body of my church. Like a surgeon, I take my knife to the stomach drugged with poppy.'[118] One workman is killed, another falls to his death through the hole above the crossways 'and left a scream scored all the way down the air.' There was hysteria in the choir, sniggers during the service, the boys quarreled without knowing why. Big boys were heavy-eyed from nightmares of noseless men....[119] The misshapen Pangall is the sacrificial scapegoat, buried in the creeping pit with a stake of mistletoe between his ribs.'[120] Goody dies in childbirth, with Aunt Alison's blood money strewn about in a scene of hair-raising horror and pain. Jocelin is smitten with spinal tuberculosis and Roger Mason stricken with consumption. Truly as Hilda Spear says, 'The glory of the cathedral has been built on human ruin.'[121] Evil and sin are rife. Life is held of little account; men die horribly in the course of the work and the latent animosities among the cathedral clergy rise to the surface and Jocelin's own life is finally destroyed by his dedication to the building.'[122]

Jocelin's obsessive pride and arrogance is seen in the openly lecherous, Wilfred Barclay, his prototype in the modern age. Lewd and farcical scenes are shot like pellets from Golding's gun. The Outraged Householder armed with his shotgun to kill the bloody badger at his dustbin surprises Rick Tucker, a full-professor of English Literature rifling through his trash in the early hours of the day![123] Furious at the American's persistence, he yells, '"I wish to God I *had* shot you!"'[124] The paradox of this outcry is completed when Rick takes a potshot at the porno-novelist for humiliating and deceiving him at the end.[125]

Wilfred is impressed and intimidated by Rick's massive physique, 'He must be strong, of course. One of those hands could squeeze-made into a fist could hit—or wielding an axe—but they had never done so. The typewriter was their weapon.'[126] The weird experience in the cathedral on the Lipari island mirrors Wilfred's physical and metaphysical terror. '...I stood there with my mouth open and the flesh crawling over my body.... Fright entered the very marrow of my bones. Surrounded, swamped, confounded, all but destroyed, adrift in the universal intolerance, mouth open, screaming, bepissed and beshitten, I knew my maker and I fell down.'[127] Wilfred hates Rick for the obligation he owes him of his life, 'Ungrateful bugger'[128] that Wilfred admits he is, he cannot surrender his ego, and escapes the clutches of his would-be biographer.

Barclay's repulsive sadism in subjecting Rick to a 'rite of passage,' making him lap dole from a saucer like a dog, is brutal.[129] Halliday would like to collect Barclay as a prize specimen. Corrupt papermen can only destroy one another! The canine violence that Wilfred provokes in Rick at the Random Club is both pathetic and degrading.[130]

Golding's art in the use of the grotesque resembles Rabelais, whose grotesquery is sometimes satirically oriented, sometimes indulged in out of a spirit of exuberance and a love of the scurrilous. In novels like *Darkness Visible, Rites of Passage, Lord of the Flies*, and *The Paper Men*, Golding tries to make a choice of direction down into Nothingness and Pure Absurdity, or off into Grace and Redemption. Michael Steig tries to formulate this paradox of the grotesque saying: 'that it both liberates or disarms and creates anxiety. It is also the defeat by means of the comic, of anxiety in the face of the inexplicable.'[131] Barclay's brush with death in Weisswald is horrifyingly real, but turns out to be a calculated melodrama.[132] A futile rage engulfs Barclay as he discovers that Rick, the Prick, had decoyed him to the path in the fog, so he would stumble and allow Rick to seemingly save his life; when, in reality, the drop to the meadow was only a few feet! Comically grotesque is the ghastly slaughter of Piggy by Roger in *Lord of the Flies*. His brains are spilled onto table rock while his pig like fat body twitches in the last throes of death—a human, a beast or just a bag of guts?[133]

'Golding's art has turned directly to the grotesque because of his vision of the world as an inseparable amalgam of elements including the comic and the tragic.'[134] The yoking together of heterogeneous elements like confusion, and the fantastic, insecurity and the terror inspired by the disintegration of the world reinforces his fractured vision of the world in *Darkness Visible* and *The Paper Men*. In these grotesquely eschatological scenes of struggle, the demonic elements in the cosmos participate. Golding focuses attention on the inseparable bond between man and the cosmos, his dependency on Nature for his survival and well being. Man is a microcosm in the macrocosm as John Donne says, 'I am a little world made cunningly.'[135] His love/hate relationship with Gaia, our Earth Mother is natural. 'Our growing knowledge both of the microscopic and the *macroscopic* nature of the earth is not just a satisfaction to a handful of scientists. In both directions, it is bringing about a change in sensibility.... Those who think of the world as a lifeless lump would do well to watch out.'[136] It emerges that Golding has a wholesome respect for Nature and its caprice and whims inspite of being a scientific rationalist.

Nature is a palpable force with its elemental offspring Earth, Air, Fire and Water. Golding's protagonists are involved in a heroic struggle in which Nature is neither a silent spectator nor a passive participant, but a fearful foe to reckon with, now a vengeful wrecker in the drama of his destiny. The macabre scene of the earth creeping in *The Spire*, where the pit dug to reinforce the foundations reveals a boglike stirring of mud and stones, 'like the stirring of grubs.' The unknown terror of 'Doomsday coming up; or the roof of hell down there. Perhaps the damned stirring, or the noseless men turning over and thrusting up; or the living, pagan earth, unbound at last and waking, Dia Hater.'[137] The panic it generates in Jocelin and the workers is terrible, the din of curses and screams and the desire to fill up this hellhole is violent.[138]

The primitive Neanderthalers in *The Inheritors* fear the new men, Ha's disappearance is shocking and Mal's pneumonia caused by his near drowning impels Fa to approach the dread Oa, the female earth deity in the mountains, with the ice women, glacier still melting. Lok follows her and cannot bear the blue and terrible caverns, the benumbing cold, the fierce light blinds him. Fa remarks, '"It is too much Oa for a man."'[139] In this strangely animistic world, the poor creatures with their cosmic piety dread, not Man or Nature, but evil human nature of the bloodthirsty, looting, abducting new men. By a curious ironic twist of comparative fears known to them, Lok and Fa's final judgment of the new people is honest but harsh: '"They are like the river and the fall, they are a people of the fall;

nothing stands against them.'"[140] Injured Lok suffers the pangs
of hate and pain, they would prefer nature to the evil new
people, 'The water is a terrible thing. The water is better than
the new people.'[141]

Golding clearly states, 'I would call myself a universal
pessimist but a cosmic optimist.'[142] No matter how modern,
rationalistic or scientific man may be, he cannot escape his
primitive sensibility, this 'tyranny of the flesh.'[143] Shaw poses
this in the devil's rhetoric, 'And is Man any the less destroying
himself for all the boasted brain of his? Have you walked up
and down the earth lately? I have; and I have examined
Man's inventions. And I tell you that in the arts of life Man
invents nothing; but in the arts of death *he outdoes Nature
herself*, and produces by chemistry and machinery all the
slaughter of plague, pestilence, and famine.'[144]

The parachutist in his tangle of lines—'the mechanics of
parody' with its 'colours of corruption'[145] is the Beast from
the air, which is the crystallisation of the boy's fears in
concrete form. As if in answer to a prayer, the riddle of the
beast is resolved by a creature dropping out of the skies on
to the mountain, with 'the ruin of a face.'[146] The complex web
of loathing and fear woven round the multiple symbols of the
beast in *Lord of the Flies* has a lurid fascination.

Fire, the red monster or the flaming spirit revered by the
ancients, reviled by the beast is synonymous with heat, light,
death and disaster. Golding invests fire with a gruesome and
awesome significance. When Ralph suggests a signal fire, the
ebullient boys stoke a huge pile, it becomes 'a great beard of
flame'[147] 'a river of sparks'[148] 'a savage with smoke and
flame' 'the drum-roll'[149] is soon an infernal beast, a hell that
claims a few littleuns. The destructive blaze is an execution
fire, a savage power mocking the boy's imprudence.

The mythical inference of the modern Prometheus (Ralph
and Pincher Martin) punished for his theft of fire is traced in
the torture of the protagonists. Ralph is vengefully smoked
out of hiding by satanic Jack and his hunters, who set the isle
ablaze in their fury.[150] Pincher as Prometheus spurns death,
God and compassion in a scene of macabre violence,[151] till out
of a black sky a thunderbolt of lightning scorches into oblivion

his locked lobster like claws. The defiant, depraved sinner sees mercy, and love of God as 'black lightning,' a darkness of fear and despair projected by himself.[152]

The very concept of hellfire and purgatory is a horrifying reality for the Christian believer.[153] Golding explained that 'Just to be Pincher is purgatory; to be Pincher for eternity is hell.'[154] Epitomised by the deadly vice of greed, Pincher is drowned, but rejects the 'selfless act of dying' and his 'ravenous ego' fabricates a rock to cling to till the black lightning, the compassion of God'[155] annihilates him. The incendiary fires of the war in blitzed London, out of whose burning maw Matthew is symbolically born in *Darkness Visible* is damned hellfire. 'The great fire...was a glare, a burning bush. It shivered constantly but with an occasional diminution or augmentation of its brightness as walls collapsed or roofs caved in. Through it all—the roar of the fire, the drone of the departing bombers, the crash of collapse—there was now and then the punctuating explosion of a delayed-action bomb going off among the rubble, sometimes casting a kind of blink over the mess and sometimes so muffled by debris as to make nothing but noise.'[156] Don Crompton describes it as 'a firestorm redolent of Milton's hell and Dante's Inferno—a hideous ruin and combustion.'[157] Matty, the burnt offering, is born 'from the sheer agony of a burning city,'[158] to see and experience terrible darkness like Aeneas of Virgil. 'His birth is accompanied by his own experience of violence in which he is horribly burnt. His appearance from the flames is as though man's suffering had coalesced at one point and produced Matty.'[159]

The whirlwind of flame that rushes out of the garage at the kidnapper is none other than Matty. In the arson plot that incinerates the garage and the bookstore, Sophy's evil scheme of diverting attention from the abduction, is achieved. But she had reckoned without the fire-monster. 'The fire-monster jigged and whirled. After a time it fell down; and after some more time it lay still.'[160] We can hardly endure the stark horror of Matty's supreme sacrifice in saving the child. Peter Green praises Golding's art, 'He is intensely, blindingly aware of physical immediacy...he has an intimate, concrete, cosmic awareness of nature in the raw, and a poet's gift of words for describing it.'[161]

Another catastrophe at the end of *Fire Down Below* is the blaze below decks of the *L'Orient,* kindled by Benét, who is involved in repairing the mast. Talbot seeing the holocaust rushes through the avalanche of sparks to rescue his friend Summers, but it is futile. Summers dies a heroic death like Matty. Boyd points out how this is anticipated by a clue in *Close Quarters* by Anderson:

'"There is too much fire below... I cannot like the things. If they should explode, they might touch off a fleet like tinder."'[162] 'Benét's scheme is thus associated with a scientific or technological development which will prove successful, despite Anderson's misgivings. And yet those misgivings have their force, because such a development will lead to greater power in *destructiveness*....'[163]

Frank Kermode finely observes that 'His characters live in a world of rock and sea and amoebae heaving in the pull of the moon, refusing to be locked fast by human imaginings of good or evil, obstinately talking its own language of sucking, plopping and roaring, against the human language which gives it another kind of life.'[164] This participation of Nature as a persona is Golding's novels finds its parallels in Melville's *Moby Dick,* in Conrad's *Heart of Darkness* and Hardy's *The Return of the Native.* The futility of man's bitter struggle against the blind impersonal force of Nature is described in *Moby Dick.* Ahab's heroism in the teeth of a seemingly hostile and malevolent creation—the white whale and the watery waste is incredible.

Conrad's *Lord Jim* mirrors the collusion between ideals and earthy empirical reality in Jim's cowardly jump as the *Patna* was sinking. He cannot confront the terrors of drowning. Hardy's fatalistic creed paints the pathological link between man and a despotic universe. In *Jude the Obscure* and *The Return of the Native* a dramatic struggle of man vis-à-vis the evil in things is waged. Hardy's characters like Golding's seek succors like wounded animals in the primitive raw earth. The striking difference is that Hardy's characters are victims of fate, while Golding's protagonists suffer and give battle to the grim elements of the sea, sky, and earth.

Golding's poetic evocation of the myriad moods of the protean ocean comes from his long love-affair with the sea during the Second World War. Nature becomes a despotic enemy in *Lord of the Flies* where the boiling sea, the impenetrable jungle and the oppressive skies entomb the boys. In Ralph's search for the illusory beast he sees the leviathan as a stupendous creature. 'There was one flat rock there, spread like a table, and the waters sucking down on the four weedy sides made them seem like cliffs. Then the sleeping leviathan breathed out—the waters rose, the weed streamed, and the water boiled over the table rock with a roar.'[165] In 'the shield of the quiet lagoon' Ralph dreams of rescue but the 'brute obtuseness of the ocean, the miles of division, one was clamped down, one was helpless, one was condemned, one was....'[166] 'For Ralph the sea typifies the insensitivity of the universe...the island, the sea, the sacrifice of Simon all show Ralph the truth of the human situation.'[167] With its inexorable tidal Movements, the Pacific waves drag Simon's battered body into a deep grave.[168] Piggy's shattered corpse is sucked up like a fragment of flotsam from the sacrificial altar of table rock.[169]

James R. Baker observes that '...*Lord of the Flies* is a forecast that humanity is involved in an explosive crisis and is on the edge of disastrous violence. *Lord of the Flies* forces us to recognise the likelihood of an apocalyptic war as well as the wanton abuse and destruction of environmental resources.... It also demands an examination of the genesis of crisis and violence. We must learn to rescue ourselves.'[170]

Whatever the technique of fantastic realism, nowhere will we find a more spine-chilling tale of survival at sea than in *Pincher Martin*. A shipwrecked sailor is found on a tiny rock on the vast Atlantic, buffeted by the briny waves, crushed by agoraphobia, the murderous gulls wheeling, bruised and lacerated with urticaria, surrounded by 'the blackness of deep water going down to the bottom of the deep sea.'[171] He evokes within us the power of empathy, as 'the pressures of sea, sky, and rock on unaccommodated man...an epic of human endurance,.... The man is an Atlas holding up an alien world that threatened to crush him; but the scene is not facile because we can feel the strain on the physical muscles. There is about his predicament, and his response to it, the stature of Man against the Elements.'[172]

The metaphor of the jam jar conveys his precariously balanced state, the ruthless pressure on the membrane would sink the figure within.[173] The violence of Pincher's death by drowning is a trifle compared to the purgatory of his past outrages. Pincher believes that Man is 'a freak, an ejected foetus robbed of his natural development, thrown out in the world with a naked covering of parchment....'[174] Dr. Tiger observes that 'his emergence on the rock is like the emergence from the birth canal.'[175] The birth trauma is incomplete until 'at the point of his mind-death he breaks the waters which support his imagined life, and suicidally destroys his source of fresh water,'[176] 'It wriggled like a seal.... There was a scraping and breaking sound and then the cascade of falling stones and water.'[177] The dam breaks free and Pincher is now newborn vulnerable prey to the black lightning that absorbs him. His macabre surreal birth is in glaring contrast to Goody's torturous pangs of labour, which are real.[178] The Romantic Wordsworthian image of 'Our birth is but a sleep and a forgetting:'[179] evades the fact of our brutal entry, which is just what Golding grimly reminds us of. The roots of our violent behaviour are linked with our nativity.

The curious motif of the dual voice of the waterfall in *The Paper Men* is symbolic of the superficial voice of the exterior and the Dread Power of the interior. 'The stream,...had two voices, not one. There was the cheerful babble, a kind of frivolity as if the thing, the Form, enjoyed its bounding passage downward, through space. Then under that was a deep,...secret of the mountain itself.'[180] Redpath analyses it as the 'surface existence, the daily life we lead.... It can also be the surface plot of the novel: the story of the relationship between Wilfred Barclay, 'well known author,' and Rick Tucker, literary critic. Beneath this is the meaning behind the Form, the 'deep secret,' and in *The Paper Men* this is a metaphysical question of being, or, as Barclay calls it of 'isness.'[181] In his fall, Wilfred becomes keenly aware of the other deeper voice 'that was what the water spoke of, not *Gaia Mater* but the space rock balanced between forces so that gravity exhibited itself with this ghastly indifference.'[182] The combined emotions of hatred, fury, and fear swamp Barclay at his being rescued by Rick. He hates to acknowledge the brute in himself. When asked about man's attitude to catastrophes, Golding replied, 'They hit us in our fear centre, inspiring awe and terror in mortals. An enormous fact that will make us respect the unknown irrational. Man, the frightened survivor will begin to understand the problems of ecological damage.'[183]

The water of life can also be the water of affliction. *L'Orient* in a watery world is the stageset of a series of dramatic episodes woven through the nautical trilogy: *Rites of Passage, Close Quarters,* and *Fire Down Below.* Talbot learns to ride the wooden world as it shoulders the waves 'like a bully forcing his way through a dense crowd.'[184] Reverend Colley is consigned to the deeps and Wheeler, Edmund's valet vanishes only to reappear in the next novel. But 'Truth is stranger than fiction.'[185]

The ship is becalmed maybe near the Sargasso sea and the weeds have to be scraped. Mr. Benét informs Talbot that 'she is hogging like a wounded stick.'[186] Rain and spray lash Talbot as the ship rolls onwards, the leaky vessel begins to render like an old boot. Panic spreads like wildfire. Edmund sees a strange thing as the dragrope is hauling the keel—'The thing rose, a wagonload of weed festooned round and over it. It was a head or a fist or the forearm of something vast as Leviathan.'[187] Could it be Colley's body dredged up? To cap it all Wheeler blows his brains out just as Talbot enters his cabin.[188] The superstitious tars deem Colley's cabin cursed with the ill omen of death. The voyage grows more perilous with a tempest brewing '...a gulf opened under the stern—there was no light in that abyss...that blackness of water a welter of black flint.... Light lifted off the earth so that the sea itself collected blackness wherever there was allowed a temporary hollow.'[189] A monstrous drifting Antarctic iceberg now confronts the ship, the crisis is near fatal as the ship steers dangerously through the barrage of falling ice crags. Jones and Tommy Taylor are lost with the lifeboat.[190] This blood-curdling experience leaves Talbot shaken. 'Columns of green water and spray climbed the ice cliff and fell back from it. Wind against wind, wave against wave, fury feeding on itself—I tried to think of my parents, of my Beloved object, but it would not do. I was a present panic, an animal, in the article of death...explosive falls of ice...I recognised that Nature—...had now finally gone mad.'[191] We recollect the terrorizing encounter of the Ancient Mariner's ship with the towering icebergs.[192] Endurance and perseverance give strength to a human being. 'In Golding's fiction both patterns of allegorical action—progress and battle—are evident. The double force of Golding's allegory is particularly effective in his dramatic use of the battle motif, where physical struggles, realistically convincing in their own right, enhance the implied symbolic conflicts.'[193]

It is the untamable beast that lurks within us that erupts into violence, terror and selfish hate. Contemporary man can boast of having ancestral links with Cain, Sodomites, Hitler, Idi Amin besides the anthropoid ape! He cannot evade the ugly truth of fear psychosis triggering off outbreaks of savage violence, the increasing wave of war-mongering that keeps us teetering precariously on the brink of a Third World War.

Desmond Morris studies the depraved nature of man linking it to his own confinement. 'Under normal conditions, in their natural habitats, wild animals do not mutilate themselves, masturbate, attack their offspring, develop stomach ulcers, become fetishists, suffer from obesity, form homosexual pair-bonds, or commit murder. Among human city-dwellers, needless to say all these things occur. Does this, then, reveal a basic difference between the human species and other animals? ...animals behave like this when they have been confined in cramped captivity. The zoo animal in a cage exhibits all these abnormalities that we know so well from our human companions. Clearly, then, the city is not a concrete jungle, it is a human zoo.'[194] Modern psychology with its emphasis on subjectivism has made man such an insular self-centred being that he is inclined to give undue importance to himself and tends to resort to violence as an end in itself.

Peter Green regards Golding primarily as a religious novelist. He says, 'his central theme is not the relationship of man to man, but the relationship of man, the individual, to the universe; and through the universe, to God. He is going back behind our distracting modern clutter of physical impedimenta to search for the basic truths that have been obscured by material progress. He is a spiritual cosmologist.'[195]

Golding points out the folly of attempting to deny the

existence of the beast that lurks within man, and 'he discovers through Simon and Jack, through Lok and Fa that the beast-man is neither all good nor all bad; for it is a paradox of human existence that good and evil are so tightly entangled in man's experience that it is impossible to separate them or at times, even to recognize them clearly.'[196]

Violence is a part of the cycle of creation and destruction. The very origin of the universe is linked with primordial violence. The Big Bang theory describes the violent birth of the earth. Violence can never be divorced from life, while man is a biological instinctual being. Asking him to eschew violence is as futile as asking him to surrender his élan vital. He glories in diverting his turbulent energies to sports like surf-riding, hang-gliding, sky-diving that slake his thirst for adventure and achievement.

In artistic creation, violence is analogous to regeneration. Golding paints the intense fire of artistic emotions in Oliver, Talbot, Jocelin, Samuel and Matty. Coleridge, describing the function of the Secondary Imagination says, 'It dissolves, diffuses, dissipates, in order to re-create; or where the process is rendered impossible, yet still at all events it struggles to idealize and to unify. It is essentially *vital* even as all objects as objects are essentially fixed or dead.'[197]

'Golding is a child of "two cultures." His steadfast opposition to the outworn public myths of the modern age is not simply negative or nihilistic. His fiction shows us the possibility of a new mentality struggling to be born against the terrific odds imposed by the patterns of our social heritage and the limitations of our species. Golding implies a psychological ecology, a synthesis of perspectives....'[198] Man's ebullient energy can be diverted to aesthetic, humanitarian works, but he must rid himself of selfishness first.

'To be in a world which is a hell, to be *of* that world and neither to believe in nor guess at anything *but* that world is not merely hell but the only possible damnation; the act of a man damning himself. It may be—I hope it is—redemption to guess and perhaps perceive that the universe, the hell which we see for all its beauty, vastness, majesty is only part of a whole which is quite unimaginable. I have said that the act of human creativity, a newness starting into life at the heart of confusion and turmoil seems a simple thing; I guess it is a signature scribbled in the human soul, sign that beyond the transient horrors and beauties of our hell there is a Good which is ultimate and absolute.'[199] Man is a blessed creature for he can wield and use to great powerful good all 'the three instruments of knowledge.'[200]

Samuel Mountjoy expiates his crime by killing his selfishness within him in the prison cell (broom closet), thus redeemed, his artistic vision is restored and he is reborn. 'I was surrounded by a universe like a burst casket of jewels....'[201] '...I was visited by a flake of fire, miraculous and pentecostal; and fire transmuted me, once and forever.'[202] The dead thing inside him is his cruel self-centredness; he is free and unburdened and finds a new thing. 'This substance was a kind of vital morality...the relationship of individual man to individual man—...this live morality was, to change the metaphor, if not the gold, at least the silver of the world.'[203]

NOTES

1. Bertrand Russell: 'I believe,' *The Gates of Wisdom*, (ed.) V.D. Salgaonkar, Bombay, Macmillan, 1967, 114.

2. C.E.M. Joad: *The Story of Civilization*, The How and Why Series, London, A & C Black, 1935, 19.

3. P.S. Fry: *History of the World*, London, Hamlyn, 1972, Introduction, viii.

4. *Ibid.*, viii.

5. W. Golding: 'Fable,' *The Hot Gates*, 92.

6. *Ibid.*, 93.

7. W. Golding: *Free Fall*, Ch.12, 226.

8. W. Golding: *Lord of the Flies*, Ch.12, 205.

9. *Ibid.*, 215.

10. W. Golding: *The Paper Men*, Ch. 8, 86-87.

11. *Ibid.*, Ch. 8, 87.

12. W. Golding: *Free Fall*, Ch. 9, 183-185.

13. *Ibid.*, 184-185.

14. S.J. Boyd: *Op. cit.*, 8.

15. In *Who's Afraid of Virginia Woolf*, New York, Pocket Books Inc., Cardinal Edition, 1962. When George tries to strangle his wife, Martha, Honey enjoys the spectacle and eggs him on crying, 'Violence! Violence!'

The two pairs thrive on violence in their depraved 'Fun and Games.' Act II, 135.

16. The question asked at a public lecture sponsored by the British Council in March 1987, Bombay, was: "'Would you say that an escalation of the cult of violence and repressed sexuality in the twentieth century are the key factors in the decline of spiritual values in society?'"

17. C.S. Lewis: *A Preface to Paradise Lost*, London, Oxford University Press, 1942, 132.

18. M. Bradbury: 'The Novel,' *The Twentieth Century Mind*, Vol. 3, 1945-1965, (eds.) C.B. Cox and A.E. Dyson, London, 1972, 343.

19. Frank Kermode: 'William Golding.' *On Contemporary Literature*, (ed.) Richard Kostelanetz, New York, Avon Books, 1964, 386-387.

20. W. Golding: 'A Moving Target,' in *A Moving Target*, 168.

21. W. Owen: 'Insensibility,' *The Penguin Book of Contemporary Verse*, (ed.) Kenneth Allott, 121.

22. W. Golding: A Personal Interview in Cornwall on June 26, 1990.

23. W. Golding: *Free Fall*, Ch. 4, 95.

24. *Ibid.*, Ch. 5, 131-132.
     Even today, we are never free from the evil threat of a Third World War. War hysteria is being deliberately engendered in the explosive Middle East, the centre of oil and power. When Iraqi president, Saddam Hussein declared that, "'Cutting necks is better than cutting means of living. O God Almighty, be witness that we have warned them.'" His open pledge to kill ruthlessly is a hallmark of this Age of Outrage.— President S. Hussein: Quoted in *TIME*, August 6, 1990.

25. W. Golding: *Darkness Visible*, Ch. 11, 167.

26. W. Golding: Quoted in the report of a Press Conference in *The Times of India*, Saturday, March 9, 1987.

27. O.V. Vijayan says, 'Whether at Mai Lai or Velvettithurai the object of war is the same brutal affront—IPKF—not Indian Peace Keeping Force (in Sri Lanka), but Innocent People Killing Force—the children screamed at the young soldier, who went berserk and pumped lead into the lot.' 'Ballad of the Soldier,' *The Illustrated Weekly of India*, October 15, 1989.

28. W. Golding: 'Belief and Creativity,' *A Moving Target*, 187.

29. P.B. Shelley: 'Ode to the West Wind,' *Shelley's Prose and Poetry*, Oxford, Clarendon Press, 1931.

30. Charles Darwin: *The Origin of Species and the Descent of Man*, New York, Random House, 1872, 920.

31. B.F. Skinner: *Beyond Freedom and Dignity*, Harmondsworth, Penguin, 1974, 172.

32. F.T. Prince: 'Soldiers Bathing,' *The Penguin Book of Contemporary Verse*, (ed.) Kenneth Allott, 250.

33. W. Golding: 'Utopias and Antiutopias,' *A Moving Target*, 181.

34. W. Golding: 'Belief and Creativity,' *A Moving Target*, 199.

35. W. Golding: *Close Quarters*, Ch. 4, 44.

36. Pascual Duarte in *The Family of Pascual Duarte* violates his fiancée, Lola, as Samuel violates Beatrice in *Free Fall*.

37. W. Golding: *Lord of the Flies*, Ch. 4, 77.

38. *Ibid.*, 69.

39. *Ibid.*, 34.

40. *Ibid.*, 53.

41. *Ibid.*, 73-78.

42. *Ibid.*, 76.

43. The Death of Adolf Hitler: BBC film screened September 1, 1990. Hitler explains to Eva Braun why he wished to exterminate the Jews. '"Hate! Hate! It gives energy and power to me!"'

44. W. Golding: *Lord of the Flies*, Ch. 9, 168.

     F. Karl tells us how physical force overwhelms religion, creativity, humanity itself. The boys are caught in a chaos of violence and fear...the blood thirst of their chant has poked through the veneer of civilization, and they are helpless within the throes of a primitive passion.—Frederick Karl: *Op. cit.*, 257-258.

45. *Ibid.*, Ch. 12, 210.

46. *Ibid.*, Ch. 4, 65.

47. *Ibid.*, Ch. 11, 201.

48. Quoted from Nietzsche's *The Genealogy of Morals* by P. Redpath in *William Golding—A Structural Reading of his Fiction*, London, Vision, 1986, 86.

49. B.F. Dick: *William Golding*, New York. Twayne Pub. Inc., 1967, 223.

50. U.G. Krishnamurthy: An Interview with Frank Noronha, *The Times of India*, August 6, 1990.

51. W. Golding: *The Inheritors*, London, Faber and Faber, 1955, 218-219.

52. *Ibid.*, Ch. 7, 138.

53. S.J. Boyd: *Op. cit.*, 36-39.

54. W. Golding: *The Inheritors*, Ch. 6, 114.

55. *Ibid.*, Ch. 7, 147.

56. *Ibid.*, Ch. 10, 195.

     B.F. Dick describes the new people, their family consists of '...a ruthless despot, Marlan; a potential murderer, Tuami; a deranged child, Tanakil and an adulterous mother, Vivani.... Although a sunburst christens their journey, it has occurred at the expense of a genocide.'—B.F. Dick: *Op. cit.*, 44.

57. *Ibid.*, 197.

58. Mary Loften Grimes maintains that the Great Mother is a Jungian symbol of the collective unconscious and man today has become detached from this source.—M.L. Grimes—'The Archetype of the Great Mother in the novels of William Golding,' *Dissertation*, University of Florida, 1977, 10.

59. W. Golding: *Pincher Martin*, Ch. 1, 7.

60. *Ibid.*, Ch. 13, 200-201.

61. *Ibid.*, Ch. 3, 42.

62. *Ibid.*, Ch. 5, 70.

63. *Ibid.*, Ch. 3, 40.

64. *Ibid.*, Ch. 9, 136.

65. *Ibid.*, Ch. 9, 139.

66. *Ibid.*, Ch. 11, 163-164.
   '"Why drag in good and evil when the serpent lies...in my body?"'

67. Michael Bell: *Primitivism*, The Critical Idiom Series, (ed.) John D. Jump, London, Methuen, 1972, 44.

68. Quoted by M. Kinkead-Weekes & I. Gregor: *Op. cit.*, 154, from *Pincher Martin*, Ch.14, 207.

69. W. Golding: *Free Fall*, Ch. 7, 148.

70. M. Kinkead-Weekes & I. Gregor: *Op. cit.*, 184.

71. W. Golding: *Free Fall*, Ch. 7, 144.

72. *Ibid.*, Ch.2, 48.

73. *Ibid.*, Ch.5, 115.

74. 'Nought loves another as itself
   Nor venerates another so
   Nor is it possible to thought
   A greater than itself to know'
   William Blake: *Collected Works*, Nonesuch Edition, 1927, 78.

75. Pete, his producer tells him, '"So you're wanted for the seven sins, Chris."' Malice, Lechery and Sloth are cast aside in favour of Greed. W. Golding: *Pincher Martin*, Ch. 8, 118-119.

76. W. Golding: *Free Fall*, Ch. 13, 246.

77. W. Golding: *The Spire*, Ch. 5, 108.
   Jocelin realizes the folly of his enterprise. 'I thought the spire would complete a stone bible, be the apocalypse in stone. I never guessed in my folly that there would be a new lesson....' 108.

78. *Ibid.*, Ch. 11, 210-211.

79. W. Golding: *The Paper Men*, Ch. 14, 170-171.

80. W. Golding: *The Inheritors*, Ch. 9, 176-177.

81. *Ibid.*, Ch. 12, 226.

82. Louis J. Halle: 'Small Savages,' *Saturday Review*, October 15, 1955, 15.

83. V.S. Pritchett: 'Pain and William Golding,' *New Statesman*, August 2, 1958, 146-147.

84. W. Golding: *The Pyramid*, 30-31.

85. *Ibid.*, 42.

86. *Ibid.*, 58.

87. 'This broken, heavily secreting gargoyle—he had struck those weaker blows with his left hand across the other weals.' Wilmot's frustrated flagellation is shocking. *The Pyramid*, 90.

88. *Ibid.*, 91.

89. Howard S. Babb: *The Novels of William Golding*, Ohio, Ohio State University Press, 1970, 177.

90. W. Golding: *The Pyramid*, 164.

91. *Ibid.*, 165.

92. David Skilton: 'The Pyramid and Comic Social Fiction,' *William Golding—Novels, 1954-67*, Casebook (ed.) N. Page, London, Macmillan, 1985, 177.

93. In a personal discussion at the University of Kent on June 6, 1990.

94. W. Golding: *Darkness Visible*, Ch. l, 16.

95. M. Kinkead-Weekes and I. Gregor: *op. cit.*, 279.

96. W. Golding: *Darkness Visible*, Ch. 2, 36-37.

97. *Ibid.*, Ch. 3, 43.

98. *Ibid.*, Ch. 16, 259.

99. *Ibid.*, Ch. 8, 109.

100. *Ibid.*, Ch. 9, 146.

101. *Ibid.*, 147.

102. *Ibid.*, Ch. 10, 166-167.

103. A.H. Maslow: *Religions, Values and Peak Experiences*, Columbia, Ohio State University Press, 1964, 25.

104. W. Golding: *Darkness Visible*, Ch. 5, 75-76.

105. W. Golding: *The Spire*, Ch. 3, 65.
     'He woke in the darkness, full of loathing. So he took a discipline and lashed himself hard.'

106. W. Golding: *Rites of Passage*, 126-127.

107. *Ibid.*, 278.
     Golding would agree with Sisir Kumar Ghose who acidly says: 'We do not know how to die because we do not know how to live. Only a few are capable of the noblest act of "Iccha Mrityu," the voluntary giving up of the body which is the highest mark of self-conscious being.'—Quoted from 'Science without a Soul,' a review of Fritjof Capra's book, *The Turning Point: Science, Society and the Rising Culture*, Flamingo, 1987 in *The Times of India*, September 20, 1987.

108. P. Redpath: *Op. cit.*, 72.

109. W. Golding: *Rites of Passage*, 205.

110. *Ibid.*, 221.

111. *Ibid.*, 237-238.

112. Nietzsche, it was, who called man 'the sick animal,' (das kranke tier), for we are open, undefined in the patterning of our lives. Our nature is not stereotyped. A human being can—adopt many roles—astronaut, artist and sculptor. He can play and actualise in his life anyone or any number of hugely differing destinies; and what he chooses to incarnate in this way will be determined finally neither by reason nor even by common sense; but by infusions of excitement: with 'visions that fool him out of his limits,' as the poet Robinson Jeffers said, 'Humanity is the mould to break away from, the crust to break...the coal to break into fire, the atom to be split.' Quoted in Joseph Campbell's *Myths to live by*, London, Paladin Books, Granada, 1985, 194.

113. W. Golding: *Rites of Passage*, 117.

114. *Ibid.*, 251.

115. *Ibid.*, 153.

In Joseph Conrad's *Heart of Darkness*, Marlow views with awe the Congo native workers subsisting on meagre bits of dough or hippo meat '"Don't you know the devilry of lingering starvation; its exasperating torment, its black thoughts, its sombre brooding ferocity? Well, I do. It takes a man all his inborn strength to fight hunger properly...some kind of primitive honour?"'—J. Conrad: *Heart of Darkness* in *The World's Classics*, (ed.) R. Kimbrough, Oxford, O.U.P., 1984, 10.

116. W. Golding: 'A Moving Target,' *A Moving Target*, 166-167.

117. W. Golding: *The Spire*, Ch. 1, 8.

118. *Ibid.*, 13.

Jocelin imagines himself to be a healing artist.

119. *Ibid.*, Ch. 3, 54.

120. *Ibid.*, Ch. 4, 90.

121. Hilda Spear: *William Golding's The Spire*, Beirut, Longman York Press, 1985, 33.

122. *Ibid.*, 38-39.

123. W. Golding: *The Paper Men*, Ch. 1, 10-12.

124. *Ibid.*, Ch. 1, 14.

125. *Ibid.*, Ch. 16, 191.

126. *Ibid.*, Ch. 8, 80.

127. *Ibid.*, Ch. 11, 123.

128. *Ibid.*, Ch. 8, 91.

129. *Ibid.*, Ch. 12, 150.

130. *Ibid.*, Ch. 15, 182.

131. Michael Steig: 'Defining the Grotesque: an attempt at Synthesis,'
      Journal of Aesthetics and Art Criticism, Summer, 1970, 26.

132. W. Golding: *The Paper Men*, Ch. 8 & 12, 86 & 135.

133. W. Golding: *Lord of the Flies*, Ch. 11, 157.

134. Quoted from William Nelson's 'The Grotesque in *Darkness Visible* and
      Rites of Passage' by Johnn Stinson in 'Trying to Exorcise the beast'
      Grotesque in the Fiction of William Golding, Cithara, Vol. 11, No. 1,
      1971, 28.

135. John Donne: Divine Poems, No. 5, *The Poems of John Donne*, (ed.)
      H.J.C. Grierson, Oxford, Clarendon Press, 1912.

136. W. Golding: 'Gaia Lives, O.K.?', *A Moving Target*, 86.

137. W. Golding: *The Spire*, Ch. 4, 79-81.

138. This fear is similar to that of Eustace, Mr. Sandbach and others in
      E.M. Forster's 'The Story of a Panic,' *Collected Short Stories*,
      Harmondsworth, Penguin, 1954.

      Forster says it was not the spiritual fear that one has known at other
      times, but brutal, overmastering, physical fear, stopping up the ears...
      I had been afraid not as a man, but as a beast, 15.

139. W. Golding: *The Inheritors*, Ch. 4, 85.

140. *Ibid.*, Ch. 10, 195.

141. *Ibid.*, Ch. 10, 197.

142. W. Golding: 'Belief and Creativity,' *A Moving Target*, 201.

143. G.B. Shaw: *Man and Superman*, Act 3, 525.

144. *Ibid.*, Act 3, 525.

145. W. Golding: *Lord of the Flies*, Ch. 9, 161.

146. *Ibid.*, Ch. 7, 136.

147. *Ibid.*, Ch. 2, 45.

148. *Ibid.*, 45.

149. Ibid., 49.

150. *Ibid.*, Ch. 12, 218.

151. W. Golding: *Pincher Martin*, Ch. 13, 192-201.

152. *Ibid.*, Ch. 12, 181.

153. J. Milton: 'Paradise Lost,' *The Poetical Works of John Milton*, (ed.)
      Helen Darbyshire, Oxford, Clarendon Press, 1978, Vol. 1.

      Milton powerfully describes the darkening gloom, the lake of fire as
      'A Dungeon horrible, on all sides round
      As one great Furnace flam'd, yet from those flames
      No light, but rather darkness visible
      Serv'd only to discover sights of woe,
      Regions of sorrow, doleful shades, where peace
      And rest can never dwell, hope never comes
      That comes to all; but torture without end

Still urges, and a fiery Deluge, fed
With ever-burning Sulfur unconsum'd:': Bk. I, 11, 61-69.

154.   W. Golding: *Pincher Martin*, in *Radio Times*, March 21, 1958.

155.   *Ibid.*

156.   W. Golding: *Darkness Visible*, Ch. l, 9-10.

157.   Don Crompton: *A View from 'The Spire' William Golding's Later Novels*, London, Blackwood, 1984, 20.

158.   Don Crompton: *Op. cit.*, 20.

159.   P. Redpath: *Op. cit.*, 164.

160.   W. Golding: *Darkness Visible*, Ch.15, 248.

161.   P. Green: 'The World of William Golding' in *William Golding—A Casebook*, (ed.) Norman Page, London, Macmillan, 1985, 96.

162.   W. Golding: *Close Quarters.* Ch.7, 99.

163.   S.J. Boyd: *Saltwater Soap*, Unpublished Papers, 24.

164.   Frank Kermode: *Spectator*, August 22, 1958, quoted in Peter Green's 'The World of William Golding,' 96.

165.   W. Golding: *Lord of the Flies*, Ch. 6, 115.

166.   *Ibid.*, Ch. 7, 122.

167.   C.B. Cox: 'On *Lord of the Flies*,' in *Critical Quarterly*, Summer, 1960, No. 2, 112-117.

168.   W. Golding, *Lord of the Flies*, Ch. 9, 170.

169.   Ibid., Ch.11, 200.

170.   James R. Baker: 'The Decline of *Lord of the Flies*,' *South Atlantic Quarterly*, N. Carolina, Duke University Press, Vol. 69, No. 5, Autumn, 1970, 446-447.

171.   W. Golding: *Pincher Martin*, Ch. 4, 65.

172.   M. Kinkead-Weekes and I. Gregor: *Op. cit.*, 126.

173.   W. Golding: *Pincher Martin*, Ch. l, 9.
        Carl Jung points out that hollow objects such as ovens, jars, cooking vessels are associated with the mother archetype.—*Archetypes and the Collective Unconscious*, trans. R.F.C. Hull, Routledge and Kegan Paul, London, 1959, 81.

174.   *Ibid.*, Ch. 13, 190.

175.   Dr. V. Tiger: *Op. cit.*, 103.

176.   Dr. A. Henry: 'The Pattern of *Pincher Martin*,' *Southern Review*, Vol. 9, No. 1, March 1976, 10.

177.   W. Golding: *Pincher Martin*, Ch. 13, 199.

178.   W. Golding: *The Spire*, Ch. 7, 136.

179.   W. Wordsworth: 'Ode: Intimations of Immortality,' *William Wordsworth*, (ed.) J. Butt, London, O.U.P., 1964, 181.

180.   W. Golding: *The Paper Men*, Ch. 8, 83.

181. P. Redpath: *Op. cit.*, Ch. 9, 143.

182. W. Golding: *The Paper Men*, Ch. 8, 89.

183. W. Golding: A Personal Interview in Cornwall, June 26, 1990.

184. W. Golding: *Rites of Passage*, Ch. 2, 16.

185. During a personal interview in Cornwall on June 27,1990, Golding related the strange story of a crewman who had fallen overboard. On finding him missing four hours later, the ship's captain ordered the ship to retrace its course and the sailor was rescued badly blistered but alive!

186. W. Golding: *Close Quarters*, Ch. 12, 181.

187. *Ibid.*, Ch. 16, 257.

188. *Ibid.*, Ch. 17, 262.

189. W. Golding: *Fire Down Below*, Ch. 14, 179-181.

190. *Ibid.*, Ch. 18, 251.

191. *Ibid.*, 242-243.

192. 'And ice mast-high, came floating by,
      As green as emerald. Nor shapes of men nor beasts we ken
      The ice was all between.
      The ice was here, the ice was there,
      The ice was all around:
      It cracked and growled, and roared and howled,
      Like noises in a swound!'

      S.T. Coleridge: 'The Rime of the Ancient Mariner,' Part I, *The Poetical Works of S.T. Coleridge*, Vol. 2, London, W. Pickering, 1840, 3-4.

193. L.L. Dickson: *The Modern Allegories of William Golding*, Tampa, University of Florida Press, 1990, 9.

194. Desmond Morris: *The Human Zoo*, London, Jonathan Cape, 1969, 8.

195. P. Green: 'The World of William Golding,' *William Golding—Casebook*, 79.

196. Evon Nossen: 'The Beast-Man Theme in the work of William Golding,' *Forum*, 9, Ball State University, Spring, 1968, 60-69.

197. S.T. Coleridge: *Biographia Literaria*, (ed.) George Watson, London, Everyman's Library, 1967, Ch. 13, 167.

198. James R. Baker: *Op. cit.*, 446-460.

199. W. Golding: 'Belief and Creativity,' *A Moving Target*, 201-202.

200. Swami Vivekananda explains how in Hindu philosophy there are three instruments of knowledge—Instinct, Reason and Inspiration. Instinct belongs to the beast, reason to man and inspiration to Godmen.—*Hinduism*, Sri Ramakrishna Math, Madras, 1946, 99.

201. W. Golding: *Free Fall*, Ch. 10, 187.

202. *Ibid.*, Ch. 10, 188.

203. *Ibid.*, 189.

3

SEX AND SEXUALITY

◆

If to Blake, experience is a prison-house, as it implies guilt and tyranny,[1] to Golding, experience is a stepping-stone to knowledge that can drive man to do evil deeds.[2] In his novels, Golding ruthlessly explores the depraved aspects of human nature—lust, greed, violence, fanaticism and repressed sexuality—the darkness of man's heart.[3] Golding's concept of evil is all-embracing, for the evil inside a man responds to the evil in the universe. Our modern wasteland civilization, nurtured on war, violence, rigid beliefs, social taboos and multiple "isms" has scarred man's psyche. It has warped man's simple sexual urges, his glorious instinct, into a perverted ugly phenomenon, to be guilty and ashamed of. Like any other orthodox moralist, 'Golding insists that Man is a fallen creature, but he refuses to hypostatise Evil or locate it a dimension of its own.'[4] As a reaction to his father's Wellsian rationalism, Golding became an avowed non-conformist.

The restraints of modern times created by the Industrial Revolution, urbanisation, decay of spiritual values, the Darwinian theory of the origin of man and changing psychological studies have influenced the sexual portrait of modern man. Sexual crimes, acts of arson and terrorism provide an outlet for repressed sexuality. Affluence and permissiveness can cause aberrations in one's sex life that leave permanent scars.

Man is a complex being and sex plays an important role in his life. It is part of the universal pattern of creation that the two sexes are complementary to each other. Sex is both for procreation and pleasure. When does the pleasure of sex become evil? When it is used as a weapon to hunt, exploit

and ruin other human beings then sex is an ugly evil power
of man.[5] Golding studies this seamy side of man with searing
honesty...he presents a starkly pessimistic picture of man, as a
creature whose proud sense of civilisation cannot save him
from the destructive forces of greed, lust, and cruelty within
himself.[6] At some point in his life, a fine sense of balance is
lost and the glorification of sex becomes the bane of man's
life. 'A young man certain of nothing but salt sex; certain that
if there was a positive value in living, it was this undeniable
pleasure. Be frightened of the pleasure, condemn it, exalt
it...did they not say that the root of art was sex? ...the little death
shared or self-inflicted was neither irrelevant nor sinful but the
altar of whatever shoddy temple was left to us.'[7] Sammy's rape
of Beatrice is a descent into hell. Pincher is the genuine
psychopathic manic-depressive who plots to kill Nat. This
travesty of sexual mores, this idolisation of sinful sex for its
own sake is the evil that wrecks man's peace of mind.

Golding is deeply disturbed by the sexual depravity in
man which causes him to indulge in bestial acts to let off
steam. Pincher Martin's male predatoriness is aroused by the
prim Mary Lovell's refusal to be seduced.[8] We witness the
birth of evil in his maddening desire to break, conquer her.
His abortive attempt to rape her in the speeding car is a
culmination of his sexual frustration at her persistent rejection
of his advances.[9] His passion becomes a 'corrosive acid in his
guts,' full of insane jealousy at Nat's engagement to Mary.[10]
For him love has become loathing, he uses sexual power to
take revenge on Nat and Mary for depriving him of his pleasure.

Behind the mask of so-called civilization bubbles a seething
cauldron of primitive, barbaric and distorted energies waiting
for an escape.[11] Golding's novels explore the hidden springs
of man's socio-sexual desires and needs and their turbulent
conflict with conventional mores. Pincher Martin is shocked
at Mary's prudish fear of him in the twentieth century! Golding's
irony is implicit. Only a moralistic Mary or a timid Beatrice
would consider pre-marital sex an outrage.[12] 'We are commonly
dressed, and commonly behave as if we had no genitalia....
Taboos and prohibitions have grown up around that very
necessary part of human anatomy. It seems to me that in the
nineteenth century and early twentieth-century society of the

West, similar taboos grew up around the nature of man. He was supposed not to have in him, the sad fact of his own cruelty and lust.'[13] It is seen in the hypocritical attitude of the society in Stilbourne. Robert Ewan, Oliver and his family, choose to ignore the travails of the flesh of Evie Babbacombe and Bounce Dawlish. In *Rites of Passage*, Edmund Talbot's amorous peccadilloes with Zenobia are overlooked, while poor Parson Colley's sexual misdemeanour is condemned. So if 'beauty is in the eye of the beholder, why then, so is everything else.'[14] We can invert it and say ugliness or evil lies in the eye of the beholder. So the greatest evil is not just violence, war, sexual depravity or fanaticism in religion, but intolerance of folly in erring humans. The charity child, Samuel Mountjoy, is scared of the furtive advances of Father Watts-Watt, the homosexual clergyman, who, in turn, is suspicious of the boy switching on the light bulb. The ugly mistrust and the child's fear of being molested are felt.[15]

Whatever the nature of the sexual impulse in whatever direction it is pointed, it seems, in Golding's works, to be as much pain as it is pleasure. Moreover, sex never seems is to be integrated as part of the whole man or woman. It remains something which takes over, subdues the will, and forces the subject, often against his own intention, to comply with a compulsion over which he has no control.[16] We see that it is invariably a degradation, a descent into the nether world of instinct (Id) and bestiality, never an exalted feeling or an act of grace. It is part of the sinful nature of man, secretive, shameful and seamy, to be suppressed and indulged in against his better self. Young Edmund Talbot pens a veritable rhapsody in honour of the frivolously dressed whore, Zenobia Brocklebank. He foresees that 'we were about to embark on a familiar set of steps in an ancient dance.'[17] Viewed through his own libidinal eyes, his seduction of Zenobia in his hutch (cabin) is only a 'tropical madness.'[18] His sexual ardour cooled, he scorns Zenobia's fear of the French and records pompously in his journal, 'I must rouse myself from too dull a view of the farmyard transactions by which our wretched species is lugged into-daylight.'[19] The psychological effect of Edmund's permissiveness is a feeling of guilt, remorse, and disgust that leads him to question whether the brief, feverish pleasure was worth it? A moral degradation of the sex act is evil. Reviewing Zenobia's coy, theatrical manner of surrender, Edmund deduces that she would suit the servile chaplain, Colley, and he wantonly pairs them as 'Beatrice and Benedict' of Shakespeare's *Much Ado about Nothing*.

Sex is a complex socio-biological activity compounded of love and lust. Love is profoundly animal and yet beautiful in the sentiments of tenderness, chivalry and romance, while lust is carnal passion, bestial and often destructive.[20] It is shouted that animals have instinct and men, in that place, have intelligence...instinct should be unconscious; intelligence conscious. Love is the supreme instinct.[21] Have men then lost their instinct to live, preserve and protect life? Man is a prey to his own progress and environment. Our minds, it seems, are the playthings of our bodies, our bodies of their environment.[22] Golding traces the link between a diseased society and a sick man. 'I believe that the condition of man was to be a morally diseased creation.'[23] So he goes on to analyse his diseased nature in his novels. From the authoritarian killer, Jack, pitted against the idealist Ralph in *Lord of the Flies*, to Sophy, the sadist, in *Darkness Visible*, we have a rich harvest of eccentric egocentrics who wreck the lives of those around them. Wilfred Barclay, the pompous porno-novelist, whose alter-ego is Tucker, his would be biographer financed by Halliday, the molester-Satan incarnate. Each unique character is a carefully researched type of personality, whose abnormality becomes both a strength and weakness in a crisis.[24]

A personality reacts, explodes, undergoes cataclysmic changes due to causality in human experience. In Wilfred Barclay's adamant refusal to fulfil Rick Tucker's aspiration to be his Boswell, we can sense a novelist's deep-rooted dislike of being pigeon-holed! Money and sex can be used as a weapon to blackmail and oppress others. In his relentless pursuit of Barclay, Rick would offer his girl-wife, Mary Lou, the double entendre in '"Wilf, you and Mary Lou should have a beautiful relationship. After all she majored...."'[25] Barclay, the callous, ageing artist evades any attempts at exposing his erotic personal life. Tucker exploits his weakness for women. Mary Lou tries to seduce Barclay on the starlit balcony, so that her husband, Rick, will get biographer's rights. Barclay

almost falls into the 'Venus flytrap'...'Right from the soles of
my feet, there swelled...rage. To know myself accepted, endured
not even as in honest whoredom, for money, but for paper!'[26]
It is fear of being shown up as a hollow pulp writer that sends
Barclay fleeing in terror from young Rick Tucker. The evil of a
depraved sex life in his youth hounds Barclay. His amours with
Lucinda, the sex genius—the very memory of it makes him
shrink in horror from publicity. The knowledge that it is too
late to reconcile morality and sex in his life dawns on Barclay.
What example can an immoral man set for his readers?

Boyd feels that Barclay deserves to be killed 'a fittingly
rotten end for a rotten novelist.' 'Barclay tries to escape, run
away from the darkness of revelation, the knowledge that he
is leading inexorably toward damnation after death, comes to
Barclay on an isle, one of the Lipari Islands, to which he
has fled in his mad fugue from Rick Tucker and his own
past.'[27]

Golding's nautical trilogy has raw realism in the poetic
description of the smiles and furies of the Protean ocean, the
vitality of the shipboard dramas and the sea-change the
characters undergo. Parson Colley is drawn into a whirlpool
of vulgar rites of passage while 'crossing the line'[28] resulting
in the evil torture of a nightmare darkness, judgement and a
guilt induced suicide. Young Talbot comprehends the horror
of Colley's mental persecution only as he reads his letter to
his sister. 'What a man does defiles him, not what is done by
others. My shame, though it burns, has been inflicted on
me.'[29] Colley regrets committing fellatio with Roger the burly
sailor, below deck, under the influence of rum. Colley's daring
act of liberating himself from the cassock, drinking with the
crew, singing with them, and the final display of manhood in
his public micturation is part of breaking free from convention.[30]
The existence of the unconscious is the result of repression.
According to psycho-analysis, the unconscious is a region of
the mind, the content of which is characterised by the attribute
of being repressed, conative, instinctive, unreasoning and
predominantly sexual.[31] Golding ruthlessly explores the lapses
(sexual) of his ecclesiastical characters, who, beneath the
gown of God, are as weak, vulnerable and erring as any
ordinary mortals. Jocelin's phallic fantasy (the spire) is more

real when we understand his secret lust for red-haired Goody Pangall, the impotent cripple Pangall's wife.

Havelock Ellis scientifically exploded psychological myths of spirits and liberated the Victorian age from its thraldom of sex taboos. He rightly states that 'So, foolish and ignorant persons may deplore the full development which the sexual instinct has reached in civilized man; to a finer insight and indissolubly linked...to all that is best in human life.'[32] Such people have a dry and shrivelled personality; their attitude towards life is unbalanced and their sex tendencies are generally abnormal.

Edmund Talbot's physical voyage to Sydney from Liverpool is more of a psychological voyage of self-discovery. His casual attitude to sex is drastically changed by the deaths of Colley and Wheeler. Edmund's envy of Lieutenant Benét's secret amours leads him to investigate the young man's poetic passion for Lady Somerset, Mrs. Prettiman and the ship! He freely condemns Benét to be a flirt. He finally gets the truth from Marion, that the golden-haired boy penning panegyrics is only a sentimental mother-complex boy like Sammy, who craves for affection from older women.[33] Edmund realizes that his sexual jealousy of Benét's popularity made him presume ill of his conduct. The devious cunning human projects his sexual fantasies on another![34]

His assessment of a number of people like Colley, Benét and the Prettimans backfires on him! Edmund feels disgusted with the engagement of the middle-aged Miss Granham and the elderly Prettiman. 'Christening, marrying, and burying— they are the marks which distinguish men from beasts, that is all.'[35] His cynical approach is part of his own sexual frustration at losing Marion Chumley, his beloved. 'There was something particularly disgusting about the furtive middle-aged sexual congress! He might well be fifty years old, and she—...Filthy, beastly, lecherous!'[36] Lusty Talbot can only see sex in marriage. He is ignorant of the need for companionship, tenderness, and love in wedlock! This constant prejudice and condemnation of Edmund confirms our knowledge of his own inadequacy. Presumption is evil! Edmund revises his hasty opinions about his fellow-men.

He learns from Lt. Summers about the archetypal nature of ships—the mother-image (ships carry the crew in their womb to safety). '"Ships ar you know. But I understand women. I understand their passivity, gentleness, receiving impressions as in wax—most of all, their passionate need to give."'[37] The sensuous imagery of the sea as a powerful force is masterfully figured by Golding in *Lord of the Flies*, (the wild sea at Castle rock is the earth mother Oa, who takes Simon into her womb).[38] In *Pincher Martin*, 'the sucking, gurgling...liquid-like appetite...a singing hiss..., subtle, unending friction' has disturbed sexual overtones to Pincher lying on the rock.[39] Golding has publicly acknowledged his admiration for the Swedish psychoanalyst, Carl Jung. 'He gave the freedom that I wanted.'[40] The interrelated nature of life in modern times includes the 'hierarchic order, this includes sex and death as the alternative rhythms of Gaia, the earth mother.... As Jung put it, the psyche and matter dwell in the same world. That is, they react as well as co-exist. Jung related this to the world of dreams, archetypes and the racial unconscious.'[41]

Every novel of Golding's becomes a life voyage of self-discovery, a journey from innocence to knowledge and awareness. He begins at the point of pre-knowledge, before self-awareness, science, rationality, Freud and evolution made man journey into himself and lose his joy of life to Evil, without and within. Golding is fascinated by the evidence 'that human consciousness is a biological asset purchased at a price, the price is the knowledge of evil. This evil emanates from the human mind, a product of its action upon the environment.'[42]

Golding's years as a school master in Bishop Wordsworth's school at Salisbury,[43] gave him the penetrating psychological insight into the behaviour and minds of school boys at the pre-puberty and adolescent stages of life. He defends the innocent, ignorant child. His perspective almost all along is that of the victimised child in an adult world of evil knowledge. We see Ralph, twelve plus, not 'old enough for adolescence to have made him awkward,' strong, but with a 'mildness about his mouth that proclaimed no devil.'[44] There are serious repercussions of the games the 'Biguns and the Littleuns' play. 'The games that "Biguns" and "Littleuns" play become more and more grim and serious as we advance, through the novel.'[45] Idealist Ralph, who stands for Ego and intelligence cannot understand the incipient sadism of the (Id and Lust epitomised) boys Jack and Roger in breaking Piggy's specs. Ralph tries to rationalise the dread of the beast neither the snakes, nor the creepers but, the dead parachutist on the hill.[46] He tries to exorcise the terrors of the littleuns and discovers 'dirt' and 'decay' in their bunch of 'salt caked savages.'[47] He realises with 'a fall of heart'[48] that this enchanted Eden is soured; trapped as they are in the evil web of their own lust, barbarism and hate. He suffers a crisis of conscience as fear of the evil beast engulfs him.[49] Ralph longs to be rescued and escape the evil fate of Simon and Piggy.[50]

We have two great vital drives in us, the self-preservation drive and the procreation drive. The sadism of rebellious youngsters is a form of latent sexuality that has not yet developed physiologically and psychologically. But, the thrill of the pig-hunt has explicit sexual undertones of the kill '...and the hunters followed, wedded to her in lust...she squealed and bucked and the air was full of sweat and noise and blood and terror...the sow collapsed under them and they were heavy and fulfilled upon her.'[51] Having satisfied their blood-lust, Jack and the hunters go from outrage to outrage in their regression from civilization to barbarism.

The twentieth-century psychologists exploded the Victorian dictum that children should be seen and not heard. It brought about a revolution in our comprehension of the child, who is a passionate being with sensuous drives and fantasies that make his life dramatic.[52] Samuel Mountjoy the precocious bastard-hero of *Free Fall* implicitly believes in the romantic fantasies that his existentialist mother weaves about his father that he is a soldier, an officer in R.A.F. We neither believed it but the glittering myth lay in the middle of the dirty floor, accepted with gratitude as beyond my own timid efforts at invention.[53]

A mother complex boy, Sammy hotly defends her morals in the Rotten Row slums. He condemns modern, aseptic intercourse as loveless and believes that 'this elephantine woman shared pleasure like a maternal pacifier,' who indulged in sex naturally 'without benefit of psychology, romance or religion.'[54] Golding's irony about the hypocrisy of permissiveness is clear. No matter how fat and unkempt she is, Sammy's sense of security is replete. 'She is the warm darkness between me and the cold light. She is the end of the tunnel, she.'[55] His present guilt (of the adult Sammy) and hate of his unknown father, 'a speck,...no heart...as soulless as a guided missile'[56] underlies his deep feeling of insecurity.

Blissfully oblivious of the squalor of Paradise Hill, Sammy lives in Shelley's 'dome of many-splendoured glass.' Poverty and dirt never bother him long as he has his mother's love. His litany on his mother echoes his worship, and fierce loyalty towards her. Sammy is thrilled and scared of Evie, (who escorts him to school) boasting that she is sometimes a boy and can pee higher than other boys. Her 'penis envy'[57] and desire to sexually dominate the orphan Sammy is evident. When Minnie, the Mongol child pisses in fear at school, Sammy is secretly delighted at the scandal, 'She was animal down there, and we all up here.'[58] The scatological reference is fraught with deep irony here.

His childhood remains unscarred. 'But there were the days of terrible and irresponsible innocence.'[59] He and Johnny trespass into the General's garden—the silvery cedar tree was 'an apocalypse.' 'This is an Eden because it is illuminated from within by the light of Innocence; it is as true of the whole world of childhood as it is true of the hospital ward that remembered they shine. Innocence is the nature of the Being described, and it cannot be changed—it is useless to look here for the beginning of responsibility.'[60] Sammy freely admits that he was 'innocent of guilt, unconscious of innocence; happy, therefore, and unconscious of happiness.'[61] '"I am looking for the beginning of responsibility, the beginning of darkness, the point where I began."'[62]

On the one hand we can bear out the Freudian argument that the child is a little criminal and pervert who only matures as his libido evolves. Hence the portrait of the 'Sinful Child' who cannot reconcile the pleasure principle with the reality principle.[63] On the other hand we have the Adlerian approach that '...every child becomes conscious of his inability to cope single-handed with the challenge of existence. This feeling of inferiority is the driving force, the starting-point from which every childish striving originates. It determines the very goal of his existence.'[64] The early stirrings of rebellion, sadism, daring and aggression are rooted in the tyranny the child is subjected to by the adult world. Sammy's friend Philip is a prime example of a natural selection a born bully who 'liked to inflict pain and a catastrophe was his orgasm.'[65] He challenges Sammy to defile the altar by outrage of pissing on it. Fear and bravado conflict in Sammy and he can only bring himself to spit on the altar.[66] Caught red-handed in the dark, Sammy is drawn into the vortex of suffering for his sin, mastoiditis, then hospitalisation, his mother's death and adoption by a homo sexual clergyman, Father Watts-Watt[67] '...a small boy's existing fear of darkness exacerbated by adult attempts to deprive him of early access to light,...a horrific bathroom , a paranoiac obsession.'[68] The very point of Sammy's confession is to contrast the physical dirt, friendly darkness, open sex of Rotten Row (that held no mortal terror for little Sammy) with the metaphorical dirt, sinister darkness of the unknown and shameful sex of the unholy house of Father Watts-Watt.

The familiar dark of the open lavatories, the pokey house of Paradise Hill do not scare Sammy like the gleaming brass bathtub, the menacing figure of the clergyman.[69] Samuel's queer memories of various darknesses are buried in his subconscious as he grows up. They are repressed, but they continue to bother him, whenever bed and darkness are experienced. The torture of the darkness of the closet in the concentration camp is a climaxing of the darkness of neurosis developed in Sammy from childhood.[70]

The psychopathology of Samuel's terror of the wet rag in the darkness of the centre (of the broom closet) is his fear of castration as retribution for his sexual outrage of Beatrice.[71] His memory recalls from the subliminal self, the 'gold mine of the happiness of Rotten Row' and the 'rubbish heap' of the priest's house.[72]

Golding mirrors the stark reality of the victimisation of children, 'born to sorrow' as he admits to John Carey, '...I didn't know it but I was thinking of them in the sixteenth or seventeenth century sense that childhood is a disease you

know; its a sickness that you grow out of.'[73] The persecution of
Samuel by Miss Pringle, the orthodox, prim, cruel, middle-
aged scripture teacher is unpardonable. She deliberately
humiliates the poor charity child and wounds his sensitive
ego in front of the whole class.[74] Bounce Dawlish's father is
an evil adult, a Barrett-like monster who canes his daughter,
when teaching her music.[75] The adult Bounce suffers from
unrequited passion for Henry, goes stark raving mad and
parades the streets of Stilbourne clad only in socks and
shoes[76] (a shocking act of defiance and liberation like Colley's
in *Rites of Passage*.) Finally she immolates herself in her house
as the crowning act of outrage against her frustrated self.[77]
Mattie Michael, the burnt ugly boy is ill-treated by
Mr. Pedigree the 'gay' master who has a penchant for cultivating
sweet looking boys.[78] A healthy sexual urge in childhood can
be perverted by the evil selfish acts of adults, who impose
taboos on the child egging him on to take revenge as he grows
up. Miss Dawlish declares that 'she would rather save a
budgie than a child from a fire.'[79] Henry exploits her passion
for him to serve his own greedy ends. Golding explains how
life had warped her joy; humanity had betrayed her, and she
becomes an inhuman person.

Golding is convinced of Original Sin in the Augustinian
way. 'It is Augustine isn't it, who was born a twin, and his
earliest memory was pushing his twin from his mother's
breast? I think that because children are helpless and vulnerable,
the most terrible things can be done by children...we confuse
it with innocence.... But I still think the root of our sin is there,
in the child.'[80] It is clear that Golding cannot escape the roots
of his own Christian upbringing. For him Original Sin is
selfishness, lust, and cruelty. He admits that only through
education in acts of altruism are children capable of an 'absolute,
passionate, profound love.'[81] The 'universal pessimist' in Golding
is revealed in the degeneration of the boys into savagery,[82]
while the 'cosmic optimist'[83] is seen in Mr. Pedigree's death,[84]
Mr. Prettiman's recovery[85] and Samuel Mountjoy's newfound
freedom.[86] Golding is full of hope for the redemption of mankind,
he refuses to be insular and so some critics have found his
moral insights not particularly original or striking as his
imagination cannot cope with the dualism of matter and spirit.

It has no sense of the 'world's body.'[87] Some critics find him original and memorable among modern writers, who have analysed the dilemma of modern man. 'He simply shakes us until we feel in our bones the perennial agony of our species.'[88]

Goldings compassion for the fallen creature is infinite. The treatment of the hallucinations of Pincher Martin's consciousness—the egocentric claws terrified of God's mercy and annihilation is tragic.[89] His characters are either innocent or full of knowledge.[90] Golding's favourite protagonist is one poised on the 'brink of adolescence.'[91] He is discovered in Samuel Mountjoy, Mattie, Ralph, Oliver and Simon. At some point, knowledge casts its mantle of guilt on them and they become guilt-ridden adults, still immature. 'Knowledge and innocence exist in him (*i.e.*, Ralph) in an exquisite poise; Ralph experiences, as well as a child can the fall through the air.'[92]

In *The Inheritors*, the nexus between the savage and the 'civilised' man is explored.[93] The reader is constantly being reminded that the new men are outwardly superior, stronger, scientific but, in reality, weaker, more sadistic, full of sexual aberrations, irrational, and inferior in spirit than the Neanderthalers. They erred innocently and ignorantly, we commit crimes and revel in them.[94] *The Inheritors* is a complete subversion of H.G. Wells's view of homo-sapiens as heroes and conquerors. The picture-perception world of the Neanderthalers is a dream of innocence, rudely disrupted by the evil in the new men.[95] The cultural values of the uncivilised world can protect man against his own evil self. It is the refinement of civilisation that can lead him into greater perversions and unhealthy complexes.[96]

Every fall drives the simple-minded, good-hearted Neanderthalers towards violence, knowledge and evil. Sex and parenthood are shared without jealousy. Lok and Fa find 'lying together' natural. Only when Liku is lost, despair drives Lok to an act of violent frustrated sex with Fa. In dreadful contrast, Lok and Fa see the drunken sexual orgy of Tuami and the fat woman, a wolfish sadistic coupling, which appears to be an act of gorging rather than sharing love and tenderness more like Sodom and Gomorrah.[97] The novel is seen as, 'the tension between two stages of human growth, the sensuous subhuman, innocent Lok is contrasted with the intellectual guilt of the cunning Vivani.'[98]

As Golding speaks through Sammy, in *Free Fall*, 'But we are neither the innocent nor the wicked. We are the guilty we fall down. We crawl on hands and knees. We weep and tear each other.'[99] Man cannot escape the vortex of evolution, progress and destruction. Golding's final judgement on the conflict of innocence and sexual knowledge is impartial. 'The people's plunge to extinction by the fall is necessary to the progress of the New Men beyond it.... The Sculptor, Tuami (you love) finds a way to voyage beyond the fall to a creative knowledge of good through evil, perceptible only to a consciousness newly aware of guilt, but offering a password to go forward.'[100]

Freud understood that a paradise of instinctual satisfaction is impossible, for man cannot develop any culture completely. Culture needs conditioning of desires, a curb on one's instincts leading to sublimation. Love and understanding can help man adapt himself to the fast changing world of values and mores. Freud's sympathies are on the side of culture, not the paradise of primitivism. Nevertheless, his concept of history has a tragic element. Human progress necessarily leads to repression and neurosis. Man cannot have both happiness and progress.[101]

Golding is no longer dogmatic, having eaten of the tree of knowledge, and shed his innocence for experience.[102] He knows there are no distinct spheres of black and white; there is only grey—an amalgam of good and evil, which man has to reconcile himself to.[103]

In *Darkness Visible*, we see that despite the corrupting influence of a permissive society that uses and abuses knowledge for its own evil ends—in Sophy, who is a sadist, terrorist whore and kidnapper of children for sexual molestation, unsung saints like Matty survive, who suffer persecution and still radiate LOVE. The metaphysical implication of the tripartite, trinity-like structure of the novel, Matty, Sophy and One-is-One indicates that good and evil are not absolutes, but reconcilable. The novel is one sustained 'Walpurgisnacht' of horror starting

with the incendiary birth of Matty from a 'burning bush' of
blitzed London, to the fire monster that saves the kidnapped
child from the holocaust of the bombed school. It examines
the different thirsts and appetites that man is a prey to.
Golding traces this vulnerability of man in the novel back to
the Bible.[104]

We have a crop of psychotic characters who appear normal
outwardly. Set in the sinful sixties of permissive sex, freedom
from restraint and the rise of terrorism, Golding studies the
abuse of vulnerable children and, 'the darkness is most intense
in the realm of Eros.'[105] Golding concentrates on aspects of
human sexuality '...presents the age of free love and "doing
your own thing" as one of particular and extreme depravity,
of terrible crimes against innocence.'[106] The bottled up
repressions of the Victorian Age that injure Bounce Dawlish
burgeon in the bizarre affairs of shrewd Sophy, the malignant
witch of *Darkness Visible*.

Matthew, the scarred hero constantly runs away from
objects of desire. The chestnut haired Venus, Miss Aylen of
the florist shop rouses a 'pure hot anguish'[107] in him. He
craves for affection and love and scorns the pity and sympathy
that people offer him. He finds it difficult to comprehend his
own desire and loathing—part of any adolescent's sexual
growth.[108] Matthew escapes from the temptations of Hanrahn's
harem of seven girls to Australia, where an Aborgine's assault
is almost a ritual castration. The vet says, '"He's ruined your
family jewels."'[109] Matty has to surrender his ego, his thirsts
and serve others in love. Sophy and Toni, the motherless
Stanhope girls are delegated to the stables by the latest
surrogate mother, Winnie. The jealous girls (fiercely possessive
of their father—Electral complex)[110] triumphantly dismiss Winnie
when Toni catches her 'in flagrante delicto' with Uncle Jim.
Sophy's adolescent sexual urges drive her to ensnare a roadside
romeo into deflowering her. She wonders at the poetry
and splendour of love and sex. For her, it is a trivial act of
disenchantment.

Like Lucifer depicted in all his magnificent evil revenge
and hate,[111] Golding achieves a compelling allure in the portrayal
of Sophy, the presiding 'Rakshashi'[112] of *Darkness Visible*. This
Queen of Darkness plumbs Stygian depths of depravity by

wielding sexual power over men like Gerry, Fido, Edwin and
Sim. She kisses Fido goodbye and wills her scent into him[113]
like a bitch on heat. The canine parallels in the novel are
disgustingly apt. She makes the doglike Fido a pawn in her
deadly kidnapping game. Gerry and Sophy could be twins.
Sophy's orgasm is linked to physical outrage and Gerry's
libidinosity is aroused by dangerous crimes. Their 'wounded,
experimental, libidinous, long, slow and greedy'[114] act of
loveless coupling is triggered off by tension in contemplating
an evil act.

Sophy, 'the avenging angel' accidentally discovers that
pleasure in pain gives her an orgasm.[115] She cultivates a sado-
masochistic delight and power in sex. Her libidinous lover,
Gerry, is awed by her perverted will-power. Buried deep
within her is her perverted Electra complex for her father. She
brazenly offers herself to him, '"you'll need, I mean you can
say sex is trivial but what do you do about it, I mean...."'[116] His
cold shocked decline and confession is a harsh truth of human
depravity.[117] We see filial love crucified in hate and neglect.
The very sanctity of family ties can be muddied by the travails
of the flesh.

Sim Goodchild, the bookshop owner, is a nymphomaniac,
who lures the charming Stanhope girls into his shop, all the
better to see them! Edwin Bell, the retired schoolmaster (we
see shades of Golding in him) is wed to Edwina, a doctor.
They're an odd couple; her hair is shorter than Edwin's. He
is snore effeminate and she is more manly![118] Sim and Edwin
experience an avid curiosity about the sexual adventures of
Sophy. Golding flays Sim and Edwin for their hypocritical
morality, a veneer of refinement not even skin deep! Their
projected thirst for sex visualises a 'Brothel Pink' in Sophy's
digs, 'Sexual games' and the 'perverted chair!' Their lurid
imagination runs riot in Sophy's stables as they explore it in
sinful glee.[119]

Sophy, the sex ogress masterminds the arson and the
kidnapping of a child. Her horrible hallucination of the orgiastic
murder which she longs to commit is averted by Matty, the
Saviour. Sim admits his guilty thoughts, 'Nevertheless, I am
guilty. My fruitless lust clotted the air and muffled the sounds
of the real world.'[120] Those who have sinned in thought, word

and deed are equally indicted. Too much repression is as dangerous to a human bèing's welfare as too much licence. In Sophy's vision of the 'black sunrise,' Golding is prophetically striking a note of doom as in W.B. Yeats's *The Second Coming*.[121] Has civilisation reached its nadir? Clearly the veil of flesh screens the depravity of Sophy from Sim and Edwin. The deceptive virtues of beauty, brains and breeding are characteristic of an unholy wisdom. It is a disease of our modern age that uncaring attitudes towards children, a mechanical approach to human relations warp the individual's psychology and lead to neurosis. Sophy and Matty are the typical fanatic byproducts of our soulless age.

Sophy only cares for money and the power that it brings her. She sells her body. Whoring is a sacred act for her as begging or thieving is to some.[122] Matty sublimates his desires and achieves peace through self-sacrifice. In redeeming Pedigree, the spirit of the Messiah, Matty shows his love and tolerance. Pedigree cannot help being a 'gay.' He is a prisoner of 'life's lavatory.'[123]

Golding demands from us an evolution in the positive understanding of the riddle of man. Modern psychologists are deeply concerned with crises in human behaviour and try to find solutions to human problems. 'Modern cognitive psychology is underpinned by one of the most recent psychological metaphors—man, the computer, the information processor.'[124] Mr. Stanhope Sophy's father sits before his machine oblivious of the sexual outrages his daughters are involved in and he himself is a sex-starved specimen. Clearly the constraints and pressures of modern life warp the human's healthy sexual growth. Harmless old men like Sim and Edwin are drawn into the web of sex crimes without even being aware of it. Is Golding trying to tell us that the pleasures of sex are indulged in as a form of escapism to compensate for energies not channelised? As a custodian of culture, does Golding attribute psychomacy to the corrupting influence of a soulless society? The powerful neurotic playwright, Tennessee Williams confessed, 'All my life I have been haunted by the obsession that to desire a thing or to love a thing intensely is to place yourself in a vulnerable position to be a possible, if not a probable loser of what you most want.'[125]

On reviewing the romantic aspirations of Samuel Mountjoy Oliver, and Pincher Martin interesting tendencies are revealed. In meeting Beatrice Ifor (I for!), Sammy finds himself, darkness and responsibility in a new dimension of knowledge. Having lost Ma, Evie and childhood, young Sammy is in a frenzy of love-hate to possess the beautiful Beatrice. His artistic appreciation of 'the secret treasures of her body,'[126] is mixed up with his mad jealousy of her womanly mystery. His insane desire to divine her femininity and identify himself with her, finds expression in a carnal conquest.[127] Beatrice's 'nun-like innocence,' her fear of religious taboos makes her a 'victim on the rack.'[128] Sammy's first effort at seduction is a fiasco. Later, Beatrice clings to him, 'Her contribution, after the heroic sacrifice, was negative. Death of a maiden head pays for all.'[129] It is the detached artist in Paul and Sammy who is repulsed by the suffocating possessiveness of the women. Beatrice becomes a clinging ivy, and makes Sammy feel guilty. 'Step by step we descended the path of sexual exploitation until the projected sharing had become an infliction.'[130]

Sexuality is a central passion, a biological need of man.[131] Sammy discards the deflowered Beatrice and marries Taffy, the councillor's daughter, to satisfy his sexual passion. Golding does not celebrate the 'dark passion of man.'[132] He is serious and chastises man for his crudity, his exploitation of women, his irresponsible sexual aberrations. He analyses the evil repercussions of such crimes. Sammy's rejection of Beatrice, drives her insane, and we find the charming woman transformed into an incontinent hag in the asylum, in the end.[133] This casual brutal use of woman by man to slake his lust, is evil. 'We are all civilized people, which means that we are all savages at heart but observing a few amenities of civilized behaviour.'[134] This exploitation, persecution and remorse-guilt complex is not new to man.

'In my too susceptible mind, sex dressed itself in gorgeous colours, brilliant and evil. I was in that glittering net...as the silk moths...spurted the pink musk of their mating. Musk, Shameful and heady, be thou my good.'[135] The root cause of this animal behaviour is repression. Sammy feels a subconscious need to take revenge on the world for the raw deal he got in life.

Man seeks pleasure in the pain of others to assuage his own thirst and discontent caused by deprivation in early life. '...the contemporary generation increasingly refuses to subscribe to the sexual restraints and taboos of the last generation...the doctrine of "Let us eat and drink, for to-morrow we die," at once concrete and definite is eagerly embraced...such an attitude...involves for the youth of the twentieth century a contemptuous abandonment of those restraints which the nineteenth century complacently termed its "morals."'[136]

It is dangerous to thwart instincts, drives and repress unconscious desires, for much of the hysteria and neurosis of our age is due to the repression of natural desires in youth. Oliver in *The Pyramid* is a typical case in point. He is at the hub of the sexual wheel of Stilbourne with 'its shames and idylls.'[137] Young Oliver is depressed by his infatuation for Imogen, 'a stupid, insensitive, vain woman.'[138] Golding understands the frustration of youth, 'Eighteen is a good time for suffering. One has all the necessary strength and no defences.'[139] While he fantasises about rescuing Imogen in his dreams, he helps the erotic Evie Babbacombe to escape detection from her clandestine affair with Robert Ewan, Oliver's handsome rival and rich neighbour.[140] Evie, the tart, with her ball-bearinged walk is the Town Crier, Sergeant Babbacombe's daughter.[141] His hopeless passion for Imogen and his ennui (prior to his going to Oxford) make him pursue his secondary sexual target relentlessly.[142] Each time he is thwarted by the 'femme fatale,' Oliver vents his spleen on the piano at home.[143] He feels like a caveman primitively aroused to club his girl. Taking advantage of Bobby's accident, Oliver lures the slut into the dark woods to seduce her. Evie orders the reluctant Greenhorn to 'get on with it.'[144] Oliver feels a newfound peace and, a 'good darkness' at his 'perilous onanism.'[145]

Oliver is shocked by Evie's insatiable appetite for sex. She seems Salome, Mata Hari all rolled into one. It is only dread at the shameful consequences of his lust that curbs his passion. In helpless rage, Evie cries, '"Nobody wants me, just my damned body. And I'm damned and you're damned with your cock and your cleverness and your chemistry...."'[146] Oliver discovers with a shock that Captain Wilmot has been sadistically lashing her. He realises that lust as a cold appetite can be callous, unscrupulous and unjust to the victim. He realises that here is a woman ill-used and wretched and pities her.[147] Yet he scorns her in comparison with Imogen...'this object, on an earth that smelt of decay, with picked bones and natural cruelty—life's lavatory.'[148] 'Beasts or not,'[149] Oliver still pursues Evie and is secretly watched by his father.[150] Oliver's awareness of the monster of repressed sex is further enlightened during his music lessons with Miss Bounce Dawlish, the severe spinster.[151] Released from the oppression of her father's power, Bounce wears frills and leaves her hair loose.[152] Oliver's normal sexuality is juxtaposed against the abnormal states of Bounce, Evelyn De Tracy, Captain Wilmont, Evie and others. Evie revels in the power she exercises over Oliver with her sexual charms. She enslaves him and uses him to ventilate her grievance against the beastly world of men.

The corrosive power of evil sex and the problems related to indulgence and permissiveness are honestly reviewed by Golding. 'This is perhaps the main function of the otherwise negative list of sexual aberrations scattered through the book: fornication, pederasty, flagellation,...incest, transvestism, homosexuality...and finally, the perversions of affection produced in poor Bounce by frustration at many levels.'[153]

Set against a stagnant list of depraved humans, Oliver's, responses are healthy. Since it is his self-knowledge that is enhanced by discovering these queers, he alone evolves. Golding's message is lucid—Change is the summum bonum of all existence. Not to change, spells extinction, and stagnation is death to the human spirit. One step in the wrong direction could spell disaster, as in the case of the demented, pathetic suicide of the sex-starved Bounce Dawlish.[154] Only growing personalities like Oliver can offer hope to Stilbourne (Still born)![155] The deadness of spirit and lack of human contact is revealed through the fact that there is a large degree of voyeurism in the light opera. The gratification it gives the performers suggests that its effects are masturbatory. The great annual event of the Stilbourne Operatic society's musical concert is a battle-ground of the sexist classes. Golding's use of subtle puns and other figurative devices make the novel a Freudian frolic.[156] Bounce Dawlish's pose that Heaven is Music is exploded in her casting off her chastity belt and liberating herself from the inhibitions of the decadent world of Stilbourne.[157]

The sexual perversions hinted at in the novel, *The Pyramid*, are deliberately explored to emphasise the hypocrisy of a society that is strait-laced by outmoded conventions and that takes an evil delight in the neuroses of some of the people. Oliver's father is unenthusiastic about the musical 'King of Hearts' in which Imogen, Oliver, his mother and Evelyn De Tracy are involved. '"Bach," said my father, "Handel, what I enjoy is a good grind."'[158] As rightly observed in an illuminating review...the dimension of mystery shown in a series of brilliantly placed puns or Freudian 'double entendres'—which are very funny, and open up sudden, unexpected and savage depths of meaning.[159] The seething cauldron of repressed hates and jealousies are ventilated in Part II, in which the 'most debased and caricatured forms of class, love or (sex), and music are revealed.'[160] 'With diabolical inevitability, the very desires to act and be passionate, to show off and impress, brought to full flower the jealousies and hatreds, meanness and indignations we were forced to conceal in ordinary life.'[161]

Oliver the protagonist of *The Pyramid* takes a psychological voyage through the labyrinth of life[162] and gratifies his libidinous Id with Evie of the Erotic woods, then outgrows his calf-love for Imogen, puzzled by Evelyn's transvestite homosexuality and Bounce's frustrated passion. He emerges from the maze of the Pyramid, a rounded personality with a prosperous family! The therapeutic effects of sitting within a 1.8m high pyramid structure are being explored by yoga experts.[163] The person within experiences a beneficial effect—physiological and psychological. Perhaps the ancient Egyptians had already unlocked this secret, and Golding is well aware of its curative properties, in the metaphor of Oliver's evolution.

Bounce Dawlish's cruel impatience with young Oliver has echoes of Miss Pringle's persecution of Sammy in *Free Fall*. 'She ruled, not by love but fear. Her weapons were unfair and vicious. They were teeny arch sarcasms that made the other children giggle and tore the flesh. She was past-master of crowd psychology and momentum.'[164]

Pincher Martin is the very epitome of GREED in all respects (lust, cupidity, avarice, covetousness). He is 'a predator, I would prowl the forest of flesh and attach myself to nobody.'[165] A man of today corresponds more or less to the collective moral ideal, has made his heart into a den of murderers.[166] His material progress has driven him away from nature, his education has repressed his instinctive nature and civilised him only outwardly, leaving a polished shell with a hollow interior. 'Anything that weakens his repression may loosen an outburst of violence, or result in chaotic and disorderly behaviour.... Hence the familiar alignment of the unconscious and the conscious may lead to a neurosis or a psychosis.'[167] Pincher Martin tries to be only a mouth, a body; while Jocelin attempts to be only a soul, an instrument in the hands of God. Both suffer from the debilitating delusion of pride, power and arrogance in self. In both novels Golding explores the dark tunnel[168] of the repressed desires of Pincher and Jocelin. 'And of course eating with the mouth was only the gross expression of what was a universal process you could eat with your cock or your fists, or with your voice.'[169] Pete, the producer, offers him the role of Greed in the play as he fits the bill so well. 'He takes the best part, the best seat, the most money, the best woman. He was born with his mouth and his flies open and both hands out to grab. His is the cosmic case of bugger who gets his penny and someone else's bun.'[170]

Jocelin, the Dean of Salisbury, is full of pride and joy at planning the four hundred foot spire. As he prays, he feels a presence behind him, his guardian angel! *'Lord: I thank Thee that thou hast kept me humble!'*[171] Golding's italics clearly indicate that Jocelin is hardly humble. He is wrapped up in himself and his folly that he has no time to talk to Father Adam. '"...One forgets you are there so easily!"—"I shall call you Father Anonymous!"'[172]

He senses the secret undercurrents of attraction between Goody and Roger—'But there was no angel; only the tides of feeling, swirling, pricking, burning—a horror of the burgeoning evil thing, from birth to senility with its ghastly and complex strength between.'[173] He is pleased that Roger's affair with Goody will keep him building His Spire! As Jocelin prays, he cannot ignore 'his unruly member,' the model of the spire is used phallus-like by the workers to mock the impotent Pangall in an obscene dance. Pincher also recollects the idea that 'A sword is a phallus,' and then inverts it to 'A phallus is a sword.'[174] Roger Mason mocks Jocelin and the spire in the end, '"Fall when you like, me old cock!"' to Jocelin.[175]

Both Pincher and Jocelin are obsessed; the former openly, the latter guiltily. The phallic symbol is strongly stressed in *The Spire* and *Pincher Martin*. The jagged tooth-like projection that Pincher clings to in Mid-Atlantic is Rockall, as Frank Kermode points out, is reminiscent of an obscene word that rhymes with it.[176] Pincher's hallucination comes from the memory of an aching tooth. 'The tooth extracted from the mouth and rooted in the seabed, is a Freudian symbol of castration, and hence, signifies a loss of manhood, a loss of self, and a loss of centre.'[177] Pincher's fear of annihilation is a dread reality in his hallucination.[178] Is the spire a diagram of prayer or a club, a phallic symbol of Jocelin's sublimated lust for Goody Pangall? The church itself is compared to a man lying down with the spire 'bursting, erupting, springing' from the centre of the building.[179]

While Christopher, the Christ bearer, realises he is a Pincher, a pair of claws, Dean Jocelin, the rapturous priest of God realises he is a mere pagan lecher. Pincher uses others for his own selfish ends. Alfred's girl-friend, Sybil, is laid by him, he tries to rape Mary Lovell and manoeuvers an accident with Peter on his new motorbike to disable him.[180] Pincher is the biggest Maggot in the Maggot Club. He ill uses the young boy, and finally, murders Nat, his best friend, on board the wartime destroyer, *Wildebeeste*.[181] '"Christ, how I hate you. I could eat you. Because you fathomed her mystery, you have a right to handle her...because in your fool innocence you've got what I had to get or go mad."'[182] Jocelin uses Roger, Pangall, Goody, Father Anselm for his folly, Pincher's bold wooing of sex is Jocelin's fear and revulsion of it, though he longs to indulge in it. He feels a 'superior compassion' for Goody, red-haired, beautiful, in the tent of Roger, now 'enciente.' But when he tries to convey his sympathy at Pangall's murder, she backs away in horror, '"Not you, too!"'[183] She can sense his lust and is terrified of the bestiality of Jocelin, the good father being a mere man besieged by earthly desires. Jocelin becomes sullen, moody, haunted by the blazing red hair, 'a mixture of dear love and prurience...a wet-lipped fever to know....'[184] As the spire grows precariously, so does Jocelin's dimension of lust and pride. The spire sways and needs the 'Holy Nail' to fix it.[185] Jocelin dreams of Goody 'naked and sweet in the uncountry.'[186] This experience provokes critics to conjecture '...is he a saint or a destructive monomaniac, self-deceived?'[187]

We can hear Jocelin's unspoken cry of anguish like Hamlet's 'O, that this too solid flesh would melt, Thaw and resolve itself into a dew!'[188] Jocelin's awareness of the frailty of his flesh makes him a human 'man of God.'

The manner in which Pincher and Jocelin exploit others to achieve their ends is part of their psychopathology that blinds them to anything but their own ambitions. Jocelin's repentance is not too late for grace, Pincher faces black lightning and Sammy is partially freed from guilt. 'The mere life of the body, like Pincher's is only half the story. To be only a Mouth is not to be fully human. The denial of the body, on the other hand, and the escape into false spiritual adventures such as Jocelin lives by are equally a lie.'[189] We need to try to live with our weaknesses and reconcile our loyalties, says Golding. We are neither of Heaven (all spirit and perfection), nor are we of Hell (all flesh and imperfection), we, are of this earth, where we have to live with the dichotomy of good and evil. Suffering, pain, and self-discovery are steps towards knowledge that makes for wisdom.

Golding chastises those who adopt a Puritan attitude towards sex. Edwin Bell unctuously declares that Edwina would have 'castrated Pedigree with her own hands if she'd caught him in flagrante delicto.'[190] Pedigree's homosexuality is definitely a lesser evil than Sophy's sexual outrages. And yet we wonder whether this pedophile can be exonerated for his crime in molesting children?[191] His spirited self-defence is pitiful—'"You—talk about my condition—It's a beautiful condition—nobody knows. Are you a psychiatrist? I don't want to be cured...."'[192]

The novelist deliberately embroils himself with a nit-picking finesse in studying the evil traits in human nature. In the characters of Sophy, Evie, Lucinda, he examines the psycho-pathology of sexual love. Generally the portrait of Golding's woman is of the seductress, the eternal Eve. The historic world-view of woman is abysmally low and unheroic at times. She is either a virgin or a whore! It is she who entices man to sin.[193] In the evil grip of middle-aged lust, Wilfred Barclay quakes at the prospect of Lucinda the sex-genius writing her memoirs. 'Dear God, *Domine defende nos!*'[194] With her jiffy camera she captures their amorous poses to gloat over them soon after. It is only the dire threat of contracting venereal disease that makes him flee in terror from this obsessive creature. Barclay wonders why the 'memory of Lucinda in this most permissive age' makes him quiver.[195]

Wilfred Barclay had prostituted his literary genius to become a whore's clown. His attempts to retrieve the obscene letters he wrote to a married woman, Margaret, end in humiliation for him.[196] Paper men like Barclay go to pieces when the battle lines are drawn with their critics, because they lack spiritual strength. One recalls the psychological experience of T.S. Eliot's *The Hollow Men*. The full horror of spiritual stagnation is felt in the 'actively dramatised inner struggle between compulsion and revulsion towards personal change,' as Elizabeth Drew describes it.[197]

A number of critics have pointed out that the prevailing trend in contemporary writing with its obsessive concern with sexuality is not only the result, of a wish *épater le bourgeois* but, more the reflection of a serious battle between the society man has constructed so illogically and badly and the needs of human nature to express themselves more freely sexually and emotionally than the economics or morality of this age will allow.[198] In *Free Fall*, love is replaced by brutal lust and barren sexuality. It is the war that drives men to live only in the present. 'Nothing was permanent, nothing was more than relative. Sex was a private business. Sex was a clinical matter and contraception had removed the need for orthodox family life.'[199]

Does Golding offer any solution? Has he shown the light at the end of the long, dark tunnel of modern sexual perversion, the young angst of the eighties and permissiveness in the twentieth century?[200] He points to the God-given faculty of

'Reason Divine'[201] that can liberate man from the travails of the flesh. Man can sublimate his sexual urges, like Matty in *Darkness Visible*. Nick, the science master sums up the issue neatly. '"But if the Devil had invented man he could'nt have played him a dirtier, wickeder, a more shameful trick than when he gave him sex!"'[202]

Man cannot ignore it but he can live with it as a friendly enemy! If the evil of repressed sexuality is not understood, the price of regression and sudden release is Death or Disaster.[203] A healthy approach is seen in the characters of Oliver and Edmund. Golding favours a Live and Let Live policy in life. Regression is the antithesis of Progression, but it can serve the forward going tendency of personality according to modern psychologists.[204] A radical negative approach is wrong '"this man what d'you call him—these books,—cinema—papers—this sex—its wrong, wrong, wrong!"'[205]

In *Pincher Martin*, Pincher's friends taunt him when drunk. She said, '"Chris, my child, let the ten commandments look after themselves.... But don't drink and don't smoke. Only foke."'[206] Jocelin's feverish curiosity about marital sex makes him listen to Rachel, Roger Mason's wife in *The Spire*. 'When she and Roger went together, at the most inappropriate moment she began to laugh—it wasn't that she was barren.... She stripped the business of living down to where horror and farce took over...striking out in the torture chamber with his pig's bladder on a stick.'[207] A more liberal but firm attitude towards sex is eminently desirable today.[208]

NOTES

1. Edwin Mullins: 'The Visions of William Blake,' *Sunday Telegraph*, 26 February 1978.

2. W. Golding: *Darkness Visible*,

   '"We think we know. Know? That's worse than an atom bomb, and always was."' Ch. 16, 261.

3. W. Golding: *Lord of the Flies*, Ch. 12, 223.

4. John Peter: 'The Fables of William Golding,' Fall, 1957, *Kenyon Review*, xix, 577-592.

5. W. Golding: *The Pyramid*, 63.

   Robert Ewan, the doctor's son in Stilbourne carries on an illicit love affair with sex-pot Evie Babbacombe. She dares him to jump the chalk pit on her red motorbike, resulting in a terrible accident. Rich Robert's

psychological damage to Evie's psyche and her physical injury caused
by her egging on his intemperate passion are part of sexual perversions
caused by permissiveness.

6. David Lodge: 'William Golding,' *Spectator*, No. 7085, Friday, April 10,
    1964, 489.

7. W. Golding: *Free Fall*, Ch. 5, 108.

8. W. Golding: *Pincher Martin*, Ch. 9, 153.

9. *Ibid.*, Ch. 9, 155.

10. *Ibid.*, Ch. 10, 162.

11. *Ibid.*, Ch. 11, 173.

    Christine Manon the ravishing wife of General Ezra Manon in Eugene
    O'Neill's trilogy, *Mourning Becomes Electra* has an adulterous affair
    with Adam Brant, in her husband's absence, involving his puritanical
    New England family in a shocking scandal. This desire to break out of
    the shackles of morality and liberate oneself sexually and socially is
    seen in Golding's Bounce Dawlish, Evie Babbacombe and Sophy.

12. W. Golding: *Free Fall*, Ch. 5, 118.

13. W. Golding: 'Fable,' *The Hot Gates*, 87.

14. W. Golding: 'Belief and Creativity,' *A Moving Target*, 191.

15. W. Golding: *Free Fall*, Ch. 8, 157-161.

16. Anthony Storr: 'Intimations of Mystery,' *William Golding, The Man and
    his Books*, (ed.) John Carey, 140.

17. W. Golding: *Rites of Passage*, 57.

18. *Ibid.*, 90.

19. *Ibid.*, 92.

20. The difference appears in William Shakespeare's 'Venus and Adonis,'
    The Complete Works, 1278.

    'Love comforteth like sunshine after rain,
    But lust's effect is tempest after sun;
    Love's gentle spring doth always fresh remain;
    Lust's winter comes ere summer half be done;
    Love surfeits not: lust like a glutton dies,
    Love is all truth: Lust full of forged lies.' (11. 799-804.)

21. 'And now abideth, faith, hope, charity, these three; but the greatest of
    these is charity.' 1 *Corinthians*: 13:13.

22. Quoted from *Point Counter Point* by Aldous Huxley in C.E.M. Joad's
    Guide to Modern Thought, London, Faber and Faber, Pan Books Ltd.
    1943, 322.

23. W. Golding: *The Hot Gates*, 87.

24. Reverend James Colley in *Rites of Passage* is chastised by Neptune in
    the pagan rites. He is outraged by the lurching brutalities of Deverel
    and company and confronts Captain Anderson, 224.

25. W. Golding: *The Paper Men*, Ch. 3, 31.

26. *Ibid.*, Ch. 7, 74-75.

27. S.J. Boyd: *Op. cit.*, 189.

28. W. Golding: *Rites of Passage*, 235.
    Conrad's *Lord Jim* comes to mind. Edmund suffers pangs of remorse on misjudging Colley like Tuan Jim who suffers for his neglect of duty. Conrad clearly views the primitive, which has a definite fascination for civilized man, as an undesirable extreme.

29. *Ibid.*, 236.
    Henry Fielding in *Tom Jones*, tells us '...drink in reality doth not reverse nature, or create passions in men which did not exist in them before. It takes away the guard of reason...it heightens and inflames our passions...that the angry temper, the amorous, the generous...and all other dispositions of men are in their cups heightened and exposed.' Ch. 5, 44-45.

30. *Ibid.*, 105.

31. S. Freud: *Introductory Lectures on Psychoanalysis*, trans. J. Riviere, London, George Allen & Unwin, 1949. Lecture, 19, 248-252.

32. Havelock Ellis: *Studies in Psychology of Sex in Relation to Society*, New York, Random House, 1942, Vol. 1, Part 2, 276.

33. W. Golding: *Fire Down Below*, Ch. 23, 300.
    Edmund is enlightened by Marion that the truth of Benét's affaire du coeur with Lady Somerset was only a worship of her as a mother. Marion, in keeping cave was caught by Sir Henry. He misunderstands the accidental embrace of Benét and his wife to be passion. The rolling ship had got them entangled in each other's arms!

34. *Ibid.*, Ch. 23, 299.

35. *Ibid.*, Ch. 7, 77.

36. *Ibid.*, 79.

37. *Ibid.*, Ch. 8. 95.

38. W. Golding: *Lord of Flies*, Ch. 9, 170.

39. W. Golding: *Pincher Martin*, Ch. 4, 57.

40. W. Golding: A Newspaper report in *The Times of India*, of a Talk at Pune University, March 10, 1985.

41. Sisir Kumar Ghose: 'Science without a soul.' Review of Fritjof Capra's book: *The Turning Point: Science, Society and the Rising Culture* (Flamingo 1987) in *The Times of India*, September 20, 1987.

42. Frank Kermode: *Puzzles and Epiphanies*. London, Routledge and Kegan Paul, 1962, 198-213.

43. Dr. V. Tiger: *Op. cit.*, 9.

44. W. Golding: *Lord of the Flies*, Ch. 1, 10-11.

45. Dr. S. Kandaswami: 'The Games "Biguns" and "Littleuns" play in *Lord of the Flies*,' *Aspects of William Golding*, Kerala, University of Calicut, 1986, 28-29.

46. W. Golding: *Lord of the Flies*, Ch. 6, 109-110.

47. *Ibid.*, Ch. 5, 88.

48. *Ibid.*, Ch. 7, 121.
    Herbert Spencer spoke of life as a process of continual adjustment of internal to external reality. Any failure to achieve this balance results in frustration.

49. *Ibid.*, Ch. 6, 118.

50. *Ibid.*, Ch. 12, 211.
    According to Freud, fears are expressions of unconscious desires, a conscious fear is the expression of an unconscious wish—J.A.C. Brown: *Freud and the Post Freudians*, Harmondsworth, Montana Books, 1961, 19.

51. *Ibid.*, Ch. 8. 149. Ironically this ritual murder is committed Simon's candle bud church-like glade.

52. Erich Fromm: *The Crisis of Psychoanalysis*, Harmondsworth, Penguin 1970, Ch. 2, 62.

53. W. Golding: *Free Fall*, Ch. 1, 11.

54. *Ibid.*, 15.

55. *Ibid.*, 15.

56. *Ibid.*, 14.

57. S. Freud: *The Complete Introductory Lectures on Psychoanalysis*, trans: & (ed.) James Strachey, London, George Allen & Unwin Ltd., 1971, Ch. 33, 590.

58. W. Golding: *Free Fall*, Ch. 1, 35.

59. *Ibid.*, 25.

60. M. Kinkead-Weekes & I. Gregor: *Op. cit.*, 173.

61. W. Golding: *Free Fall*, Ch. 4, 47.

62. *Ibid.*, Ch. 3, 78.

63. Erich Fromm: *The Crisis of Psychoanalysis*, Ch. 2, 63.

64. Alfred Adler: 'Understanding Human Nature,' quoted in C.E.M. Joad's *Guide to Modern Thought*, 248.

65. W. Golding: *Free Fall*, Ch. 2, 48.

66. *Ibid.*, 61.

67. *Ibid.*, 76.

68. Dr. A. Henry: 'The Structure of *Free Fall*,' *Southern Review*, Vol. 8, No. 2, June, 1975, 108. Dr. Henry is disappointed that Dr. V. Tiger in *William Golding: The Dark Fields of Discovery* has not examined Ch. 8 of *Free Fall* conclusively.

69. W. Golding: *Free Fall*, Ch. 8, 158-159.

70. *Ibid.*, Ch. 9, 176-183.

71. *Ibid.*, 181.

72. F.W.H. Myers: *Human Personality*, London, Longmans & Co., 1903, Vol. 2, 307.

73. W. Golding: 'Interview with J. Carey' in *William Golding—The Man and his Books*, (ed.) John Carey, 173. Desmond Morris observes that 'next to animals, children are the most vulnerable subordinates and, despite greater inhibitions here, they too are subjected to a great deal of re-directed violence. The viciousness with which animals, children and other helpless subordinates are subject to persecution is a measure of the weight of the dominance pressures imposed on the persecutors.' *The Human Zoo*, London, Jonathan Cape, 1969, 76.

74. W. Golding: *Free Fall*, Ch. 11, 200-201.

75. W. Golding: *The Pyramid*, 207.

76. *Ibid.*, 207.

77. *Ibid.*, 215.

78. W. Golding: *Darkness Visible*, Ch. 2, 22

79. W. Golding: *The Pyramid*, 212.

80. William Golding: *The Man and his Books, A Tribute on his 75th Birthday* (ed.) John Carey, 174.

81. *Ibid.*, 175.

82. W. Golding: *Lord of the Flies*, Chs. 9 & 10.

83. William Golding: 'Belief and Creativity,' *A Moving Target*, 201.

84. W. Golding: *Darkness Visible*, Ch. 16, 265.

85. W. Golding: *Fire Down Below*, Ch. 17, 219.

86. W. Golding: *Free Fall*, Ch. 14, 250-251.

87. Dennis Donaghue: 'The Ordinary Universe,' *The New York Review of Books*, December 7, 1967, 21-24.

88. V.S. Pritchett: 'Pain & William Golding,' *William Golding Novels 1954-67*, A Case Book, 47.

89. W. Golding: *Pincher Martin*, Ch. 13, 194.

90. William Blake: Contrast 'The Divine Image' with the poem 'The Human Abstract.' *The Poetical Works of William Blake: Songs of Innocence and Experience*, (ed.) John Sampson, London, Oxford University Press, 1948, 75 & 105.

91. W. Golding: *Lord of the Flies*, Ch. 1, 7.

92. Barbara Everett: 'Golding's Pity,' *William Golding: The Man and his books—A Tribute on his 75th Birthday*, (ed.) John Carey, 122.

93. In the novel, *Friday,* by the modern French mystical writer, Michel Tournier the popular concept of the civilized man is examined satirically.

94. Sophy's sadism in *Darkness Visible*. Ironically, her name stands for wisdom in Greek.

95. Friday appears on Crusoe's island in Tournier's novel, and everything 'civilised' is open to debate, and is ultimately negated.

96. Mr. Pedigree's 'affairs' with the beautiful boys of his boarding school, leading to the suicide of young Henderson, in *Darkness Visible*, Ch. 2, 27.

97. W. Golding: *The Inheritors*, Ch. 6, 174-177.

98. Dr. V. Tiger says 'We not only experience a consciousness that twentieth century man has lost in which instinct, intuition and pictorialisation predominate; we participate in its loss,' *Op. cit.*, 84.

99. W. Golding: *Free Fall*, Ch. 14, 251.

100. M. Kinkead-Weekes & I. Gregor: *Op. cit.*, 116.

101. Erich Fromm: *The Crisis of Psychoanalysis*, Ch. 2, 66.

102. Golding was awarded the Nobel Prize for 'illuminating the human condition in the world today.' As he told Craig Raine in an interview, '"he couldn't now speak with such authority of good and evil."'

103. 'Knowledge comes, but wisdom lingers, and I linger on the shore,
    And the individual withers, and the world is more and more,
    Knowledge comes, but wisdom lingers and he bears a laden breast,
    Full of sad experience, moving towards the stillness of his rest.'

    From 'Locksley Hall,' *Tennyson: Selected Poems*, (ed.) M. Millgate, London, O.U.P., 1963, 11. 141-144. Maybe Golding agrees with Tennyson.

104. Christ himself had cried out on the cross: 'Dipso!' ('Δψω!' means 'thirst' in Greek.) 'The thirsts of men were not to be controlled so men were not to blame for them.' W. Golding: *Darkness Visible*, Ch. 2, 32.

105. S.J. Boyd: *Op. cit.*, 127.

106. *Ibid.*, 127.

107. W. Golding: *Darkness Visible*, Ch. 3, 49.

108. *Ibid.*, Ch. 3, 50.

    This suppression of instincts involves the risk of neurotic illness. Thus education has to find its way between the Scylla of non-interference and the Charybdis of frustration. S. Freud: *The Complete Introductory Lectures on Psychoanalysis*, 613.

109. *Ibid.*, Ch. 4, 65.

110. *Ibid.*, Ch. 8, 128.

    Electra complex refers to the attachment of a daughter to her father, with hostility to her mother. The Greek story of Electra, who helped avenge her mother's murder of the father.—*Chamber's Dictionary*, Cambridge, Chambers, 1988, 299.

111. John Hilton: 'To reign is worth ambition though in Hell Better to reign in Hell than serve in Heaven.' *Paradise Lost*, Bk. I, 11. 262-263, *The*

Poetical Works of John Milton, (ed.) Helen Darbyshire, Oxford, Clarendon Press, 1978, Vol. 1, 12.

112. A hideous female and evil spirit in Hindu mythology.

113. W. Golding: *Darkness Visible*, Ch. 11, 169.

114. *Ibid.*, Ch. 11, 180-181.

115. *Ibid.*, Ch. 9, 146.

P. Garnier notes that 'Pathological sadism is an impulsive and obsessing sexual perversion characterised by a close link between suffering inflicted or mentally represented and the sexual orgasm, without this necessary and sufficing condition frigidity usually remaining absolute'.—Quoted by Havelock Ellis in *Studies in the Psychology of Sex*, Part 4, Vol. 1, 105. Sophy is cold blooded in normal sex, it is only violence and cruelty that evokes an orgasm in her.

116. *Ibid.*, Ch. 11, 186.

117. *Ibid.*, 187.

'"What do I do?"' Then with a hissing kind of hatred—'"You want to know? You do? I masturbate."' Sophy's father is full of venom at his own weakness.

118. *Ibid.*, Ch. 12, 197.

119. *Ibid.*, Ch. 15, 244-245.

120. *Ibid.*, Ch. 16, 257.

121. W.B. Yeats: 'The Second Coming' from *The Faber Book of Modern Verse*, London, Faber and Faber, 1965, 58.

'Things fall apart; the centre cannot hold;
Mere anarchy is loosed upon the world,
The blood-dimmed tide is loosed and everywhere,
The ceremony of innocence is drowned;

....

Surely the second coming is at hand.

....

And what rough beast, its hour come round at last,
Slouches towards Bethlehem to be born?' (11. 3-6 & 10, 21-22.)

122. *Moll Flanders*, the petty thief in Defoe's novel steals with great pride and makes a career of harlotry, even incest. Her journey is from innocence to evil.

123. W. Golding: *The Pyramid*, 91.

The deep irony of Golding's portrayal of Pedigree, the much misunderstood homosexual, who needs no cure. We know that the world view of such men is more liberal and compassionate today.

124. Paul Kline: *Psychology Exposed or The Emperor's New Clothes*, London & New York, Routledge, 1988, Ch. 1, 6.

125. Tennessee Williams: Foreword to *Penguin Plays*, Middlesex, Penguin, 1962, 10.

126. W. Golding: *Free Fall*, Ch. 5, 109.

127. *Ibid.*, 117.

   In Sammy and Beatrice, we see Paul Morel and Miriam. The pre-
   marital love affair of the former is a parallel to that of the initiation
   of Paul and Miriam into the secrets of sex in D.H. Lawrence's, *Sons
   & Lovers*, Harmondsworth, Penguin, 1971, Ch. 11, 353.

128. *Ibid.*, Ch. 5, 118.

129. *Ibid.*, 119.

130. *Ibid.*, 123.

   Sammy says, 'I was trembling,...as if love and sex and passion were a
   disease,' 109.

131. Paul Morel abandons the chaste virgin Miriam for Clara Dawes in
   D.H. Lawrence's *Sons and Lovers*, Ch.12, 375.

132. Unlike D.H. Lawrence who venerates the act of sex in *Lady
   Chatterley's Lover*, Bombay, Jaico Publishing House, 1961, Ch.12,
   308.

133. It is reminiscent of the brutal sexual assault of the virile Stanley
   Kowalski on the neurotic decadent refinement of his sister-in-law,
   Blanche Dubois (Sc. 10). When Stella, Stanley's wife returns from the
   hospital after her delivery, she has to take the painful decision of
   letting Blanche be taken away to an asylum. (Sc. 11)—Tennessee
   Williams: *A Streetcar Named Desire*, Middlesex, Penguin, 1962.

134. *Ibid.*, Foreword, 9.

135. W. Golding: *Free Fall*, Ch. 12, 231-232.

136. C.E.M. Joad: *Guide to Modern Thought*, Ch. 8, 273-274.

137. W. Golding: *The Pyramid*, 141.

138. *Ibid.*, 145.

   Don Crompton: Op. cit., 56-57. Oliver, the hero, is the common factor
   of the Triadic groups of the characters, focusing attention on sex,
   music and class, the three sides of the pyramid in the S.O.S.—
   (Stilbourne Operatic Society), also (Save Our Souls)!

139. *Ibid.*, 12

140. *Ibid.*, 12.

141. *Ibid.*, 13.

142. *Ibid.*, 49.

143. *Ibid.*, 67.

   'I slammed the dining room door brutally. I stood still, trembling... I
   swung my left fist with all my force into the shining walnut panel...and
   it cracked from top to bottom.'

144. *Ibid.*, 71.

145. *Ibid.*, 71-72.

Here we are reminded of Paul Morel's frenetic love-making with Clara Dawes in the sweet-scented woods in *Sons and Lovers*, Ch. 12, 376.

146. *Ibid.*, 88.

147. *Ibid.*, 90.

148. *Ibid.*, 91.

149. *Ibid.*, 94.

Oliver's mother and father are talking about Evie. '"Beasts," said my father "All men are beasts. That's what she said."' Mutual contempt born of mutual need is a salient feature of the battle of the sexes! Evie both hates and needs the affection of young men like Robert and Oliver.

150. *Ibid.*, 99.

151. *Ibid.*, 168.

152. *Ibid.*, 184.

153. Dr. A. Henry: 'William Golding: "*The Pyramid*,"' *Southern Review*, Vol. 3, No. 1, 1968, 13-14.

154. W. Golding: *The Pyramid*, 215.

155. Tagore envisages: 'Where the clear stream of reason has not lost its way into the dreary desert sand of dead habit.' From *Gitanjali* (Song Offerings), London, Macmillan, 1989, St. 35, 17.

156. Philip Redpath: *Op. cit.*, Ch. 5, 146.

Olly is in an agony of embarrassment when he has to climb with his halberd onto the stage from the front, "What are you going round in front?"'—W. Golding: *The Pyramid*, 150. Again the association of sex with the play 'King of Hearts' is noticed on 152—'"My halberd '...I can't get it up!"'

157. P. Redpath: *Op. cit.*, 207.

158. W. Golding: *The Pyramid*, 140.

159. A.S. Byatt: 'Of Things I sing,' *The New Statesman*, June 2, 1976, 761.

160. Don Crompton: *Op. cit.*, 114.

161. W. Golding: *The Pyramid*, 114.

162. Change is the greatest good and only Bounce and Oliver progress towards an enlightened awareness of self in the latter part of the novel.

163. Mr. Chandrabhanu Satpathy in 'Cosmic Energy in Pyramids,' *The Illustrated Weekly of India*, February 11, 1990, has demonstrated the power of cosmic energy in the 1.8m high pyramid to cure hypertension, high blood pressure etc.

164. W. Golding: *Free Fall*, Ch. 10, 195.

Here we recall other unhappy children in literature like David Copperfield in Dickens, who is tortured by Mr. and Miss Murdstone. And the jilted Miss Havisham's indirect needling of young Pip, through Estella in *Great Expectations*.

165. Dom Moraes: *My Son's Father, An Autobiography*, London, Bell Books, 1971, Ch. 12, 217.

166. C. Jung: *Two Essays on Analytical Psychology, Collected Works*, (ed.) Constance Long, London, Tindal & Cox, 1953, Vol. 7, 240.

167. *Ibid.*, 240.

168. W. Golding: *Pincher Martin*, Ch. 9, 146.

169. *Ibid.*, Ch. 6, 88.

170. *Ibid.*, Ch. 8. 120.

171. W. Golding: *The Spire*, Ch. 1, 22.

172. *Ibid.*, 26.

173. *Ibid.*, Ch. 3, 62-63.

174. W Golding: *Pincher Martin*, Ch. 6, 95.

175. W. Golding: *The Spire*, Ch. 11, 208.

176. Frank Kermode: *Op. cit.*, 209.

177. P. Redpath: *Op. cit.*, 145.

178. W. Golding: *Pincher Martin*, Ch. 13, 200.

In his analysis of dreams with a dental stimulus, Freud says 'A tooth being pulled out by someone else in a dream is as a rule to be interpreted as castration.' *The Interpretation of Dreams,* trans. J. Strachey, 1900, Harmondsworth, Pelican Freud Library, 1976, Vol.4, 509.

179. W. Golding: *The Spire*, Ch. 1, 8.

180. W. Golding: *Pincher Martin*, Ch. 10, 153.

181. Ibid., Ch. 7, 100-101.

Pincher's sexual jealousy goads him to kill Nat, his rival in love.

182. *Ibid.*, Ch. 5, 100-101.

183. W. Golding: *The Spire*, Ch. 5, 100.

184. *Ibid.*, Ch. 7, 127.

185. *Ibid.*, Ch. 9, 176.

186. *Ibid.*, 178.

187. M. Kinkead-Weekes & I. Gregor: *Op. cit.*, Ch. 5, 207.

188. W. Shakespeare: 'Hamlet,' *Complete Works*, Act I, Sc. 2.

189. Leighton Hodson: *Op. cit.*, Ch. 6, 98.

190. W. Golding: *Darkness Visible*, Ch. 15, 242.

191. *Ibid.*, Ch. 2, 35.

Young Henderson commits suicide in despair when his master, Pedigree, camouflages his passion for him by involving innocent Matty.

192. *Ibid.*, Ch. 13, 230.

Havelock Ellis observes, 'In the opinion of some, English homosexuality has become much more conspicuous in recent years, and this is sometimes attributed to the Oscar Wilde case.... The development of urban life renders easier the exhibition and satisfaction of this as of all other forms of perversion.'—Havelock Ellis: *Op. cit.*, Part 4, 63.

193. 'So saying, her rash hand in evil hour,
Forth-reaching to the fruit, she plucked, she eat,
Earth felt the wound, and Nature from her seat,
Sighing through all her works, gave signs of woe,
That all was lost,'—John Milton: *Paradise Lost*, Book IX, 11. 780-784, 202.

194. W. Golding: *The Paper Men*, Ch. 5, 51.

195. *Ibid.*, 52.

196. *Ibid.*, 52.

197. E. Drew: *T.S. Eliot—The Design of his Poetry*, 119.

198. Gore Vidal: 'Ladders to Heaven,' *On Contemporary Literature*, (ed.) Richard Kostelanetz, New York, Avon Books, 1964, 31.

199. W. Golding: *Free Fall*, Ch. 6, 129.

200. Luke M. Grande: 'The Appeal of Golding,' *Commonweal*, January 25, 1963, 457-9.

201. As Kant said the exercise of this God-given power can lead man to Truth. Man comprehends the world mentally and emotionally through love and through reason.

I. Kant: *Critique of Pure Reason*, trans. J.M.D. Meiklejohn, London, J.M. Dent & Sons, 1950, 460.

202. W. Golding: *Free Fall*, Ch. 12, 231.

203. Golding shows this in the deaths of Colley, Pincher Martin, and Bounce Dawlish.

204. Erich Fromm: *Op. cit.*, 66.

205. W. Golding: *The Pyramid*, 100.

A rigid approach to Oliver is unhelpful.

206. W. Golding: *Pincher Martin*, Ch. 9, 134.

207. W. Golding: *The Spire*, Ch. 3, 59-60.

208. C. Bent: 'Let us be behaviourist for one type of problem, introspective interactionists for another, naive realists in this context, subjective idealists in that and silent mystics or agnostics in regard to the remainder.' 'Brain and Consciousness,' *Bulletin of British Psychological Society*, 1969, No. 22, 29-36.

4

CLASS-CONFLICT AND MODERN SOCIAL ETHOS

$\blacklozenge$

Man is born free but is soon enchained by his social class. At birth certain identity tags such as sex, class and religion are inescapable. Even in modern times, the fate and fortune of a man are determined largely by such decisive factors like the legitimacy of his birth, class, race and religion. If a man were not branded by the stigma of his social class he would have a better chance of thriving as a human entity in society. Lieutenant Summers in Golding's *Rites of Passage* is a classic case in point. He comes of a humbler class than Deverel and so lacks his niceties. He tells Talbot bitterly that '"a man's original is branded on his forehead never to be removed."'[1]

He cannot wish society away for he is a gregarious animal. And society is an intricate network of social relationships. 'The core element of any social structure, and the basis be class rule, is functioning property, the economic system of ownership and dependence.'[2] Now a class is an important unit of society. And Gerhard Lenski defines a class as 'an aggregation of persons in a society who stand in a similar position with respect to some form of power, privilege or prestige.'[3]

Class-war is inevitable when large numbers of individuals cannot realise their goals by individual behaviour. Oliver in *The Pyramid* cannot marry Imogen of a higher class. His middle-class respectability prevents him from making public his illicit love affair with Evie, the town crier's daughter as he is the dispenser's son! Golding examines the evils of class war in England, which lead to disintegration and disruption in human relationships in *The Pyramid, Rites of Passage, Darkness Visible* to mention a few.

Young Golding had visualised a classless paradise on reading H.G. Wells's *Men Like Gods*; but this was rudely shattered as he grew up. Utopias are a myth, an escapist clause, a pipe dream that idealistic writers in a class-ridden society like to envision. We have come a long way from More's *Utopia* and Plato's *Atlantis*. Social regression in contemporary society arouses anti-utopian sentiments. Orwell's *Nineteen Eighty Four* and E.M. Forster's *The Machine Stops* paint grim portraits of the abyss between political power and humanity. Golding belongs with these writers by virtue of the prevailing 'Zeitgeist.' 'It is a sad knowledge that anti-Utopians share among them. Their hearts are not ebullient as the satirist's, not savage either, but broken.'[4]

Class-conflict is an endemic evil in most societies and this is particularly true of English society in the nineteenth and twentieth centuries. In his later novels, Golding emerges as a serious social novelist embittered by the issue of social divisiveness in different historical frames. In *Darkness Visible* and *The Paper Men* the issues of current class-struggle like economic hardships of the lower middle-class facing problems of poverty and unemployment together with their envy and hate of the upper class are dealt with in Sophy's maladjustment, her desire to bleed the rich, earn money somehow. Gerry, her accomplice, is like her, '"No, dear thing. It's social security or paff paff."'[5] The welfare state only widens the gulf between the secure rich and the idle deviants like Gerry and Sophy. Sophy plots to kidnap a kid from the posh Wandicott public school to claim a ransom that would secure them forever. '"We could be rich for life."'[6]

Satirizing paper men, writers, journalists and critics Golding presents another gruesome frame of a modern society like Sophy's world where outrage, crime, deception, hyper-violence are rooted in class hatreds. Popular, wealthy porno-novelist Barclay experiences a paroxysm of fury, hate and fear when the persistent professor Rick saves his life in the fog.[7] How could he ruin his current image and reputation by divulging the sordid facts of his having been 'a real bastard, an ithyphallic bank clerk, 'nature's comic...right from the cradle. The first time I shot over a horse's head my fall was broken by a pile of dung.'[8] Coldly, in his wife's honest opinion, Barclay is '*the sacre monster outside the accepted rules, a national treasure, the point about you being words that the world would not willingly let die whereas what you write is—*' not popular as Barclay says but 'inferior' as Liz opines.[9] In the masquerade of an intellectual who is a successful writer, Barclay is embittered and terrified of exposure about his real class roots.

Shades of Dickens and Austen are detected in the complex class hierarchy in *The Pyramid* with its trigonal elements of class, property and status, Victorian middle-class was aware of its obligation to solve the problems of society. Working-class violence in Dickens's *Hard Times* poses a threat to the middle-class faced with a welter of issues emerging from social stratification. In Golding, Evie Babbacombe's family and friends like Captain Wilmot, who belong to the lower strata are involved in violence and jealousy. Evie's amorous affairs with Oliver and Robert Ewan of the Middle and Upper class respectively, threaten their repeatability by encroachment, generating fear, hate and problems. Robert is injured while showing off to Evie on the motorbike. Dickens's impassioned attack on the anti-human elements in the smug middle-class is seen in *Dombey and Son* where he focuses on the nexus between wealth, power and human relations. 'It is Dombey's aim to use money to distance human connections and exploit the poor while feigning charity.'[10]

Jane Austen gently satirizes the irresponsible opportunistic attitudes of a decadent society in *Pride and Prejudice* using countless moral antitheses—propriety and snobbery, liberality and excess—a fine balance is seen in Darcy and Mr. Gardiner as against the social climbing of Mr. Collins.[11] Austen demonstrates like Golding, that bitterness between classes is a reality and deviation from traditional values causes clashes.

In Golding's nautical trilogy, we see the corroding effect of capitalism on human relations. The crisis in bourgeois values and the cultural sterility of the middle-class, exploitation of the working-class for its pleasure—Talbot's casual seduction of Zenobia in his hutch is a prime example.[12] The modern world desires to break down class barriers and minimise the evil effects of social stratification through inter-class marriages, like that of Lord Talbot and Marion Chumley, by fostering positive attitudes to human values.

Since Fielding fathered the English novel in the eighteenth century, depiction of society has become part of the aesthetics of the classic English novel. Recent critics like Dr. A. Henry, P. Redpath, S.J. Boyd, and David Skilton have appraised Golding's skill in examining human relationships against a coherent social fabric and the rhythms of social change which give rise to corrosive animosity between classes. M. Kinkead-Weekes and I. Gregor observe that '...in Sammy's search for the pattern of individual self-determinism, what had never really come into focus was the social determinism of the English class-system, about which, as we now know, Golding felt strongly.'[13] Golding declares, 'I think that an Englishman who is not aware of the classic disease of society in this country, that is to say, the rigidity of its class-structure—he's not really aware of anything, not in social terms.'[14]

The pathology of class-war, symptomatic of hate in our modern civilization is rooted in the ancient traditions of class, culture and ritual. In every human being, there is a constant conflict between the individual and the herd. Generally, the self-impulses win over the herd-impulses. As Russell observes 'The only social group that has a really profound instinctive hold is the family.'[15] 'Sexual domination and parental affection form the basis of the kinship system. Conflict situations gave rise to the fear that women might become sexual property in their own families, thus giving rise to the incest taboo.'[16]

Golding presents a brilliant study in contrast between a pre-social primitive group and our ancestors, the homo sapiens in *The Inheritors*. The former are a close-knit, passive people with no tensions or turmoil. Lok and Fa share the children of Ha and Nil. Each individual in the tribe has his allotted task. The old woman tends the fire, while Mal, the old patriarch is the counsellor. They share responsibility, pain, sex, food, and picture perceptions with singular goodwill unlike the new People bristling with animosity and mutual hate. Tuami, Vivani's lover, contemplates killing Marlan, her husband to usurp his leadership.[17] His lust for Vivani is curiously mixed up with envy at seeing her splendid figure sprawled in the boat on the sail. 'She was covered with a magnificent skin, the cave-bear skin that had cost two lives to get and was the price her first man paid for her. What was a sail, thought Tuami bitterly, when Vivani wanted to be comfortable?'[18] Their mutual reactions when they meet are significant—while the Neanderthal Lok wishes to befriend the new people,[19] Tuami considers them 'forest devils,'[20] who should be destroyed.

The new people launch a belligerent fatal attack on the innocent red creatures[21] as they fear annihilation themselves. Golding seems to sadly ask if this is the price of progress? Freud in his *Civilization and its Discontents* explains to us that no civilization, no society and no culture can wholly express man's nature, as the existence of such an ideal society depends on the altruistic principle of sublimation of certain instincts. The social world is dominated by the reality rule that expects man to curb his instinctual pleasures. 'Civilised society is perpetually menaced with disintegration through this primary hostility of men towards one another.'[22] Conflict theorists view society to be in a constant state of conflict between groups and classes. The rhythms of social change are detrimental to peace and human welfare. They can disrupt the equilibrium causing everyday life to become dysfunctional as we see in riots, bombings, religious wars and terrorism.

Such is the story of *The Spire*. Dating back to the fourteenth century, the Salisbury Cathedral spire is both an engineering marvel and a miracle. Golding narrates the dreadful human cost of building this four hundred foot spire. 'The power of the Latin Church emerging from the dark middle ages was diluted by the "Great Schism" which had reduced its religious and political prestige to negligible proportions.'[23] The socio-religious conflict of the period is mirrored in the plot of *The Spire* and in the reformation in Jocelin's character.

The clash between Dean Jocelin of the cathedral and Roger Mason, the architect-builder is not merely one between a clergyman and a mason, but symbolises the conflict between Christianity and Paganism, ruling class and the working-class.

Blinded by pride and power of position, Dean Jocelin lords it over the humble cleaner, Pangall, the dumb man, Father Anselm, Roger and Father Adam. Jocelin deludes himself that he is humble, 'Lord; I thank Thee that Thou hast kept me humble.'[24] Yet, his condescension and presumption in his dealings with his subordinates proves otherwise. '"I ask your pardon, Father Adam. One forgets you are there so easily!... I shall call you Father Anonymous!"'[25] In the heated exchange with Father Anselm, the Sacrist, it emerges that Jocelin is unconventional in his approach to the problem of the workers defiling the church, filling it with dust and rubble.[26] The malicious Sacrist initially votes against the spire but retracts ungraciously, leaving a sting, 'an indefinable rebuke that was a sort of insolence, so that the thread snapped.'[27]

Roger feels the pressure of the ruling class in Jocelin's arrogance and resists it. Jocelin is embroiled in an unholy alliance, when Rachel brazenly confesses why she and Roger are not compatible bedfellows and Roger is attracted to the red-haired Goody. Jocelin is secretly glad that Roger is caught in Goody's tent and will not abscond.[28] Jocelin wields an evil power over the pawns, who can be sacrificed for his Folly. Roger loses his best stonecutter in a fight,[29] a worker falls to his death,[30] Pangall is crucified in the pit,[31] and Goody dies in childbirth.[32] The question is what godly power does Jocelin exercise when he asks Roger to send a man to whip a drunkard on the streets, when his own house, the cathedral is sullied by 'murderers, cut throats, fornicators, sodomites and atheists?'[33] At the inquiry into Jocelin's transgressions it is clear that he has evaded confession for two years and kept company with men, 'who, are more than merely wicked!'[34] He is branded as an outcast by his churchmen.

Such stupendous projects require money. The construction of the spire is an act of profanity for it is financed by tainted money. Jocelin's aunt Alison happily explains how the king paid for his pleasure by presenting her nephew with money, '"We shall drop a plum in his mouth."'[35] In his obsession, Jocelin chooses to ignore the scandalous rumours and Father Adam's warning 'They say that if it had not been for her wealth, you would never build the spire...even if your sins are as scarlet, money can buy you a grave next to the High Altar.'[36]

Class-war within the ranks of the clergy in medieval times is brilliantly studied by Golding. The petty jealousies, the envy and the desire to pull Jocelin, the rebel individual down is depicted. The precarious balance between pagan beliefs, superstitious fears on the one hand, and rigid faith and orthodoxy in Christianity in the dark ages on the other, is keenly felt.

In the eighteenth and nineteenth centuries, English novelists like Fielding, Defoe, Thackeray, Swift, Austen, and others were concerned with social realism. They painted English society in its true colours with its hypocrisies and its middle-class morality. Lionel Trilling suggests that the novel from its birth was involved in questions of social mobility, which implies stations of birth and snobbery. Since this social change is linked with the birth of capitalism the novel has the issue of materialism as its basic subject. The fantasies engendered by money and status are shocking—Trilling defines the novel as 'a perpetual quest for reality, the field of its research being always the social world.'[37]

Golding was sensitised by this class-distinction as his father was a master in a local grammar school. His parents could not afford to send their boys to a public school. He observes that 'In the dreadful English scheme of things at that time, a scheme which so accepted social snobbery as to elevate it to an instinct, we had our subtle place.... In fact, like everybody except the very high and the very low in those days, we walked a social tightrope, could not mix with the riotous children....'[38] Golding must have experienced the bitterness of class hate felt by young Stephen Spender, echoed in:

'My parents kept me from children who were rough
And threw words like stones and who wore torn clothes
....
I feared the salt coarse pointing of those boys.
....
They were lithe, they sprang out behind hedges
Like dogs to bark at our world...'[39]

in *Rites of Passage*, the wooden world of the ship has invisible lines that demarcate the different classes. Representing the upper echelons of Her Majesty's administrative service is Edmund Talbot, a lordly buck flaunting his aristocratic powers and patronising Lieutenant Summers, humble Parson Colley and the other officers of the L'Orient. Though Talbot apologises politely to young Summers for injuring his sensibilities, Summers cannot conceal his hurt. '"But true, Sir, in our country, for all her greatness there is one thing she cannot do and that is translate a person wholly out of one class into another. Perfect translation from one language into another is impossible. Class is the British language."'[40] While mollifying Summers, Talbot harshly condemns Reverend Colley for stepping out of his station. '"I swear he has got out of the peasantry by a kind of greasy obsequiousness...Colley plied...with spirits there in the fo'castle, had neither the strength to refuse it nor the breeding to resist its more destructive effects."'[41] Blake Morrison observes that the novel is not so much a sea story as a modern post-Auschwitz allegory where the sea represents a larger social order. 'The conflict of Colley and Captain Anderson symbolises the perennial conflict of Church and State and their glances at such topics as class, justice, authority and the virtues and limitations of verisimilitude in art.'[42]

Rites of Passage is significantly concerned with the evils of social stratification leading to injustice and persecution of less fortunately ranked individuals like Colley, Summers, Wheeler and Janet. At the top of the social ladder, Edmund Talbot, the Byronic dandy, blusters about the *L'Orient* highly intolerant of the 'decrepit vessel,'[43] his cramped 'hutch' of a cabin, the stink and fetor of the sand ballast. Wheeler's subtle smile when Talbot brags to him that he is a good sailor stirs his aristocratic ire at his impertinence. 'I made an immediate resolution to teach the man a lesson in manners at the first opportunity.'[44]

Talbot is almost upbraided for his uppity behaviour by Captain Anderson on the quarterdeck. His timely mention of his high connections stalls the rage of the Captain. 'Our Captain squinted first,...down your lordship's muzzle, decided you were loaded, cast a fearful eye at the ambassador in my other hand and reined back with his yellow teeth showing!... I swear Captain Anderson would have shot, hanged, keel-hauled, marooned me if prudence had not...got the better of his inclination.'[45]

While Anderson condescends to converse with Talbot, he clouts the servile Colley for venturing onto his sacred domain.[46]

Edmund cannot bear the 'little tyrant's'[47] overbearing orders
of forbidding a service. He resolves to assert his authority.
'The brooding Captain should not dictate to me in this
manner! What! Is *he* to tell *me* whether I should have a service
to attend or not?'[48]

Talbot is repelled and amused by Parson Colley's servility,
his crudity of dress and demeanour, but patronises him to
flaunt his power of class before Anderson. Talbot is outraged
by Summers' attack on his social duty to visit Colley lying ill
in his cabin. '"I? Go in that stinking hole?"'[49] is his initial
negative reaction. Summers accuses him saying, '"...you have
used your birth and your prospective position to get for
yourself an unusual degree of attention and comfort—I do not
complain—dare not! Who am I to question the customs of our
society or indeed, the laws of nature? In a sentence, you have
exercised the privilege of your position. I am asking you to
shoulder its responsibilities."'[50]

Summers is unafraid of Talbot's status and openly condemns
him for Colley's lapse of conduct. He analyses that if it were
not for Talbot's bold provocation of Captain Anderson's wrath,
he may not have assaulted poor Colley soon after. '"But had
you not acted as you did at that time, he would never in the
very next few minutes have crushed Colley with his anger and
continued to humiliate *him* because he could not humiliate
you."'[51]

Despite Talbot's smugness it is obvious that he is insecure
in his position, cowardly, when really tested in a crisis. The
prospect of being killed is 'oppressive' when a strange ship
is sighted.[52] He blunders onto the gundeck and is soundly
concussed. His pompous view that civilized nations will rule
the backward ones and his conviction that an elite body will
govern better reflects his brash confidence. '"...A civilized
community will always find ways of healthfully limiting the
electorate to a body of highly born, highly educated,
sophisticated professional and hereditary electors who come
from a level of society which was born to govern, expects to
govern, and will always do so!"'[53] Redpath finds the 'egotistical
snobbishness and overconfidence of Talbot's class superiority
a defensive reaction to a world of political and social upheavals

threatening the old class hierarchy which is in danger of collapse.'[54]

The nonpareil Lord Talbot can be forgiven any trespass-venturing to call on the surly Captain Anderson, enjoying coitus interrupts with Zenobia Brocklebank, insulting Summers, looking down on the marine artist, Brocklebank's rough and ready manners, and sceptical of the romance between Miss Granham and Mr. Prettiman. Talbot's wealth and status render him immune to criticism, while the peasant parson Colley is laughed at by all, doused in the badger bag by Deverel, mocked at for his sexual misdemeanour, attacked by Anderson, all because he comes of a lowly class! So, class is not merely a station in life, it is a dangerously vulnerable shifting sand for the less fortunate.

Golding pessimistically proves that any violent switch from one class to another is fatal. Colley risks trying to cultivate Captain Anderson, Talbot and others. Badly snubbed and humiliated by Deverel and crew, in the barbaric rites of passage, he retreats in humiliation. He does not recognise the hierarchy of classes, for him it is the ideal community of God. He approaches the common folk below decks as a rebuke to the superior classes who have alienated him. Drinking rum and socialising with the sailors is his act of liberation. In a moment of excess, he outrages his clerical status and, subsequently commits suicide, rather than bear the disgrace of taunts in the rigid society aboard the *L'Orient*.

Miss Granham inspires both awe and contempt in Talbot, being a canon's daughter, a free thinker who makes no distinction between officers and seamen.[55] Mr. Prettiman, the social philosopher and rationalist, holds his own in his arguments with Talbot. Fear of exposure pressurises Captain Anderson to host Talbot and make friendly overtures after Colley's death—such hypocrisy! "'Ah! the journal. Do not forget to include in it, Mr. Talbot, that whatever may be said of the passengers, so far as the people and my officers are concerned, this is a *happy* ship!'"[56]

The wild rites that Parson Colley is subjected to in *Rites of Passage*, are anticipated in the bedevilled pranks played on Parson Adams in Fielding's *Joseph Andrews*.[57] Adams' spiritual dignity is unimpaired by the evil crudities of the affluent. Abuse of parsons is a deadly game played to insult clergymen.

Like Henry Fielding who parodies Richardson's *Pamela* in *Joseph Andrews*, Golding parodies Jane Austen's *Pride and Prejudice* and *Persuasion* in his *Rites of Passage*. Fielding's realism and morality were a satirical reaction to Richardson's facile classist sentiments. Golding, like Fielding, registers the need of the middle-class in England to eschew the affectations of the rich. Boyd observes critically, that Austen often camouflaged or implied the social problems created by class barriers. 'To Golding such classist values are an obscenity and...such values are glaringly visible in the pages of Austen. The ship with its rigid segregation of classes, its lines on the deck which are dangerous to cross, is manifestly Britain in miniature, and it stinks:...'[58] Talbot's blind arrogance and pride are like Dean Jocelin's, for both treat human beings as objects. They are hateful and hurting in thought, word and deed. Men like Talbot cocooned in comfort lack breadth of vision and a broad-minded sympathy for the other classes; from their lofty position, they can have only a warped view of humanity.

Could an aristocrat like Talbot endanger his class by marrying a piano teacher like Marion Chumley?[59] Sir Henry Somerset in *Close Quarters* is thoughtlessly impatient and rude to Janet Oates, Lady Somerset's companion and a distant kinswoman. '"Oh, come straight in, for heaven's sake, Janet! You need not be scared nor say anything, for you was only brought in to make up the numbers."'[60] Such deliberate cruelty in the cultured classes is fairly common.

It is interesting to note that Marion Chumley has achieved a measure of respectability and gentility by dint of her perseverance. When Edmund is easily moved to tears by the sentimental song of Mrs. East, Marion is critical of her technique and style of presentation. She confesses that she prefers Art, though it is fashionable to believe in Nature in the nineteenth century '"...I believe I was the only young person in the school who saw that orphans are the victims of Nature and that Art is their resource and hope."'[61] In a fast changing society, the low born Marion can set her cap at Lord Talbot of the landed gentry. She has the charming graces of a social climber, who, through matrimony, acquires a higher status in society!

The battle between Summers and Benét is subtly different. Summers is the steady, loyal, intelligent non-conformist, while Benét is sophisticated with a brilliant engineering proclivity and a penchant for poetry. Sent on board the *L'Orient* from the *Alcyone* in exchange for the drunken Deverel, Benét promptly wins the favour of Captain Anderson by organising the scraping of the weeds off the keel. Edmund Talbot compares two officers, who vie with each other for his favours. '...the one brilliantly putting us at risk, the other soberly and constantly taking *care*.'[62] Clearly Summers is intimidated by the bold scientific attitude of Benét. Summers is deeply hurt by Anderson's admiration for Benét and his cutting remark, which he relates to Talbot. '"I am to cease my obstruction."'[63] How could Anderson favour a young new officer over him so unfairly? The evil of class barriers can never be wiped out.

The metaphoric import of Captain Anderson's remark about steam tugs, in a discussion on board the *Alcyone* is significant. '"There is too much fire below... I cannot like the things. If they should explode they might touch off a fleet like tinder."'[64] Benét's negligence in Sydney harbour causes an uncontrollable conflagration on board their ship that consumes poor Summers. Class-conflict is equally deadly in its disastrous consequences.

Benét even stirs Lord Talbot's bile. His charm and passion for poetry rouses Talbot's envy and jealousy. He resents the very thought of his beloved Marion in the company of Benét. '"Just because he has yellow hair and a face like a girl's—God damn and blast my soul to eternal bloody perdition."'[65] His fancy French airs irritate Talbot. After a bitter altercation outside Prettiman's cabin Benét gives vent to his spleen. '"Ah, the English! When one gets to know them, dislike turns to genuine loathing!"'[66] Wheeler's violent manner of blowing his brains out in Colley's cabin with Brocklebank's brass blunderbuss is a form of deviant behaviour.[67] Socially insecure and unstable, Wheeler is frustrated in his job as cabin attendant. He cannot stand the strain of another brush with death as the ship is in danger of sinking.

Talbot wisely rejects Prettiman's Utopian schemes of building an ideal community in the Australian desert. He is a realist and has very definite ideas about how to achieve happiness, materially and socially. Boyd observes that the promises and ideals of egalitarianism and socialism, however exalting, are misleading for the world can defeat such ideal dreams.[68] One fact emerges from the long voyage, storms, stresses shared by the crew and passengers have made them shed their cláss consciousness to a great extent, breaking down invisible barriers. 'The rigid system of separation which had been so moderated by time and adventure that I could now walk among them without comment.'[69]

In *The Pyramid*, Golding is a sterner Dickens[70] castigating man in social groups for his intolerance. He is a more militant Shaw in establishing the shams and illusions of a capitalist civilisation. Shaw clearly proved that bourgeois society was a sham, a society in which honest and generous impulses were incompatible with success. As a socialist, he detested the anarchical scramble for money, which point is driven home by Golding with his sharp incisive criticism of English society in Stilbourne. *The Pyramid* is Golding's most powerful indictment of the English class-system.

Since man is an economic being at base, the cash nexus becomes the determining factor in a society's growth and development. Social philosophers like Ruskin, Carlyle and Morris advocated the nationalisation of industry in the nineteenth century to check the evils of monopoly in England. Ruskin denounced man's enslavement by the machine and castigated the spirit of individualism that preached the profit motive at the cost of human relationships. Golding symbolically uses various vehicles like Bounce's twin-sealer, Bobby Ewan's motor-bike, Oliver's bicycle as clear status symbols representing their upper class, upper middle-class and lower middle-class respectively. Dr. A. Henry points out the import of the vehicle symbol when she writes, 'Throughout, control of vehicles has implied control of events, reason or passion, and failure to control them is inadequacy or imbalance, like Phaethon modernised. The last words of the book are "I concentrated on my driving."'[71]

Oliver imagines his romantic idol, Imogen Grantley driving her fiance, Claymore's 'green, open Lagonda across the downs, her long reddish hair flying back from her pale face.'[72] The novel closes with Oliver driving away in his superior sealed saloon. Oily vividly recalls, as a three-year old in his push chair seeing the eccentric failed musician, Mr. Dawlish, smash the poor man's 'honkety tonk' in its battered pram.[73]

The novel registers the illusion that snobbery generates with its uneasy pride in status. Modern society is based on the pride of false appearances which cannot always hide the sordid reality beneath. Bounce partially frees herself from the despotic power of Mr. Dawlish by buying a two-seater and incurring his wrath for wasting money. Henry Williams rises by sheer perseverance from a poor garage mechanic to Bounce's chauffeur, and thereafter to owning an automobile showroom. 'There was a forecourt of concrete where old Mr. Dawlish had lived and lounged, there was a garage and a pit for inspecting the entrails of cars... Henry wore a suit at work and was cloistered in the little office.'[74] Oliver is amazed at Henry's rapid ascent into the upper echelons of society. Henry has been driven by Mammon to exploit Bounce for his own avaricious ends.

The title of the novel conveys the pyramidal structure of class ossification in a small English town, Stilbourne. At the apex of the hierarchy are Imogen Grantley and Claymore.[75] Bounce Dawlish by virtue of her property also belongs to the prestigious upper strata. Robert Ewan's father is a doctor. In the wavering middle ranks is Oliver, whose father is Ewan's dispenser. Though David Skilton says that from *The Pyramid* it would be hard to extract the model of a satisfactory social system, past, present or future, he himself mentions the emphasis on army ranks.[76] The impressive list includes Sergeant Babbacombe, Beadle, Town Crier in his eighteenth-century uniform, Captain Wilmot, a war veteran in his wheel-chair, Sergeant Major O'Donovan and Henry Williams with his garage. Comic controversy rages about Oliver's title in the Stilbourne Operatic Society's annual musical, *The King of Hearts*. His mother argues hotly with Norman Claymore that he should be called general or colonel. Finally, a compromise of 'Captain' is reached, thus placing him a step above Sergeant Babbacombe and others.[77] Evelyn de Tracy is the professional producer, an eccentric artist. Evie Babbacombe is the town crier's luscious daughter with no moral scruples or fear of breaking social codes in her sexual liaisons with Robert Ewan and Oliver by virtue of her low status.[78]

Oliver's efforts to break free from the suffocating conventions of his class are linked with the trauma of his social maladjustment in Stilbourne—a stagnant provincial town. It is a fact that Post-Darwinian man tends to feel alienated from his environment. 'Class-conflict will be more disruptive and bitter in closed groups and rigid social structures. Tensions, and antagonisms, seething hatreds and jealousies will thrive.'[79] The degree of intolerance increases with the rigidity within the framework as we see in the society in Stilbourne.

The petty people slaked their thirst for the sensational from *The News of the World*. Each year the Stilbourne Operatic Society organised a concert. Innumerable conflicts, undercurrents of hate accompanied the performance. As Oliver says, 'The SOS rose from a vein that wandered through society beneath the surface. We had no rituals...no eloquence, no display. We were our own tragedy and did not know we needed catharsis.'[80] Invisible lines of class forbade people like Evie, who sang well and was attractive, from joining the concert. The affronts and humiliations caused terrible wounds and it took time for the 'scar tissue'[81] to form again. This strife was an annual event in Stilbourne!

Oliver's head on clash with Robert Ewan over gorgeous Evie springs from his deep-rooted hatred for the son of his father's employer. He grudgingly helps Ewan to tow Bounce's car out of the pond. Eighteen year old Olly still recollects a childhood altercation. '"You're my slave." "No I'm not." "Yes you are. My father's a doctor and yours is only his dispenser."'[82]

Olly strains against the fetters of his class, envying Robert's motor-bike which he cannot afford, afraid of the scandal of his affair with Evie. Olly realises that the disastrous consequences of his concupiscence would set all the tongues wagging, ruin his studies at Oxford and kill his kind parents. 'To be related even if only by marriage, to *Sergeant Babbacombe*! I saw their social world, so delicately poised and carefully maintained, so fiercely defended, crash into the gutter. I should drag them down—Yes. I should kill them.'[83] Olly is concerned with his own integrity in the social world of Stilbourne.

Oliver suffers the scorn of Bounce Dawlish, the repressed spinster, during his music lessons. Even her mocking nickname 'Kummer' has a sexual aside. Naturally, Oliver hates this warped woman, who twists his body into a torturous stance for his violin lesson.[84] Thwarted in love and life—Bounce fails to find love with the lower class Henry, the cunning social parasite. As an act of revolt Bounce parades Stilbourne's streets stark naked and then kills herself.[85] 'Bounce was like the long-dead Ophelia with her hatful of leaves—a Stilbourne eccentric, assimilated and accepted.'[86] Oliver admits the truth of his raw emotions only at her graveside. '*I was afraid of you, and so I hated you. It is as simple as that. When I heard you were dead I was glad.*'[87]

Only outsiders like Evelyn de Tracy with an objective critical eye can judge the worth of individuals in the 'crystal pyramid.'[88] His advice and candid opinion of the high-born Claymore and Imogen is '"Never let her know your calf-love. It would just go to feed her vanity. And insolent, the pair of them! Not ten guineas' worth, a hundred, a thousand—."'[89] He tears the veil of awe and ignorance from Oliver's eyes. '"Everything's *wrong*. Everything. There's no truth and there's no honesty. Life can't—I mean just out there, you have only to look up at the sky—but Stilbourne accepts it as a *roof*...that *stuff* they call music—It's a lie! Don't they understand? It's a lie, a lie! It's—obscene!"'[90] The curse of a stagnant society enclosed in the tomb of *The Pyramid* with its evil inter-class hates and jealousies is obvious to the impartial percipient onlooker.

Oliver's parents on the lower middle-class rung, hoard their culture, status and morality zealously. Oliver's mother is nosy, parsimonious and a notorious gossip. 'My mother had a secret weapon as well as radar. She had me. I was a kind of inter-planetary probe,.....'[91] She condemns Bounce for her wasteful maintenance of the big house after her father's death. '"She ought to let part of the house. I don't think a woman ought to live by herself like that. And the money."'[92] She envies and maligns those above her class and scorns and pities those below her. When Ewan is injured she acidly remarks on Evie's escape '"Nobody else was hurt—more's the pity!"'[93] Olly's father is a phlegmatic soul who does not fight his status, he buys himself a wireless and listens to music, which Bounce thinks is terrible and common. He feels hurt at Evie's power over Oily and her contempt—'"...Laughing...Hysteria, I thought...Laughing and sneering."'[94] He chides Oily and warns him of contracting a disease. However Olly's parents are proud that he will not accept charity from Mr. Wertwhistle. 'I knew I was not a Poor Boy. I backed away shaking my head, and shut the door.'[95]

The predicament of individuals trapped in a web of social intrigues generates tension. Howard S. Babb rightly remarks, '*The Pyramid* is decidedly sombre in depicting the power of human environment to mould imperceptibly the values of the individual and in effect annihilate him.'[96] Evie's case is pathetic, this lower class angel in disguise exhibits both malice and perversity. Though she lives in one of the tumbledown cottages of Chandler's Close, she holds her own with Robert Ewan, Oliver and others. She aspires to learn classical music like Olly. She hates the town for exploiting her, using her as a sex object. Oliver thinks of her as 'our local phenomenon, this bit of hot stuff.'[97] 'This object, on an earth that smelt of decay, with picked bones and natural cruelty—life's lavatory.'[98] She gets her sweet revenge by exposing his lust in public. Two years later, on vacation from Oxford, Olly meets a sophisticated London returned Evie and takes her for a drink to the local pub, the Crown. She boasts of her conquests and, finally, ruins Olly. '"It all began when you raped me."'[99] She thus gets her pound of flesh. Olly is shocked at the gross sexual abuse of this woman from the age of fifteen by her father, Captain Wilmot, and the local lads.

Golding's complex interlacing of the themes of money, music and sex in Stilbourne's society to stress its sterility, immobility and decadence is impressive. He finds society antagonistic to man. Materialism and spiritual progress are incompatible. Olly's parents are worried that he may pursue music as a career, but he becomes a chemist. '"Money's always tight—that's money!"'[100] Money is used to muffle music when Olly inserts a penny in his violin to mute the notes.[101] As a gypsy musician, Olly has to catch a bag of money tossed to him by Claymore, the King of Hearts. '"You'll have to catch it laddy," said Mr. De Tracy. "And if you miss it you'll have to grovel."'[102] Ironically this is true of Olly, who can ill afford to miss opportunities to become prosperous and rise in society. Money may ensure power and comfort and status but never happiness. His mother darkly warns him '"Money isn't everything. You'll find that out one day, Oliver."'[103]

Golding's endeavour is to show that love and hope are buried and mummified in *The Pyramid*. 'Golding's pessimism is his greatest claim to importance. But here he turns on the social controls and withers them.'[104] Arnold Johnston compares *The Pyramid* to Dickens's *Great Expectations* which records a phase in English society, of what money can do, good and bad, of how it can change and make distinctions of class, how it can pervert virtue and ruin simple human relationships.[105]

The two World Wars were not only a shock to western culture and society, but to western cultural values! It created not only a new political, social and ideological environment, but inevitably a new intellectual and artistic environment as well[106]—changing social frames and the evils of class-conflict. Golding, Graham Greene, Angus Wilson and Iris Murdoch convey a sense of social servitude, a feeling that for modern society, despite its new consumables stifles some humanity or vitality in man. Golding speaks of this scarring effect, 'Life goes on at the conscious level, frivolous, worried, cynical, anxious, amused. But beneath, in some deep cavern of the soul, we are stunned.'[107]

Post-war literature, as Leslie A. Fiedler analyses 'mirrors a conflict between two worlds: the class world of the past and the declassed world to come....'[108] The Movement writers turn their backs on Freud, Marx and Kierkegaard and are pro-labour. They are against the alliance of high culture, fashion, Fabian socialism and homosexuality and are anti-Bloomsbury. Greene, Amis, Osborne and Golding satirize the tendency to pretend to the standards of an upper class which no longer has roots in the present world of grim realities. Their novels are in this sense, weapons, in a class war that is over.

They damn culture vultures and are driven to rage by chamber-music groups, academic flummery, amateur dramatics listing towards a true middle-class rather anti-intellectual, as Golding proves in *The Pyramid* and *Pincher Martin*. Protagonists like Pincher, Jimmy Porter of Osborne's play *Look Back in Anger* and *Lucky Jim* of Amis, reflect the rage, a fear of success and hate against the upper class. As Fiedler says, 'these new heroes are irascible men, impossible husbands and lovers, impotent bullies gifted with a rough eloquence and rage arising from their own predicament in the fractured world.'[109]

Pincher is obsessed with Mary Lovell's inaccessibility, 'her eyes...fired an ammunition of contempt and outrage.' This 'prudish and social Mary was nothing but the intersection of influences from the cradle up,...gloved and hatted for church, who ate with such maddening refinement,...who carried a treasure of demoniac and musky attractiveness that was all the more terrible because she was almost unconscious of it.'[110] Inflamed by her contempt for his actor-class, Pincher resolves to ravish her, if only to humiliate her. He is enraged at her preference for Nathaniel, his friend. He wonders, 'by what chance, or worse, what law of the universe was she set there in the road to power and success, unbreakable yet tormenting with the need to conquer and break?'[111]

Sammy's dilemma in *Free Fall* is to find the bridge between, the religious world of the spirit, of Rowena Pringle's fanatic catechism and the rational world of the science master, Nick Shales. His quest for spiritual freedom in the social chaos of twentieth century existence is desperate as 'no creeds or codes operate to sustain,' to use Dr. Tiger's phrase.[112] He can hardly be healthily transplanted from the slums of Rotten Row, Paradise Hill to the alien comfort of Father Watts-Watt's home.

Sammy's introspection leads him to his childhood to find the point of social responsibility. Johnny Spragg and he are princes in the fight for fagcards, while Philip, the cowardly bully, becomes his henchman. Sammy in a superior fashion, collects, only kings of Egypt. Caught redhanded in bullying the boys near the lavatory, Sammy takes revenge by 'battering Johnny's face.' 'I can still sense my feelings of defiance and isolation; a man against society... I was avoided.'[113] He is ostracised for his anti-social behaviour. His tendency to defy authority to boost his own power, makes him accept the challenge to piss on the altar.[114] He can only muster courage to spit and is cuffed by the Verger.[115] Sammy is doomed to suffer a chip on his shoulder as charity-child adopted by Father Watts-Watt. He reckons Rowena Pringle is more cruel to him as his adoption thwarted her romance with Father Watts-Watt![116] She makes life a public hell for him in the catechism class. '"We all know where you come from, Mount-joy, and we were willing to regard it as your misfortune.... But you have brought the place with you...."'[117]

Naturally Sammy hates the sick deluded spinster who confuses religion with class-consciousness and idolises the socialist science master, Nick Shales. Having risen from a slum, this self-made scholar symbolised the decay of class hierarchy and hope for orphans like Sammy. As Boyd neatly sums up, 'in Golding's English landscape religion very often seems to be the handmaid not of the Lord but of the class system: "Church of England was top and bottom; chapel was middle, was the class grimly keeping its feet out of the mud."'[118] Sammy furtively conceals his lower class status from Beatrice, so that he can woo and win her. He is jealous of the privileges of her class, her chic clothes, a fury at his own inferior status and helpless passion for her. 'She could marry the Prince of Wales. Be Queen. Oh God, myself on the pavement.'[119]

It is Samuel Mountjoy's envy of prim and pretty Beatrice and her upper class that attracts the slum boy to conquer her sexually. He deceives Beatrice about his drinking habit, his slum origin and poses as the artist bent on success. 'In her little village, three miles beyond Rotten Row, all the boozers were Church of England and all the boys in broad cloth, chapel.... I kept an awful lot of things from Beatrice.'[120] Beatrice's guilt at Sammy's seduction, is part of her class upbringing that views pre-marital sex as sin. Sexual exploitation of women is an ageless social evil. Sammy deserts Beatrice without marrying her and finds the daring, violent comrade Taffy, more to his taste. 'So Taffy and I went our way regardless. She was a lady by my low standards. She was fastidious except when she remembered that we were the spearhead of the proletariat.'[121]

Even in the Egyptian fable *The Scorpion God*, a romantic relationship between Princess Pretty Flower and the Liar, an outsider and commoner is a social evil. They defy the taboo of sex outside the family and carry on an illicit affair. The Liar is a rebel who breaks rigid social laws by violently refusing to be entombed with his monarch, 'Great House in the Motionless Now.'[122]

Violating social codes is punishable by death. The Liar is bound and dragged to the pit, where the blind man is languishing. The Liar's love of life is tenacious, he escapes the ruthless sentence of death for his presumption and disobedience, by killing some guards and stinging the Head Man 'like a scorpion.'[123] Golding gives us an insight into the quaint social customs of the ancient Egyptians. Their faith in the evil superstition that the river Nile's flooding is imminent because the Liar defied the law of entering the House of Life with the deceased Great House.

In *Envoy Extraordinary*, the persecution of inventors like Phanocles, whose brain-children like the steamship, which runs wild and damages the fleet of Posthumus, the heir and the brass butterfly destroys Posthumus by causing an explosion. Both these novelettes depict ancient cultures at points of crises and the consequences. *Clonk Clonk* portrays a matriarchal society where dominating aggressive women like Palm rule the roost, shouldering all social responsibilities like providing food, initiating sex-rousing awe and terror among the men-folk. Palm only fears the power of the dark potent brew that she is addicted to.[124] Charging Elephant's weak ankle alienates him from the hunting men and his passion for poetry links him to Palm and the woman. Chimp brings change to the static society of the Leopard men in *Clonk Clonk* by his ambiguous sexual role.[125]

The radical forces of upheaval within individuals *vis-à-vis* society in Samuel Mountjoy, Colley, Oliver, Pincher and Jocelin are seen to go beyond the social into the darker world of the self. Cataclysmic changes like war, can cause a disorientation of the spirit, a displacement or personal crisis, social insecurity and a feeling of rootlessness.

Defects of human society can be traced back to defects in human beings and this is clear in *Lord of the Flies* where Golding drags us into the vortex of the contemporary horrors of a nuclear war and beyond it past civilization into a primitive world of blood and anarchy which finds expression in class-war in a group of boys. Jack Merridew and his choir group feel superior to Ralph and the rest of the boys. As Walter Allen observes, 'One sees what Golding is doing. He is showing us stripped man, man naked of all his sanctions of custom and civilisation, man as he is alone and in his essence,...and the collapse of morality, goodness, kindness in the absence of restraint.'[126]

Here we have a powerful portrait of the social and moral regression of a group of English schoolboys. Class barriers ruin goodwill between the individual boys right from the beginning, causing tension and disenchantment in the tropical paradisaic isle. Superiority of class breeds insecurity and hate. Ralph and Piggy introduce themselves. '"I could swim when I was five. Daddy taught me. He's a commander in the Navy. When he gets leave he'll come and rescue us. What's your father?" Piggy flushed suddenly. "My dad's dead, and my mum—."'[127] Fat Piggy is a social misfit among the boys with his practical, pessimistic philosophy and the strange maturity of a loner in society. Evil stems from the arrogant confidence in status flaunted by Jack and his choir boys. Piggy is 'intimidated by the uniformed superiority and the offhand authority in Merridew's voice.'[128]

Jack's potential for despotism makes him abuse the power of democracy enshrined in the conch and the leadership of Ralph. The clash of individual wills of the two boys arises from their lack of co-ordination of priorities on the isle. Ralph wants the signal-fire and shelters while Jack is bent on pig-hunting and primitive survival. '"I was talking about smoke! Don't you want to be rescued? All you can talk about is pig, pig, pig!" "But we want meat!"'[129] Conflict leads to disintegration of the group.

Jack symbolises the forces of unreason, confusion, violence and terror within the individual which wreck social institutions and hinder the progress of virtues like peace, harmony and unity. As the tribal chief-hunter Jack savours the heady power of providing food. Primeval fear of the unknown beast permits Jack to externalise the evil and identify it with a physical thing. He goads his hunters to paint their faces and pursue the pig with spears. Group meetings are a kind of social machine that transform the energies by plugging into group situations. Social rituals demand rhythmic regular actions like chanting to focus attention on the object. 'Jack thinks that evil and destruction are live forces. In a world of power there are powers at work that are stronger than man. But these powers (Beast, Devil or God), can be propitiated by ritual, ceremony, sacrifice.'[130] From pig-hunt to man hunt it is just one step. The chant changes from '"Kill the pig! Cut his throat!... Bash him in!"'[131] to '"Kill the beast! Cut his throat! Spill his blood!"'[132] And Simon is ritually sacrificed in the orgy. Emile Durkheim explains how 'society and rationality rest on a non-rational foundation.'[133]

Critics have reacted sharply to Golding's grim image of society and his portrait of children as worse than adults. In truth, children being uninhibited, immature are likely to be more violent and uncontrolled when the brakes of civilization are taken off.[134] David Spitz recognises 'Piggy as Socrates, the voice of reason.' He is the "outsider" and in his death madness of anarchy and chaos set in! Authority must be found elsewhere, for men accept Reason no more than they do Revelation.[135] Golding's belief that human nature is diseased is only partially true. 'He has forgotten that the state of nature is not necessarily a state of political and moral innocence. The boys are carefully chosen products of an established middle-class society of the twentieth century.'[136]

J.D. O'Hara is equally damning when he observes defensively that 'Golding's images of society are erroneous. Our society, though bad, is not as corrupt as Jack's; our society's morality is not as impotent as that of Ralph's society. Even a skeptic must admit that society refrains from barbarity more often than it licenses it.'[137] In fact, similar situations like Jack's rise to tyranny are being witnessed in the second half of the twentieth century in countries like Iran with Ayatollah Khomeini, Romania with Ceausescu and Uganda with Idi Amin. It is fear and panic of life that unleashes the primitive forces of violence in mob frenzy. The proportion of passive, civilised people like Simon, Piggy is far outweighed by the massive hordes of mindless madmen. At a personal interview, when asked if he wished to shock readers into sense by the ugly truths in his novels, Golding assented. He explained. '"I am like a doctor. I diagnose the ills of mankind."'[138]

Talcott Parsons describes our age when he says that 'We live in a time in which conflict as a deep-rooted malady of civilization, is attracting attention more strongly than ever—cold war, the nuclear menace, racism creating a rebellious world that thinks up theories of conflicts; which provide a distraction and it is felt that the evil is exorcised. Actually, it is symptomatic of a deep undercurrent of social insecurity and unrest caused by inflation, economic disparities and political instability.'[139] An escalation of crime and terrorism is a notable feature of our age. In 1941, Pitrim Sorokin viewed modern western civilization as 'rotten and soon to collapse, to be followed by a new ideational culture. His contemporary, Arnold Toynbee, also viewed the cycle of twenty-one civilizations all except the contemporary western civilisation, which he predicted is moving into the later stages of decay.'[140]

Darkness Visible is a complex novel in which Golding probes the invisible forces of good and evil along with class hatreds that corrode society. Two individuals of extreme types are examined—Sophy, the evil terrorist and child kidnapper, and Matty, the saintly scarred boy, who is martyred in the end. In between there is an entire range of social perverts and eccentrics like Pedigree, the homosexual master and pedophile; Edwin Bell, the schoolmaster, inclined to religion; Gerry, the mafia henchman of Sophy. Sim Goodchild, the bookseller is a rational intellectual blinded by the evil of intolerance and lack of perception. Sim has always been attracted by the Stanhope girls. He confesses '"I used to be in love with them."'[141] These two old men derive pleasure and experience an emotional orgasm from discussing the sordid details of Pedigree's follies.[142] Their 'deeply liberal' wives will not come to a seance with Matty as Pedegree is coming too.

Social turmoil is a phenomenon of our modern age when youth under social stress rebels against hierarchy. Sophy is a typical product of this period. Neglected in childhood, she and Toni adapt themselves quickly. She revels in the power of sadism and is more cold-blooded than Gerry, the professional killer, she teams up with. Her looks are so deceptive. Sim observes to her father, Mr. Stanhope, '"...she's so enchanting—they're both so enchanting,"' The father replies '"Be your age. That generation's not enchanting, any of it."' To which Sim remarks, "'They've always been a pleasure to us, innocence, beauty, manners—'" Stanhope explodes, "'Innocence? They tried to poison me....'"[143] Freedom to Sophy, is to put aside guards and taboos and take the brakes off—in the cosmic sense it is physical unwinding or entropy.[144] She matches Matty's divine energy of light and calm with her witch-like energy of darkness and chaos. She invokes the 'black sun'[145] in the mock murder of the child she plots to kidnap.

Golding is constantly questioning the motives and erratic behaviour of human beings. There is a vital link between crime and social-structure. Serious crimes like sexual outrages, murder, terrorism can be explained as part of the situation of a class-stratified society. It is a matter of conflict between people in a stratified society. What makes evil so alluring? Dr. Henry opines that 'Evil is a fascinating subject as it has the aura of glamour about it. Sexual perversions also arouse our curiosity about abnormal human behaviour.'[146] Wilfred Barclay in *The Paper Men* is elected mock paper-saint in his Random Club for being the most notoriously corrupt man.[147]

In the trial after the incident of arson and the abortive attempt at kidnapping the child by Sophy, Gerry and company— Sim, Edwin, Stanhope and others are all interrogated and involved in the ugly scandal. They realise that though the court has released them, they are guilty of sheer ignorance and a sick, class superiority. Sim cannot comprehend what freedom and justice Sophy as a young person lacked![148] Their warped judgement makes them damn Pedigree.

Golding puts the grand accusation into Pedigree's mouth, "'How do I know I'm not speaking to a very clever pair of terrorists who put those girls up to it?.... The judge said you were innocent, but we, the great British Public, we...we know, don't we?'"[149]

Class privileges breed hate and antagonism between people, which manifests itself in all kinds of clashes. Pedigree hates their complacency, their money power and their pretended innocence. In *Rites of Passage*, Captain Anderson, Talbot, Deverel, and others are responsible for the suicide of Colley. In *The Spire* and *Free Fall* Jocelin and Sammy partly admit to the sin of exploitation and lack or tolerance. Oliver, in turn stands indicted for his casual callous use of the low class, Evie Babbacombe.

Golding clearly conveys the terrible truth that men cannot evade the social responsibility of crimes and outrages in society. They have to take the rap and bear the burden of guilt. Along with social change, changes in values take place. Individualistic, hedonistic, and materialistic viewpoints are being fostered. This reduces social control and increases social disorganisation. Golding's world is socially relevant to the tensions, frustrations, and predicaments of the upper class and the middle-classes in flux. Wilfred Barclay's particular predicament is well posed by his friend, Johnny. '"You intrigue me. Why a man ostensibly so indifferent to society should be, if I may coin a phrase, so shit-scared of critical opinion—"'[150] That is the very crux of the problem, that Barclay cannot stand exposure.

The seething cauldron of class antagonism is revealed at the party that Barclay throws at the Random Club for Rick. Gabriel and Johnny are curious about Rick's status and wealth, '"The day of the rich Americans is past, I'm afraid." "No sir, it isn't, sir!" "I am looking for a rich American. Arabs don't go in for sculpture except as an investment." "He's not wealthy, Gabriel. He's a poor white like the rest of us."'[151] This enlightens one about the attitudes across the Atlantic. Barclay refuses Rick the rights of a biographer and in the ensuing brawl people are hurt in the melée. Apparently a normal pastime for the stinking rich to shed their social inhibitions! Barclay has to accept responsibility for the damage to the club property and the statue of Psyche.[152] Barclay's bloated ego is at peace but vengeful Rick has the last word or rather, the last card.[153] Golding shows honestly how diseased modern society is, especially, the elite, the academics—the paper men!

Not all conflict is injurious to progress. T.S. Eliot in *The Idea of a Christian Society* explains how the functions of individuals become hereditary and this hardens into class or caste distinctions soon leading to conflict. So religion, politics, science and art reach a point of conscious struggle for dominance. This friction can be highly creative[154] in Jocelin's building of *The Spire* in the teeth of fear, fury, and envy.

The conflicts between reality and fantasy in the delusions of class, snobbery, money, status are a natural sign of growth and development. A static society like the sterile bourgeois society of Stilbourne must learn from Golding's feeling epigraph in *The Pyramid* of PTAH-HOTEP '"If thou be among people make for thyself love, the beginning and end of the heart."'[155] A full-blooded society's culture will encompass its strengths and weaknesses, its greeds and illusions, and its rise and fall.

To the charge that Golding does not show social responsibility in a period of crisis,[156] M. Kinkead-Weekes answers that it is very unfair as it robs the writer of his freedom. He maintains that Golding on the contrary had taken pains to expose social evils in his novels.[157] Twentieth century novelists cannot help but mirror the moving graph of class struggle in their realistic novels.

The Cambridge critic F.R. Leavis' view of the world of new novelists befits Golding brilliantly: 'a religious yet moralistic, non-political yet aggressively class-conscious, the faith of a British Last Puritan.'[158]

The rigid class-structure had its own worth as a splitting device but it was a wasteful, ugly system which is being broken down gradually. Desmond Morris opines that for 'the development of a super-tribe a high proportion of frustrated status-seekers is a must to make it a mobile one.'[159]

Golding shows the impossibility of a static society. 'For the cruel fact is that had that boy walked into the perfected society, to him would have come out of his blood the hates and loves...the antipathies and greeds, the jealousies and ambitions, the misdirected energies and deadening sloths; not just his but those of other people all working with, through and against each other.'[160]

Utopias are static dreams on paper—for reality and life spell change. Golding's metaphor of the bicycle in a snapshot rings the doom of stagnation in real life. When 'It no longer relies on the balance between change and stability, will fall in the road; and a society of the same sort would fall clean off the world and vanish with the dinosaurs.'[161] A dynamic or vibrant society requires conflict, growth, and decay, to thrive. Class-conflict is therefore a necessary evil.

NOTES

1. W. Golding: *Rites of Passage*, 124.

2. Ralf Dahrendorf: 'Conflict after Class: New Perspectives on the Theory of Social and Political Conflict,' *The Third Noel Buxton Lecture*, University of Essex, March 2, 1967, London, Longmans, 1967, 2.

3. Gerhard E Lenski: 'A Theory of Inequality' in *Three Sociological Traditions*, (ed.) Randall Collins, Oxford, Oxford University Press, 1985, 102.

4. W. Golding: 'Utopias and Antiutopias,' *A Moving Target*, 182.

5. W. Golding: *Darkness Visible*, Ch. 10, 153.

6. *Ibid.*, 160.

7. W. Golding: *The Paper Men*, Chs. 8-9, 89-93.

8. *Ibid.*, Ch. 5, 47-49.

9. *Ibid.*, Ch. 5, 55.

10. Mary Eagleton and David Pierce: *Attitudes to Class in the English Novel*, London, Thames and Hudson, 1979, 41-42.

11. Mary Eagleton and David Pierce: *Op. cit.*, 26-27.

12. W. Golding: *Rites of Passage*, 86-89.

    Lord Talbot calls Zenobia's plea for reassurance after seduction 'act three of an inferior drama.' He treats her as a tawdry bit. 'Do not pretend that these circumstances even our somewhat inelegant posture are unfamiliar to you.' Calling her a fool only shows his aristocratic power of class, in according a low esteem to people like Zenobia. The battle between Gertrude Morel's genteel ways and Walter's working-class values mirrors class-conflict in the Bestwood village in D.H. Lawrence's *Sons and Lovers*.

13. M. Kinkead-Weekes and I. Gregor: *Op. cit.*, 262.

14. Quoted from Interview, 'Twentieth Century Literature,' Summer, 1982, by M. Kinkead-Weekes and I. Gregor in *William Golding: A Critical Study*, 262.

15. Bertrand Russell: *New Hopes for a Changing World*, London, George Allen and Unwin, 1951, 59.

16. Claude Levi-Strauss: 'Kinship as Sexual Property Exchange,' 1949, reviewed in *Three Sociological Traditions*, by Randall Collins, 198-200.

17. W. Golding: *The Inheritors*, Ch. 12, 226.

18. *Ibid.*, 225-226.

19. *Ibid.*, Ch. 5, 102.

20. *Ibid.*, Ch. 12, 224.

21. *Ibid.*, Ch. 11, 216.

22. S. Freud: *Civilization and its Discontents*, trans. Joan Riviere, London, The Hogarth Press, 1949, 86.

23. H.G. Wells: *A Short History of the World*, Pelican, Harmondsworth, Penguin, 1956, 219.

24. W. Golding: *The Spire*, Ch. 1, 22.

25. *Ibid.*, 26.

26. *Ibid.*, Ch. 2, 32-35.

27. *Ibid.*, 35.

28. *Ibid.*, Ch. 3, 64.

29. *Ibid.*, Ch. 2, 39.

30. *Ibid.*, Ch. 3, 54.

31. *Ibid.*, Ch. 4, 90.
    The dumb man shields Jocelin from certain murder in the orgy.

32. *Ibid.*, Ch. 7, 137.

33. *Ibid.*, Ch. 9, 167.
    Father Anselm's revenge is sweet—this is how he has described the workers in his report to Rome.

34. *Ibid.*, 169.

35. *Ibid.*, Ch. 10, 184.

36. *Ibid.*, Ch. l, 27.

37. Lionel Trilling: 'Manners, Morals and the Novel,' *The English Novel*, Casebooks Series, (ed.) Stephen Hazel, London, Macmillan, 1978, 76.

38. W. Golding: 'The Ladder and the Tree,' *The Hot Gates*, 168.

39. Stephen Spender: 'My Parents kept me from children who were Rough,' *Poems*, London, Faber and Faber, 1933, 22.

40. W. Golding: *Rites of Passage*, 125.

41. *Ibid.*, 126.

42. Blake Morrison: 'Men Can Die of Shame,' *New Statesman*, October 17, 1980, 24.

43. W. Golding: *Rites of Passage*, 7.

44. *Ibid.*, 9.

45. *Ibid.*, 31.

46. *Ibid.*, 42.

47. *Ibid.*, 63.

48. *Ibid.*, 63.

49. *Ibid.*, 129.

50. *Ibid.*, 129.

51. *Ibid.*, 134.

52. W. Golding: *Close Quarters*, Ch. 3, 38.
    Talbot experiences mawkish sentimentality on realising that the enemy ship is an English vessel. His fear is dispelled and so he weeps.— Ch. 5, 55.

53. *Ibid.*, Ch. l, 11.

Karl Marx and Frederick Engels observe that 'the history of all hitherto existing society is the history of class struggles. The ideas of the ruling class are in every epoch the ruling ideas: that is, the class, which is the "ruling material force" of society, is at the same time its ruling intellectual force.' Reprinted from 'The German Ideology' and quoted in *Three Sociological Traditions*, (ed.) Randall Collins, 5.

54. P. Redpath: *Op. cit.*, 65.

55. W. Golding: *Rites of Passage*, 259.

56. *Ibid.*, 258.

The irony implicit in 'happy,' used soon after Colley's death is clear. Anderson, Prettiman and others have no respect for the church and are prejudiced against clergymen.

57. Golding follows Fielding in his symbolic parody of the outward humiliations of Parson Adams—his wig is snatched off by the hounds, his cassock torn, soup poured down his breeches, gin mixed with his ale to make him drunk and crackers tied to his cassock to make him dance like a devil. Finally, he is enthroned on a blanket suspended over a tub for a horrible ducking like Colley's. Henry Fielding: *Joseph Andrews*, New York, Random House, 1950, Book III, Ch.7, 290.

58. S.J. Boyd: *Op. cit.*, 157.

59. W. Golding: *Close Quarters*, Ch. 8, 107.

But Lord Talbot is so deeply smitten that he is willing to override class barriers to fulfill his heart's desire. He marries Marion at the end of his voyage in *Fire Down Below*, Ch. 23, 311.

60. W. Golding: *Close Quarters*, Ch. 7, 92.

61. *Ibid.*, Ch. 8, 118.

62. W. Golding: *Fire Down Below*, Ch. 5, 56.

63. *Ibid.*, Ch. 9, 116.

64. W. Golding: *Close Quarters*, Ch. 7, 99.

65. W. Golding: *Fire Down Below*, Ch. 11, 143.

66. *Ibid.*, Ch. 11, 145.

67. W. Golding: *Close Quarters*, Ch. 16, 262.

68. S.J. Boyd: 'Saltwater Soap,' Unpublished papers, 18.

69. W. Golding: *Fire Down Below*, Ch. 20, 261.

70. Charles Dickens in *Oliver Twist* exposes the evils of child labour, exploitation and proves that rotten social regulations can only create an atmosphere of hopelessness and helplessness.

71. Dr. A. Henry: 'Golding's *The Pyramid*,' *Southern Review*, Vol. 3, No. l, 1968, 16-18.

72. W. Golding: *The Pyramid*, 12.

73. *Ibid.*, 164.

74. *Ibid.*, 191-192.

75. Oliver is awed by Claymore's power and wealth. 'I saw him so secure, so old, so huge in his ownership of the *Stilbourne Advertiser*, impregnable,' *The Pyramid*, 12.

76. David Skilton: '*The Pyramid* and Comic Social Fiction,' 1978 in *William Golding—Novels 1954-1967—A Casebook* (ed.), Norman Page, London, Macmillan, 1985, 176-79.

77. W. Golding: *The Pyramid*, 131-133.

78. *Ibid.*, 88.

79. Stephen Mennell: 'Sociology' in *Twentieth Century Mind*, (eds.) C.B. Cox and A.E. Dyson, Vol. 3, 1945-65, London, Oxford University Press, 1972, 166.

80. W. Golding: *The Pyramid*, 114.

81. *Ibid.*, 115.
    In Evelyn de Tracy's words the concert is an 'outrageous exercise in bucolic ineptitude,' 146.

82. W. Golding: *The Pyramid*, 23.

83. *Ibid.*, 82.
    The middle-class protagonist's frustrations, fears, and inhibitions influence his development towards a new social responsibility, scarred by his past.

84. *Ibid.*, 168.

85. *Ibid.*, 207.

86. *Ibid.*, 206.

87. *Ibid.*, 214.

88. *Ibid.*, 178.

89. *Ibid.*, 145-146.

90. *Ibid.*, 147.

91. *Ibid.*, 177.

92. *Ibid.*, 179.

93. *Ibid.*, 58.

94. *Ibid.*, 100.

95. *Ibid.*, 178.

96. Howard. S. Babb: *Op. cit.*, 195.

97. W. Golding: *The Pyramid*, 75.

98. *Ibid.*, 91.

99. *Ibid.*, 109.

100. *Ibid.*, 83.

101. *Ibid.*, 126.

102. *Ibid.*, 127.

103. *Ibid.*, 205.

104. Wilfred Sheed: 'William Golding: *The Pyramid* in his *The Morning After*, Farrar Straus and Giroux Inc., 1971, 280-82.

105. A. Johnston: 'Innovation and Rediscovery in Golding's *The Pyramid*, in *Critique: Studies in Modern Fiction*. Vol. 14, No. 2, 1972, 97-112.

When Bounce Dawlish tries to coax Olly to choose music as a career, his middle-class caution warns him, 'All at once the *obscenity* of erratic, unpensioned music presented itself to me.' *The Pyramid*, 193.

106. M. Bradbury: 'The Novel' in *The Twentieth Century Mind*, (eds.) C.B. Cox and A.E. Dyson, Vol. 3, 319.

107. W. Golding: 'Crabbed Age and Youth.' *A Moving Target*, 99.

108. Leslie A. Fiedler: 'Class War in British Literature,' on *On Contemporary Literature*, (ed.) Richard Kostelanetz, 67.

109. Leslie A. Fiedler: *Op. cit.*, 75.

110. W. Golding: *Pincher Martin*, Ch.10, 147-148.

111. *Ibid.*, 149.

112. Dr. V. Tiger: *Op. cit.*, 141.

113. W. Golding: *Free Fall*, Ch. 2, 53.

114. *Ibid.*, Ch. 2, 59.

115. *Ibid.*, 62.

116. *Ibid.*, Ch. 11, 194.

117. *Ibid.*, 203.

118. S.J. Boyd: *Op. cit.*, 75.

119. W. Golding: *Free Fall*, Ch. 4, 80-81.

120. *Ibid.*, Ch. 4, 101.

121. *Ibid.*, Ch. 6, 128.

122. W. Golding: 'The Scorpion God,' *The Scorpion God*, London, Faber and Faber, 1971, 40.

123. *Ibid.*, 60-62.

124. W. Golding: 'Clonk Clonk,' *The Scorpion God*, 92.

125. *Ibid.*, 102-108.

126. Walter Allen: *Tradition and Dream*, London, The Hogarth Press, 1986, 289-290.

127. W. Golding: *Lord of the Flies*, Ch. 1, 14.

128. *Ibid.*, Ch. 1, 22.

129. *Ibid.*, Ch. 3, 59.

130. M. Kinkead-Weekes and I. Gregor: *Op. cit.*, 45.

131. W. Golding: *Lord of the Flies*, Ch. 7, 126.

132. *Ibid.*, Ch. 9, 167.

133. Durkheim's microsociology examines the theory of small groups and rituals. Anyone who tampers with the social-energy transforming machine runs the danger of receiving a high intensity shock. Rituals

are the coordinated actions of an assembled group that gives its members a special emotional energy; symbols being ideas, emblems, and doctrines that represent group experience—Feelings can develop from mere neutrality into outright hostility. Randall Collins: 'Sociological Insight,' *An Introduction to Nonobvious Sociology*, Oxford, Oxford University Press, 1982, 45-46.

134. Wordsworth's idealisation of the 'child,' 'the growing boy' based on a recognition of his spiritual purity is in sharp contrast to Golding's view of children today!

135. David Spitz: 'Power and Authority—An Interpretation of Golding's *Lord of the Flies* in *The Antioch Review* A.R. Inc. Vol. 30, No. 1, Spring, 1970, 25-30.

136. *Ibid.*, 33.

137. J.D. O'Hara: 'Mute Choir Boys and Angelic Pigs,' The Fable in *Lord of the Flies*, in *Texas Studies of English Literature and Language*, University of Texas Press, Vol. 7, No. 4, Winter, 1966, 411-20.

138. W. Golding: A Personal Interview in Cornwall on June 26, 1990.

139. Talcott Parsons: 'The Social System' (1951) in *Harmony and Conflict in Modern Society*. J. Pen Translated from the Dutch by Trevor S. Preston, London, New York, McGraw-Hill, 1962, 3.

140. Paul B. Horton and Chester L. Hunt: *Sociology*, Sixth edition, McGraw-Hill, 1984, 511-513.

141. W. Golding: *Darkness Visible*, Ch.13, 224.

142. *Ibid.*, Ch. 15, 242.

143. *Ibid.*, Ch. 13, 219.

144. Don Crompton: *Op. cit.*, 117.

145. W. Golding: *Darkness Visible*, Ch. 15, 252.

146. Dr. A. Henry: A Personal Interview at the University of Exeter, Exeter, June 1, 1990.

147. W. Golding: *The Paper Men*, Ch. 15, 179.

148. W. Golding: *Darkness Visible*, Ch. 16, 259.

149. *Ibid.*, 259.

150. W. Golding: *The Paper Men*, Ch. 10, 110.

Modern civilization has commercialised and debased both art and the artist. Social pressures make Barclay write potboilers for cheap success.

151. *Ibid.*, Ch. 15, 180.

The impact of class is rather weakly studied in this novel. It is Anglo-American prejudice that is examined.

152. *Ibid.*, Ch. 15, 182-183.

153. *Ibid.*, 191.

154. T.S. Eliot: 'The Idea of a Christian Society,' *Selected Prose of T.S. Eliot*, (ed.) F. Kermode, London, Faber and Faber, 1975, 292.

155. W. Golding: *The Pyramid*, epigraph, 9.
156. James R. Baker: 'Golding's Progress,' in *Novel*, Fall, 1973, 62-70.
157. M. Kinkead-Weekes: A Personal Interview at the University of Kent, Canterbury on June 6, 1990.
158. F.R. Leavis: 'Class War in British Literature,' in *On Contemporary Literature*, 74.
159. Desmond Morris: *Op. cit.*, 62.
160. W. Golding: 'Utopias and Antiutopias,' *A Moving Target*, 178.
161. *Ibid.*, 179.

5

RELIGION

◆

To label Golding as a 'deeply religious'[1] writer in the conventional sense is a sterile paternity for a man who prides himself on his 'curse of rationality.'[2] A harshly realistic, complex, and disturbing writer, Golding has no time for 'fringe religion or kitchen theology.'[3] Deeply concerned about the moral malaise of modern man, Golding yearns to solve the riddle of man faced with the problem of pain, death, social and moral responsibility. 'Man is...an eternal question mark.... What am I after? What am I trying to discover?... There is awe and terror about us, ugliness and pathos, and this finality which we cannot believe is indifference, but more like preoccupation.... We are mysterious ourselves.'[4]

From his Cornish mother he inherited a sense of the supernatural, an awareness of the terrors of darkness—'My childhood's stance, then, was romantic though terrified, even a bit religious though pagan.'[5] And from his father, a Wellsian rationalist, Golding imbibed a wholesome respect for science and a rational approach to the knowledge of man and the cosmos; finally, a healthy scepticism of the empirical limitations of dogma. As he frankly observes, 'Sometimes, when the whole cycle of Christianity had seemed simply too implausible, a fantasy and a ridiculous one from Adam onwards, in a glum way I would unearth documents which proved him no more than a man or perhaps not even that but only a compilation.'[6] He told Jack Biles that his father's critical mind did not prove an absence of religion but a profound religious feeling. And Golding himself admits he is a moralist.[7]

The venerable sage-philosopher novelist expresses his cry of hope for the evolution of a moral man in the future—'It is, then, a moral question. Well, we have had...*homo habilis, homo neanderthalensis*, Mousterian Man, Cromagnon Man, *homo sapiens*—has nature done with us? Surely we can search that capacious sleeve and find something a bit better!... We must produce *homo moralis*, the human being who cannot kill his own kind, nor exploit them nor rob them.'[8]

From a penetrating study of his novels emerges the view that the protagonist is perpetually impaled on the horns of the dilemma of moral choices. Samuel Mountjoy pays the price of his freedom of choice in *Free Fall*. The science master, Nick's universe is controlled by the law of conservation of energy, while Pringle's world is ruled by the Bible. In a choice between the physical and the spiritual, Sammy opts for the former, sacrificing everything for sex and Beatrice. He rejects religion as Pringle, the tormented spinster, misinterprets the healthy curiosity and awe of an 'earnest metaphysical boy.'[9] His intelligent mind tries to grasp and divine the truth of Moses and the burning bush on Mount Sinai, while she thinks he is searching the bible for smut! Young Sammy cringes in hate and recoils from the fanatically violent churchwoman's intolerant zeal, spirituality and religion. He makes a fetish of sex and woos it in the name of religion. Evil becomes his good. As Hodson finely observes that Sammy 'has abrogated his soul: like matter he is in free fall, apparently stable but, in fact, falling as all things fall relative to each other simultaneously in space.'[10]

Sammy realises only in Halde's interrogation sessions that he is damned. 'Once a human being has lost freedom there is no end to the coils of cruelty,..... They said the damned in hell were forced to torture the innocent live people with disease.'[11] The artist in Sammy knows he is irrational in adopting Nick's 'stunted universe.'[12] He deduces that there is 'no spirit, no absolute.'[13] Therefore right and wrong are 'a parliamentary decision like no betting slips or drinks after half-past ten....'[14] He rationalises 'why should not Sammy's good be what Sammy decides? There are no morals that can be deduced from natural science, there are only immorals. The supply of nineteenth-century optimism and goodness had run out before it reached me.'[15] Christian religion had lost its enchantment, its beauty vitiated by evil, mechanical propagation.

Ambrose Bierce remarks that 'Religion is the daughter of Hope and Fear explaining to ignorance the nature of the unknowable.'[16] Modern man's attitude is naturally cynical, curious. Golding reveals the evil of fossilized religious beliefs in characters like Rowena Pringle with her superficial faith in the tenets of orthodox Christianity. She hammers Johnny in the catechism class: '"God—"/Smack! "is"—/Smack!—"love!"'[17] And this is the evil way in which she propagates belief in Christianity. Golding is bitterly ironic in his condemnation of the stagnation and decay of true religion. The blind, cruel religious zeal of Pringle only drives Sammy and Johnny away from the love of God, and belief in a benign Being.

Golding has been called a religious writer for daring to describe man's brush with God. David Lodge speaks of his Christian pessimism, insistently anti-humanist and anti-Pelagian.[18] He is not always negative and his fables are more in the tragic frame of Kafka, Camus, Greene and Huxley than Aesop's fables. His deep compassion for man's suffering and his moral transgressions focus attention on his exposition of the evils of polluted dogmas and intolerance. Samuel Hynes calls his novels 'moral models'[19] for they trace a contour of experience and examine the consequence of human actions in a moral frame.

Golding does not smugly evade the problem of evil, for Poincaré says, to agree with everything or nothing are two equally simple solutions for they both avoid the necessity of making up your mind. Golding is neither a fanatic nor an agnostic, but pledges his faith in a religion of humanity, non-violence and peace like Edwin Bell of *Darkness Visible*.

By the end of the seventies, the spiritual surge of the age had meandered into a swamp of fake god men, psychedelic religion and sadists like Sophy and Reverend Jim Jones of the Carribean, who organised a mass suicide in 1980. And Edwin Bell's pertinent diagnosis of Sophy's weird outrages is, "...she's mad and bad! She's not human Sim. We have to face it at last. We're not all human.... We're all mad, the whole damned race. We're wrapped in illusions, delusions, confusions about the penetrability of partitions, we're all mad and in solitary confinement."[20]

The spiritual isolation of man in the welter of scientific progress in modern civilisation is stressed. Exactly when does religion become an evil or a negative force? According to Golding, it is when we violate the principle of our obedience to the performance of our duties of love and duty towards God.

Contemporary writers have traced the loss of faith to the alienations of man from God by rationality.[21] It is the meddling intellect that steals man's faith and perverts his mind.[22] Golding examines the problem of evil both from the metaphysical and the moral angle. He believes in Original Sin and the burden of man's guilt. Truly his 'bête noir' is Original Sin and he does not conceal the fact. Boyd observed that 'it is not possible to separate Original Sin from Golding's skin!'[23]

The story of man's fall from grace is linked with the tragic inevitability of mortality, the price that man pays for his disobedience, to attain the knowledge of good and evil. Golding focuses attention on this inglorious state of man, but allows in his later novels, for grace in death through redemption. This is why he calls himself 'a universal pessimist but a cosmic optimist.'[24] He recognises self-awareness in the world as hell, as the first act towards knowledge, grace and redemption. For his characters, fear of God and knowledge of God are one and the same.

Dean Jocelin accepts the evil of his arrogance in building the impossible spire as an act of folly. So Golding says, 'I prefer and at the same time fear the saying of St. Augustine, "Woe unto me if I speak of the things of God; but woe unto me if I do *not* speak of the things of God."'[25] He feels strongly the urge to record his supra-rational experiences. It is this mystic acceptance of the rationalist's faith in the awe and mystery of Nature and God, which is a fascinating trait of Golding's mind. He does not deny being 'an aging novelist floundering in all the complexities of twentieth century living, all the muddle of part beliefs.'[26] A review of this 'muddle' in the light of evolutionary theories, scientific research political and psychological advances and a revival of animism, paganism in universal religion as an antidote to orthodox Christianity, is undertaken.

Golding's vision of a world religion is seen in Prettiman's

dream in *Fire Down Below*, when he tries to convince the sceptical Edmund of the goodness of the universe, that every man can receive. '"I tell you Edmund, there is not a poor depraved criminal in the land towards which we are moving, who could not by lifting his head, gaze straight into the fire of that love, that 'xàpis' of which we spoke!"'[27] Golding speaks of the fire of human affection that glows in every human heart.[28] It is like Tennyson's 'little systems' which are 'broken lights of thee.'[29] A similar idea of a universal religion is expressed by the philosopher, Mr. Prettiman, '"Imagine our caravan, we, a fire down below here—sparks of the Absolute—matching the fire up there—out there! Moving by cool night through the deserts of this new land towards Eldorado with nothing between our eyes and the Absolute, our ears and that music."'[30] Like Butler, Golding seeks a rational religion unpolluted by the stale doctrines of the decaying Church.

The nineteenth century was an age of intellectual upheavals. Darwin's Theory of Evolution and the thesis that emergence of the human species from a common ancestor with the ape dealt a blow to the orthodox belief of genesis and the creation of man in the image of God. If the process of the evolution of life was a consequence of the operation of natural forces, then Man, the most conceited of mammals was shocked to recognise his kinship with the lower animals. If Man was merely a tenuous link in the evolutionary chain of life, how could he claim divinity? It shook the western world and struck at the very roots of Christian belief. In 'Copernicus,' Golding explains succinctly the fear and prejudice of established religions like Christianity that resented the discoveries of scientists like Copernicus in their quest of truth, knowledge and God.[31]

While blind faith in dogma is evil, blind faith in the perfectibility of man through evolution is also evil. Evil exists where ever humanity is threatened. In *The Inheritors* Golding savagely twists the biblical saying that 'the meek shall inherit the earth' to explode the myth of progress by means of the slaughter of the innocent Neanderthalers by the homo sapiens! The greater evil of the new people strikes fear and dread into the hearts of the gentle Neanderthalers. These outwardly gross creatures are really friendly and kind.

Lok, Fa, Mal and others follow the religion of Animism[32] of non-civilized peoples which includes the worship of Nature as a loving entity and the practice of ancestor-worship. Old Mal is the venerated patriarch while the old woman is the custodian of fire like the earth mother, Oa. Their reverence for the matriarch is seen in Mal's speech, '"There was the great Oa. She brought forth the earth from her belly. She gave suck. The earth brought forth woman and the woman brought forth the first man out of her belly."'[33] Their pre-lapsarian life is a paradise of primitivism, for it is one of instinct and simple rituals.

Fa has all the traits of a protector of her family. Sensing danger in the destructive evil power of the new people, she appeals to the only deities they worship like the ice woman in the cave—to save Liku. Mal's death is poignant and the Neanderthalers resign themselves to the Great Oa, for she has taken him back into her womb. Their love for Oa is compounded of fear, respect and veneration. Reluctantly, Lok kills the hyena dragging the dead doe, for destruction of any living creature saddens them. 'This natural religion contains no idea of crime or punishment, and, while it requires offering, it knows nothing of blood sacrifice. The only idea of evil they have, in fact, is the destruction of life by violence.'[34] Lok experiences a feeling of guilt and remorse at dismembering the doe. He is a Hamlet in his noble indecision. The cruel lust of the new people baffles him.[35]

Liku, Lok and Fa venture into the orgy of the camp of the new men where Lok is mercilessly attacked and chased away.[36] He bears the pain of loss and grief with a new awareness that '...the misery must be embraced painfully as a man might hug thorns to him and it sought to comprehend the new people from whom all changes came.'[37] Despite the kidnapping of Liku and the little one, Lok has no picture perceptions of revenge, no idea of violating their pacific religion by attacking or killing the new people.

Seen through the puzzled perception of Lok, the new people's religion is one that propagates ritual killing, revenge and the terror of whips. Their progress seems but a refinement of cultivated evil. Golding's polarized vision admits that to lament innocence is to reject progress in the chain of evolution.

Golding illustrates perversities in religion in various ages. The primitive blood sacrifices of the new people shifts to the pagan, Christian scatological notion of objectifying the beast or Satan in *Lord of the Flies*. In *The Spire*, the evils of medieval superstitions of witchcraft, miracles and 'religious hubris'[38] are explored, while in *Rites of Passage* the Dionysian idea of excess and the sacrifice of the scapegoat is examined.

The Christian view of purgatory and hell are examined in the Greedy Soul that rejects salvation in *Pincher Martin*. The rationalising of sin and the erotic espousal of evil versus social responsibility is seen in *Free Fall* and the worship of false gods like Mammon, and the marketing of religion through music, sex and class is reviewed in *The Pyramid*. The use abuse of religion by man is not true religion but an evil bond that man must try and break out of to achieve some link with his Creator.

A climax of sorts is attained in *Darkness Visible* where Golding grapples with the problem of evil by attempting to break down the barriers between Good and Evil and reconcile them as One is One. For man the twin realities of Good and Evil co-exist on the earth, which is his only reality! In *The Paper Men*, the gross neglect of religion and ethics has a boomerang effect on the hedonistic Barclay, who is humbled by a spiritual experience. In *Close Quarters* and *Fire Down Below* Golding sums up his ideas on religion and the moral individual's dream of a world religion based on 'caritas' or love and service-rational, yet profoundly irrational in its hope. The world as we live in has not the foggiest notion of the brotherhood of mankind, as Edwin Bell dreams of it. Gerry, Sophy's mafia associate asks her, '"Old soul! Have you got religion?"'[39] Very much as one would ask if someone had cancer or some such dread disease.

At times Golding's eschatological inquiry is very sombre. In christening his characters, he ironically uses symbolic personality traits that are appropriate.[40] Golding's focus on evil in religion springs from his Christian belief in Original Sin, and the Fall of Man. Man's loss of faith and morality in the modern age has finally led the perversion of religion in the world to breeding hate, chaos, and to foster fundamentalism.

He explained how man has been influenced in the twentieth century, which has swept away all prevailing beliefs in religion. Fanatical fundamentalists are walled in by absolute beliefs leading to religious madness causing perversions. Man needs a religion of selfless service to his fellowmen, any day nobler than the idea of reward or gain.[41]

This pragmatic philosopher respects Jung who states that 'those who view religion as an illusion, an escape from reality or a childish weakness, are too conventional to understand the power of faith and intuition. Man possesses a natural religious function, which is as potent as the instincts of sexuality and aggression.'[42]

Pincher Martin's substitute for God and religion is his greed, which displays the deeper cardinal sin of pride and self-deification allowing him to indulge in aggressive sexual assaults. 'The whole business of eating was peculiarly significant. They made a ritual of it on every level, the Fascists, a punishment, the religious as a rite, the cannibal either as a ritual or as a medicine or as a superbly direct declaration of conquest. Killed and eaten...eating with a mouth was only the gross expression of what was a universal process. You could eat with your cock or with your fists or with your voice.'[43] Martin's purgatorial atonement for his squalid sins is both terrifying and moving.

Janet Burroway examines Golding's revival of the fall from grace of Adam and Eve in *The Inheritors* by fusing Darwin and *Genesis*.[44] Each successive fall of the Neanderthalers results in a fatal calamity like Mal's fall in the water and his death.[45] Lok and Fa encounter guilt-based religion in witnessing the sacrificial amputation of Pine-Tree's finger.[46] Violence in religious rituals is evil as Golding illustrates in the comparison between the non-violent , nature-worship of the Neanderthalers and the militant, totemic, cannibalistic rites of the new people.[47] 'The novel offers an anthropological analogue of the Fall, which distinguishes between pre-lapsarian and post-lapsarian man in terms of knowledge of evil and capacity for thought.'[48] With an ironic twist Golding reveals the blinding spiritual darkness of the New People, who imagine that it is the creatures 'under the trees who live in the darkness.'[49]

In *Clonk Clonk* and *The Scorpion God*, Golding shows how primitive religions flourished by fostering the evils of the fear of natural phenomena, oppression of the ignorant and weak and the persecution of free thinkers like the Liar. Infantile men like Chimp fear the magical, mysterious power of the Sky Woman, Palm's powers of creation. She inspires awe and terror in the matriarchal community.[50]

Pretty Flower confesses her illicit passion for the Liar. She believes that her sin has caused the river to rise. Her guilty cry, 'I have shattered the laws of nature'[51] proves her superstition. According to custom, the Head Man wishes to entomb the Liar with the dead monarch, but the Liar is an immoral, bold destroyer of beliefs spurning superstitions. Evil is purely a matter of subjective judgements. The Head Man calls him 'a madman who is a peril to us all unless he agrees to serve the god.'[52] In rejecting eternal life, the Liar outrages the conventional beliefs and says the dirty thing in giving his rationale, '"Because this one is good enough."'[53]

Pursued and persecuted, the Liar stings the Head Man like a Scorpion.[54] Iconoclasts like the Liar pay the price of their non-conformism to prevailing religion and are doomed to suffer torture at the hands of the bigoted majority. Religious fanaticism or bigotry can blind man to humanity and peace. Dr. Tiger observes that in *The Scorpion God*, 'it is the free-thinker—the man who explodes religious orthodoxy who emerges as a spokesman for the imagination.'[55]

Golding speaks in 'Digging for Pictures' of the potential fire of fossilized religions to evoke terror and awe in man.[56] What is rational to the Liar, the real evils of death, murder, and lust, the evil of entombing live people is considered irrational and heretical by the fanatic Egyptians. The Head Man's religious authority is threatened by the intelligent, questioning intellect of the Liar. Golding is drawn to the darkness of the Egyptians, 'Of the Egyptians who brought life and death very close in their rituals,' He admits, 'I recognise in their relics...my own mournful staring into the darkness, my own savage grasp on life... I am, in fact, an Ancient Egyptian, with all their unreason, spiritual pragmatism and capacity for ambiguous belief.'[57]

Strangely enough Simon, the quiet boy, who seeks to dispel the primitive fear of the Beast in *Lord of the Flies* is scoffed at and killed in a ritual orgy by the mob of frenzied boys. The irrational fear of the beast has reached fever pitch among the panic-stricken hunters and in a macabre dance they pounce on crawling Simon, coming to tell them the truth about the dead parachutist-beast.[58] Martyrdom is the reward Simon gets for seeking truth and showing courage in doing so.

While Golding opposes doctrinaire religion like his father, he admits being lumbered with Original Sin 'intellectually and emotionally.'[59] He uses the Genesis myth to isolate his characters like Pincher, Sammy, Jocelin and Barclay and probes the tragic elements of human life. By eating the fruit of the forbidden tree of the knowledge of good and evil, one passed from the amoral world of the simple elemental life into the moral world of human experience. The spontaneity of sex between man and woman yielded to a guilt-ridden relationship. Good and evil haunt human experience and influence all choices that men have to make. Disobedience is the cardinal sin, but through obedience and humility man can achieve a closeness to God.[60]

Christianity emphasises moral evil as the root of man's unhappiness. It insists on loving fellowship with God as life's highest good and promises an immortal glory and blessedness with God. It offers the forgiveness of sin and the renewal of the soul of man by the grace of God and Divine grace in the sacrificial divinity of Christ and his spirit.[61] The ethical, universal, and redemptive aspects are stressed by Golding. Quite a few critics like James Gindin,[62] Samuel Hynes,[63] and M. Kinkead-Weekes[64] have reviewed the religious vision of Golding, and his preoccupation with man's proclivity to sin. Embittered by the moral atrophy of man in the squalor of twentieth century chaos, Golding studies the collision of innocence and experience, Good and Evil in his characters. Though man is prone to sin, he can fight and conquer evil. Man has to find his own God and religion by self-awareness as we see in the evolution of Sammy, Jocelin, Barclay and Talbot. Golding's world is dark and terrifying fraught with moral pitfalls and temptations and real, for a morally static world is a myth. Besides, a paradise would be dull to the free spirit of man.

Basically the true nature of evil stems from a deficiency or lack of something. It is a privation of what the being, by its-very nature needs—not physical evil but a psychic or moral evil. It hinders, falsifies or distorts individuation. Evil is vanquished once the distortion is corrected.[65] Golding is deeply influenced by this Jungian view and emphasises awareness of self as a belief. In his essay 'The Ladder and the Tree,' he explains his morbid quest for the meaning of darkness. 'There was no place in this exquisitely logical universe for the terrors of darkness. There was darkness, of course, but it was just darkness, the absence of light; had none of the looming terror which I knew night-long in my very bones.'[66] It is this psychic evil[67] that Golding examines in Jack, Sammy, Sophy and others.

Clearly there is no evil when an animal lives like a beast, but when a human being lives like one, he is evil. This moral degradation is seen in the pathological portrait of Jack Merridew, the choir leader whose power, lust and bestiality make him descend into evil paganistic rites of offering the pig's head to the Beast to appease its wrath. '"This head is for the beast. It's a gift."'[68] By painting their faces Jack and his hunters liberate themselves from shame and guilt and all the values that a human being stands for, except fear! This fear sees the evil of the beast objectified in the 'snake things' seen by the littleuns in the forest fires.[69]

The enchantment of Eden, this tropical island—a paradise of primitivity loses its charm as the psychic forces of hate, fear, lust, and jealousy work havoc among the boys. The beast motif is woven into the plot symbolising the irrational fears of the boys, fears of the darkness are thrashed out at the meeting. Piggy's rational stand that '"There isn't no beast—but I know there isn't no fear, either."'[70] Is scorned by the boys, who still believe in '"something big and horrid moving in the trees."'[71] Simon, the quiet contemplative boy ventures to talk, but his voice is drowned in a crude barrage of jokes, for the scatological minds of the young boys can only think of excrement. Simon becomes inarticulate in his effort to express mankind's essential illness. His effort at philosophic rhetoric fails miserably. '"What's the dirtiest thing there is?"'[72] While Jack quells the fears of the boys by vowing to kill the beast, and hunt it down, 'Simon thought of the beast, there rose before his inward sight the picture of a human at once heroic and sick.'[73] The visionary alone can comprehend the true nature of Evil—the beast that lurks within man.

In ironic response to Ralph's desire for adult advice,[74] a beast drops from the air in the form of a dead parachutist and terrifies, first, the twins on the mountain and then all the boys.[75] Simon alone is determined to investigate it fearlessly. As he sits in his cathedral-like glade Jack and his hunters ironically set up the dead pig's head on a stick there. In a mystical experience, Simon's supra-rational consciousness hears the Beast—the Lord of the Flies mocks him. '"You knew, didn't you? I'm part of you? Close, close, close! I'm the reason why it's no go?"'[76] In this symbolic sermon from Satan, Simon faints into his own emergent consciousness of evil and darkness. He accepts his own evil before the obscene decapitated pig's head. B.S. Oldsey and S. Weintraub observe that Simon is the real saviour of the novel, 'his voice goes unheeded, as once again, the crucifixion takes place, this time without redemption or resurrection.'[77] Later, Simon staggers up the hill to discover the Truth of the other beast—the fly infested corpse of the parachutist.[78]

Meanwhile Jack's hunters are caught in the vortex of a demented ritual dance to ward off fear of the Beast. They chant: '"Kill the beast! Cut his throat! Spill his blood! Do him in!"'[79] Simon crawling down to break the news to them is murdered ritually in an orgy of sacrificial violence and terror. *Lord of the Flies* is an incisive indictment of contemporary man's savage brutality, a story of moral regression. David Anderson rightly remarks that 'We are conspirators in the international crime of torture and destruction. The truth about Man is not merely that he is savage and afraid, but that he refuses deliverance and murders the messengers of Light ....'[80] Golding himself calls Simon 'a Christ-figure in my fable,' 'a lover of mankind going into the bushes'[81] to pray like a saint seeking seclusion from the world. This queer funny boy is gentle, kind, and patient-plucking fruits for the littleuns in the jungle.[82] We recollect Christ's words: 'Verily I say unto you, Except ye be converted and become as little children, ye shall not enter into the kingdom of heaven. And whoso shall receive one such little child in my name receiveth me.'[83]

While Golding outlines the burden of evil, he is both compassionate and honest. It is nobler for man to confront the reality of the Beast than cheat himself out of the truth of its existence within himself. Ralph weeps with the burden of this knowledge of 'the end of innocence, the darkness of man's heart, and the fall through the air of the true, wise friend called Piggy.'[84] Religion in the novel appears in the moralistic study of Good and Evil, the harsh truth that irrespective of age or so-called innocence of children, the human propensity for evil is limitless. Samuel Hynes points out that, 'Golding makes no reference to Grace, or to Divinity. The novel tells us a good deal about evil; but about salvation it is silent.'[85]

Christianity, after a period of great persecution in the Roman Empire, became the state religion under Constantine. It became fashionable, and gradually settled into a kind of culture. In the challenging, revolutionary, questioning movement that it was intended to be by Jesus himself, it became an elaborately organised structure of society. During the middle ages, a number of pagan rituals were incorporated into the lives of the people.[86]

The Spire, set in the fourteenth century Age of Faith reflects the conflict between pagan devil-worship and Christianity. Dean Jocelin's obsessive mania to erect a four hundred foot spire on the weak foundations of the existing cathedral is based on a few facts. The Salisbury cathedral is a miracle of faith as Golding tells us, built in the middle of a swamp in the thirteenth century. 'The truth is, we have a primitive belief that virtue, force, power—what the anthropologist might call mana— lie in the original stones and nowhere else.'[87]

Eccentric Jocelin's intense religious fervour is the sublimation of his sexual and worldly desires. W.S. Bunnell notes 'he cannot distinguish between Christian love and sexual love...partly because of the medieval ascetic tradition. His own sexual longings he equates with the devil's attacks on him and chastises himself. He is ignorant of the power sex wields—a dark, awesome primitive power, and becomes a mere puppet in this power.'[88]

'Satan himself,...clad in nothing but blazing hair stood over his nave...full of loathing...he took a discipline and lashed himself hard...in his pride of the angel, one time for each devil.'[89] The fanatic ecclesiast does not at first understand that as the spire grows, so does his arrogance, ambition and lust for Goody. At the level of everyday reality, dreadful accidents, quarrels among the workers, dirt and dust in the nave prevent services; disrupting the religious activities of the church. Jocelin remains as preoccupied as a pregnant woman in the act of creation, wrapped up in his own grand spiritual delusions. His will puts all else by, '"I am like a flower that is bearing fruit. There is a preoccupation about the flower as the fruit swells and the petals wither; a preoccupation about the whole plant, leaves dropping, everything dying but the swelling fruit. That's how it must be."'[90]

Wrapped up in the folly of building his 'stone bible'[91] Jocelin is blind to the trials and sufferings of humanity around him. He reasons with Roger Mason, the master builder that their spire will be 'a diagram of prayer.'[92] When Roger warns him of the unreasonableness of the whole project, he retorts that it is not his folly, '"It's God's Folly. Even in the old days he never asked men to do what was reasonable. Men can do that for themselves. They can buy and sell, heal and govern. But then out of some deep place comes the command to do what makes no sense at all—to build a ship on dry land; to sit among the dunghills; to marry a whore; to set their son on the altar of sacrifice. Then, if men have faith, a new thing comes."'[93] His supreme egotism and religious conviction that he is a chosen one of Christ is admirable! He is immune to the taunts, titters of the public, the condemnation of his brothers, even the open accusation of Roger, that he is 'the devil himself.'[94]

Symbolically the breaking open of the church exposes it not only to the physical muck of dust, rain, and wind but, to the devilish forces of superstition, pagan rituals and subterranean filth as in the pit which comes to a witch's boil terrorizing the workers.[95] The evil ritual of killing the scapegoat to ward off ill luck is seen in *The Spire* in the burial of the misshapen Pangall.[96] Jocelin can barely comprehend the complex pagan undercurrents of evil superstitions of the workers. Golding indicates how Jocelin himself is a victim of pagan fears, when he is shaken by the pillars singing,[97] the rotten berry of the mistletoe.[98] Beneath his clerical garb Jocelin is part pagan with his morbid superstitions and fears.[99] The scapegoat leitmotif links the ritual killing of Simon, to the murder of Pangall, abuse of Colley and Barclay's abuse of Tucker.

Another level of perversion of true religion can be traced in the possible biblical parallels in *The Spire*. Imprisoned in his own passion for Goody, Jocelin is glad that Roger is smitten likewise, so he will continue to build the spire. S.J. Boyd suggests that this unholy sacrament of passion distantly suggests the crucifixion. Jocelin is Judas in playing the pimp to Roger and Goody. He brings money to Goody to ransom her from disgrace but in the panic and horror of the childbirth one literally sees the blood money of betrayal.[100] Crazed with grief Jocelin admits he is 'bewitched' and 'the paving stones were hot to his feet with all the fires of hell.'[101] He is unaware then that it is as much his repressed sexuality as his expressed faith. Ignorance of self is the most dangerous spiritual evil that a man can fall a prey to. He feels the pain of the spinal tuberculosis is a spiritual chastisement.[102] Jocelin's perversity engulfs him in darkness stemming from his ignorance, evil use of others and finally his misery in realising he is bereft of God's mercy.

Glimmerings of true reconciliation emerge when Jocelin accepts humbly the reality of his evil lust for Goody. He experiences a peace in 'atonement in the uncountry.'[103] He seeks redress for his crimes when he visits Roger to ask forgiveness. On his deathbed Jocelin understands the import of God's omnipresence and the beauty beneath the ugliness of humanity. 'If I could go back, I would take God as lying between people and to be found there....'[104] He accepts the grim truth of his unscrupulousness, he perceives that *There is no innocent work. God knows where God may be.*[105] He has a sweet vision of 'a cloud of angels,' a scatter of leaves, an appletree with 'a long, black springing thing.'[106] He is the evil intruder in paradise. He realises that man must take the onus of evil perpetrated. With a mixture of despair and joy he sees a flash of blue, a vanishing[107] kingfisher, symbolic of Mary of the blue snood as explained by Hilda Spear.[108] In his terminal consciousness, Jocelin sees two eyes slide into one—the unity of perception of good and evil, symbolic of his spirit and his flesh united in the spire 'glittering like an upward waterfall.'[109] Jocelin's dying words 'It's like the appletree'[110] is symbolic of the tree of knowledge, the appletree, the singing and the gold in the *Hippolytus* of Euripides.[111]

Arguments about the knowledge of human nature which raged in the seventeenth and eighteenth centuries fuelled religious beliefs and a blend of Christian and socialist doctrines in the future ages. Darwin's *Origin of the Species* (1859) established the co-extensiveness of the human species with the rest of the animal kingdom. This shattered the time-honoured belief in the Scintillan Dei—Divine Spark of man. The sceptical mind shunned the Infinite and religion was shorn of its mystery, magic and joy. Nature was no longer the glorious handiwork of God. Empirical explanations of natural phenomena exploded the idea of a benevolent Godhead.

Julian Huxley's *Man's Place in Nature* (1863), provoked violent religious controversy, when he said that man could no longer be seen to stand alone as a uniquely created order of being. Freudian psychology further upset man's position by labelling him an instinctive creature, whose behaviour is determined by internal stimuli that arise from the organic needs of the body-hunger, sex, aggression. Freud says 'The religions of humanity...must be classified as mass-delusions. Religion succeeds in saving many from individual neuroses.'[112] The Marxist view of economic man who needs to fight against class distinction by abolishing private property in a classless society led to the emergence of religion as a non-communal form of worship in the orthodox sense. Communists believed they had found a way to deliver man from evil by removing what corrupted his nature *viz.*, private property. In a welter of 'isms' like communism, materialism and socialism, spiritualise was stamped out and the basic tenets of Christianity concerning love—'caritas' or charity, peace and tolerance[113] were lost sight of.

The disease of commercialism stemming from the Industrial Revolution determined social values, ethical norms and caused a fossilization of religious tenets. Religion was expressed by rituals of church-going, flaunting of wealth, charity done for display and the evils of class exploitation. It sullied the pure stream of Christian love, and abused the very etymology of the word 'catholic' which means 'universality' or 'liberality.' Mammon worship became fashionable. Wordsworth,[114] Goldsmith, and Ruskin,[115] bemoaned man's divorce from Nature and the dearth of spiritual values.

Golding's ethical message in *The Pyramid* is the corruption of faith and love by money, sex, and social stratification. The title symbolises the mummification of love and tolerance, the stifling hate engendered in a closed stagnant community like Stilbourne a significant pun—'Still born.' This image could convey not merely the entombment of the dead, but the malaise of man, his hunger for love which he has lost.[116] The perversions caused by wealth, and rigid moral codes leading to repressed sexuality, hypocrisy and hollowness in conduct provoke wild behaviour in the people. Erotic Evie, the Salome of Stilbourne, exudes the musk of sex to ensnare 'every male for miles around'[117] as Oliver sees her.

'In the triadic structure of the novel, the themes of class, sex, and music emerge as a musical elegy for lost harmonies or unresolved discords, deeply gloomy, a sense of death and life mingled together.'[118] The epigraph of *The Pyramid*: '"If thou be among people make for thyself love, the beginning and end of the heart,"' from the ancient Egyptian sage, PTAH-HOTEP,[119] is ironically twisted to show the hate fostered among the characters in Stilbourne. They debase love, sex, and holy passion.

Sex is not a holy consummation of love but a cheap, guilty, furtive act indulged in by Oliver and Evie, Robert and Evie. Her poverty causes her to carry on illicit affairs. Oliver does not even consider her a human being, 'this object, on an earth that smelt of decay, with picked bones and natural cruelty—life's lavatory.'[120] Evie's gold cross has 'Amor vincit omnia' inscribed on it and Oliver translates it as 'Love beats everything.'[121] The irony of it is that it is the motto of Chaucer's modest, chaste Prioress, dragged into filth by the whoring Evie. Thrilled to have it back, Evie makes the sign of the cross in mock piety.[122] Oliver is puzzled 'In our local complex of State, Church, Non-conformity, and massive indifference, I had never seen anything like them.'[123] His Protestant rationality cannot comprehend her Catholic fervour!

Roman Catholicism is a curiosity in Stilbourne for only the Babbacombes are Catholics. Sergeant Babbacombe as the town crier with his endless duties of collecting pennies from the public lavatories, hoisting the union jack shows no signs of being pious. The bird-like Mrs. Babbacombe makes futile efforts to maintain social contacts but is obviously ostracised by the Protestant community. She smiles graciously at Lady Hamilton-Smythe who was apparently unaware of her existence.[124] 'She was about our only Roman Catholic, was Mrs. Babbacombe—unless you include Evie—and that, taken with her other eccentricity, made her notable and trying.'[125] Here tolerance is unheard of!

It is tragic that Oliver egotistically exploits Evie, while jeering at her lower status and religious affiliations. He frequents Chandler's Lane, where they live and examines the church. He is amused at the notice of Mass being celebrated whenever possible '...for I had never met the Roman Catholic Church outside a history book. To come across it living, so to speak, was like finding a diplodocus.'[126] This prejudiced attitude of Oliver speaks volumes for other Protestants in Stilbourne who are narrow-minded and intolerant towards the Roman Catholics. The simile is cruel as it gives the impression of how outdated its system, faith and practice have become.

Evie is an ill used wretched girl and longs for tenderness, which Oliver reserves for the rich, heartless, vain idol Imogen. 'So did I; but not from her. She was no part of high fantasy and worship and hopeless jealousy. She was the accessible thing.'[127] The evil exploitation of human beings—the sterile loveless copulation of Oliver and Evie, the sweet revenge she takes in publicly humiliating him[128] are all caused by the perverted religion of class. Boyd admirably observes that 'the religion of class, with all its rituals, observances and commandments dominates life in Stilbourne almost to the extent that Egyptian life is dominated by religion in *The Scorpion God*.'[129] The theme of music savagely studies the battleground of various groups in the Stilbourne Operatic Society's 'biennial or triennial resurrection.'[130] Instead of Art being a meeting-point of souls in love and appreciation of music, it is a scene of ugly strife.

The long war years further alienated man from his Maker. The war machine engendered hate and callousness, human dignity and ethical values were lost. War distorts man's judgement, for it gives him the licence to kill, torture and betray others of his own kind in the ugly name of perverted nationalism. Man lost all his ideals, his faith in goodness and God. Religion lost its credibility and the world reverberated with violence, animosity and brutality. Dr. Halde, the German interrogator, pertinently remarks, '"You know, Sammy, history will be quite unable to unravel the tangle of circumstances between you and me. Which of us is right? Either of us, neither? The problem is insoluble, even if they could understand our reservations, our snatched judgements, our sense of truth being nothing but an infinite regression, a shifting island in the middle of chaos."'[131]

Sammy is tortured by being confined in a pitch dark broom cupboard because he will not betray his comrades who have escaped. War stunned the soul of man and rendered religion impotent. The scene in the Nazi prison reminds one of Christ's temptation in the wilderness, he spurns the tempter and in his hour of dark despair—Sammy cries out for help.[132] His struggle against the engulfing darkness of fear is like Pincher's agonising struggle to resist death and compassion. 'This made the fear of the centre, the rage of the centre vomit in a mode that required no mouth. It screamed wordlessly, "I shit on your heaven."'[133] Martin's rage and madness spring from his fear of the centre. As Golding explains in 'The Ladder and the Tree' of the terrors of darkness—the cellar image 'represents more than childhood terrors; a whole philosophy in fact—suggesting that God is the thing we turn away from into life, and therefore we hate and fear him and make a darkness there.'[134]

The novel is an allegory of a purgatorial experience. On the physical level, it is the tragic saga of a shipwrecked survivor on a lone rock in mid-Atlantic. On the spiritual level, it is the battle of Martin's will to resist truth—the Centre, God and

Darkness. The metaphorical implication is that his hell is the rock to which he clings for being Greedy. The paper world of nothingness[135] is torn apart by the lightning. Only Pincher's locked hands—red as a lobster's claws and the centre are left.[136] The modern myth of the spiritual torment of Christopher—Christ Bearer in a hypothetical after-life presents a character who is both grandiose and mean, for his doubtful virtue is recalcitrance.[137] The flashbacks and Six Days Creation climaxing in the final terror and the black lightning has been described by M. Kinkead-Weekes and I. Gregor as 'a maze in which all the paths lead to the centre, and the centre is a single, simple image of a Being reacting to Non-Being.'[138]

God created man in his own image and gave him freedom. Pincher's arch egotism centres the world in himself and not in that of God. His selfhood is compounded of hate and Greed—one of the Seven Deadly Sins.[139] In the theatre world, the mask of Greed fits him—ironically, he wouldn't have to play act but be himself! As Helen exclaims '"Darling, it's simply *you!*...Chris—Greed. Greed—Chris. Know each other."'[140] In his pretentious world Pincher, bereft of love, spurned by Mary,[141] betrayed by his best friend, Nathaniel,[142] is besieged by a destructive lust. Images of eating and the sin of injuring others in Greed are examined in Chris's Life. His wrath against Nat for winning Mary is dreadful, 'Christ, how I hate you. I could eat you,'[143] is highly symbolic of the Eucharist, ironically used here, for Pincher's bloated evil ego has no room for God.

'Greed' writes W.B. Easton, 'is not so much a sin itself as the external expression of a deeper sin, pride. The fundamental sin according to the Bible is pride, egocentricity, self-deification, and the insistence that each of us is the final arbiter of what is good for him...it is evidenced in the fact that...we seek the good in terms which we, in the privacy of our own selfish judgement have decided to be good.'[144]

The connection between eating and the Chinese box is recalled in Pincher's delirium. How the maggots in a box eat a fish and then one another, till 'one huge successful maggot'[145] remains. Pete offers himself to Chris '"I love you, Chris, you lovely big hunk. Eat me."'[146] As the spade hits the tin box, Martin-maggot knows he will be eaten![147] He realises the evil of eating others—it has poisoned his body and his soul. His monolithic intelligence decides to evict this poison by an enema. '"Why drag in good and evil when the serpent lies coiled in my own body?"'[148] He begins to see his corrupt self. Only once it seems, he is not the predator, that is when Nat and Mary pledge their troth—the enraged beast recognises 'Not where he eats, but where he is eaten.'[149] Can he evade mortality? Samuel Hynes calls Pincher 'the modern heir of Descartes; man proving his existence from the inside out.'[150] Martin suffers the same fate he subjected others to, he is 'pinched' in his make-believe heaven! Unlike Milton's Satan who makes a heaven of hell, Martin only makes a hell of heaven. 'Eternity, inseparable from pain was there to be examined and experienced.'[151] His religious friend Nat explains that 'heaven would be sheer negation.' Without form and void.... A sort of black lightning destroying everything that we call life,[152] he also predicts that Chris would achieve the 'technique of dying into heaven.'[153]

Golding himself has said that 'the Christian expects to see devils with forked tails or winged angels. If you're not a Christian and die, then if the universe is as the Christian sees it you will still either go to heaven or hell or purgatory. But your purgatory or hell will not have Christian attributes.'[154] Dr. Henry clearly refutes this argument by pointing out that 'He is no blessed soul being purified by pain: he is already in the hell of mere self-possession.'[155]

Pincher does feel fear, terror—but not guilt or remorse and he spurns salvation.[156] Brian Davies cites examples of such egoists who find any kind of life better than extinction. Miguel de Unamuno writes, 'I remained unmoved when shown the most moving pictures of hell, for even then nothing appeared to me quite so horrible as nothingness itself.'[157] In his madness Pincher inverts the God role of creation week on the rock—'On the sixth day he created God.' The futile battle rages against nothingness 'I have created you and I can create my own heaven.'[158] Pincher suffers the same hamartia as Jocelin of objectifying evil and giving vain battle to it.

While Pincher is damned to eternity, Samuel Mountjoy is redeemed because he accepts responsibility for his past evils, and so begins the process of regeneration. His joy at freedom regained physically and spiritually, is lyrical. He walks as '...a man resurrected in a universe of brilliant fantastic crystals, that miracles instantly supported in their being. I was surrounded by a universe like a burst casket of jewels... I was visited by a flake of fire, miraculous and Pentecostal; and fire transmuted me, once and forever.'[159] Sammy is aware that in resigning selfhood alone can man attain joy. Scientific knowledge is inadequate to study man; 'a vital morality,'[160] is necessary to change the world into a better place. God creates free humans, he cannot cause or determine them to do only what is right. For if he did, then they would not be free! Christianity recognises man's power for evil as well as for goodness.

C.B. Cox admires Golding's skill in writing twentieth century allegories. 'This success is due in part to the quality of Golding's Christianity. 'He is neither puritan, nor transcendentalist, and his religious faith is based upon his interpretation of experience, rather than upon an unquestioning acceptance of revelation.'[161] He wishes to explore not only the depravity of human nature but the causa sine qua non of human suffering and how to ameliorate it. Modern man has severer temptations than his ancestors. Golding holds the Arnoldian view that Religion is morality touched with emotion.

When Dr. Halde emotionally blackmails Sammy for information in the Nazi prison saying, '"There is no health in you, Mr. Mountjoy. You do not believe in anything enough to suffer for it or be glad,"'[162] he awakens Sammy's sleeping conscience to his evil. As a child sensitive Sammy is tortured by Miss Pringle who confuses religion with class—'I understand how I must have taxed her, first with my presence, then with my innocence and finally with my talent. But how could she crucify a small boy, tell him that he sat out away from the others because he was not fit to be with them and then tell them the story of that other crucifixion with every evidence in her voice of sorrow for human cruelty and wickedness.'[163] So he, in turn, feels justified in torturing Beatrice as a young man. 'Guilty am I; therefore wicked I will be. If I cannot find the brilliant crimes to commit then at least I will claim to have committed them. Guilt comes before the crime and can cause it. My claims to evil were Byronic; and Beatrice looked the other way.'[164] It is only when Dr. Halde grills him as an adult, does Sammy realise the vicious circle of Evil and divine retribution that he has got entangled in.

Sammy experiences his own expulsion from Eden, when he has to stake his claim for Beatrice. His plunging into the ferny forest pool[165] has been called a 'baptism in reverse'[166] by Babb. This significantly sensual experience and his decision to sacrifice everything to pursue his violation of Beatrice, 'So that there should be no doubt, I now see, the angel of the gate of paradise held his sword between me and the spices.'[167] His temptation, his fall and his descent into evil are made explicit. '"What will you sacrifice? Everything"'[168] is Sammy's firm resolve, in order to win the forbidden fruit of enthralling sex.

Dr. Henry explains that 'the parallels to Mountjoy's behaviour and experience serve to underline perceptions germane to the novel: the variable relation between merit and reward, the elusive link between reason and imagination, the thin line between goodness and madness, and even that discipline cannot command salvation as the admission of inadequacy can.'[169] Sammy understands that 'Something to forgive is a purer joy than geometry. I've found that out since, as a bit of natural history of living. It is a positive act of healing, a burst of light.'[170]

The Apollonian and the Dionysian conflict between the divine or supra-rational and the irrational world[171] is marked in Golding's works. Human life is a constant battle between the rational and irrational forces in man, typified by the noble Apollonian impulses that seek to reconcile the untameable beast impulses of Dionysius. Euripides in his tragedy *Bacchae*, dramatises the dichotomy of reason and emotion and the tragic consequences of irrational excess just as Golding has described in Colley's sexual misdemeanour and Jack's pig-hunt turning into a man-hunt in *Lord of the Flies*. Three interrelated ritual themes of the cult of a beast-god, a hunt as prefiguration of the death of the scapegoat figure and the dismemberment of the scapegoat are seen in Golding too. The boys set up a pig's head to worship and appease the Beast-Lord of the Flies-Dung.[172] They hunt the pig down and then the throb and stamp of their ritual orgy where darker passions are released climaxes in the ritual killing of the scapegoat, Simon, the saintly boy.[173]

Similarly in *Rites of Passage*, clumsy Parson Colley viewed as a 'drunken crab'[174] by Talbot, rudely snubbed by the atheist, Captain Anderson,[175] is made a crude scapegoat in the obscene pagan rites of Crossing the Line—'"Two huge figures with heads of nightmare, great eyes and mouths, black mouths full of a mess of fangs drove down at me."'[176] In the ensuing Dionysian orgy, Colley is gagged and dragged before the throne of the pagan God, Neptune, chucked into a paunch of filthy water and humiliated beyond endurance.[177] Colley relives the experience in 'most fearful nightmares of judgement and hell.'[178]

Prior to the Equatorial rites, Colley's apocalyptic pagan vision is eerie: '...the very scales of GOD...I was alone in a place where on a sudden I feared the Justice of GOD unmitigated by His Mercy! On a sudden I dreaded both GOD and man!'[179] Colley has a dreadful premonition of doomsday and primitive archaic gods reigning within. Shorn of respect by the evil Captain,[180] his clerical cloth desecrated by Deverel and company, Colley seeks the simple joy of the community below decks.

Two evils examined in *Rites of Passage* are the gross indifference to the Church and Christianity in general and to clergymen in particular. Religion seems an anachronism, a convenience necessary for rites like marriage, service, and death. Golding satirizes the phoney culture of the upper class that degrades parsons—Talbot freely admits how much he 'enjoyed these few weeks of freedom from the whole paraphernalia of Established Religion.'[181] During the simple service Colley conducts, 'Mr. Prettiman demonstrated his anticlericalism as noisily on the afterdeck as possible.'[182] Brocklebank farts after Colley's Amen![183] Their hypocritical attitude to religion is evident in their enjoyment of the vulgar revelry of the Equatorial rites. But their conventional mask registers shock at the simple act of a man urinating in public. They have neither charity nor forgiveness in them. Mocking at religion is pardonable, but mocking humanity is unpardonable. This is what Golding is upset about.

Liberated from fear, guilt and shame, Colley experiences pure joy '...he flung out his arms as if to embrace all. "Joy! Joy! Joy!"'[184] His solemn blessing is grossly misunderstood by the shocked company on deck. Jocelin also feels this innocent joy of the glory of God the Father, a beacon of light irradiating all creatures. 'And he laughed aloud for pure joy....'[185] This unbridled joy is a God-given gift of Jesus—'These things have I spoken unto you, that my joy might remain in you, and that your joy might be full.'[186]

Blind and presumptuous, Talbot understands Colley's humble overwhelming love for humanity, only when he reads his journal, his remorse at his sexual lapse—'What a man does defiles him, not what is done by others.'[187] Sin in Christianity is often linked to moral, licentiousness—Colley's submission to evil, his fall and repentance, his ultimate death are part of the cycle of sin and redemption.[188] Golding like Euripides, questions the prevailing codes of religious conduct and presents intensely moving moral crises in the irrational excesses of human beings.

Colley, Jocelin, Sammy, Pincher and Barclay are fashioned on the lines of the prodigal son straying in excess and then seeking redress through the forgiveness of a loving father, Jesus. It seems to follow the idea that the greater the sinner, the greater the saint! The parable of the shepherd who would risk ninety-nine sheep to retrieve the one stray one is significant. As *St. Luke* said, 'I say unto you, that likewise joy shall be in heaven over one sinner that repenteth, more than over ninety and nine just persons, which need no repentance.'[189] In the parable, the father rejoices on the return of the prodigal son and kills the fatted calf for him.[190]

Even the much maligned homosexual Pedigree is redeemed in the refining fire of love in *Darkness Visible*. Pedigree on the park bench has a golden vision of the deceased Matty, Christ-like, loving and terrible. 'The gold grew fierce and burned. Sebastian watched in terror as the man before him was consumed...the face was no longer two-tone but gold as the *fire and stern* and everywhere there was a sense of the peacock-eyes of great feathers and the smile round the lips was loving and terrible.'[191] The fire child offers him 'Freedom' but Pedigree resists death and salvation, like Pincher Martin. The many-coloured ball he clings to symbolises his desires, these earthly pleasures that he must sacrifice to embrace the terrible darkness of God to go through to light and salvation. This is the chiaroscuro of Life—*Darkness Visible*. One is One—the Supreme Being reconciling within him both Good and Evil.

St. Augustine has said that God permitted evil in order to bring about good, that is, a greater good; while Thomas Aquinas maintained that evil is permitted for the good of the universe. Gottfried Leibniz explained why the ancients called Adam's fall *felix culpa*, a happy sin, because it had been retrieved with immense advantage by the incarnation of the Son of God, who gave to the universe something nobler than anything that ever would have been among creatures except for it.[192] Golding demonstrates a blending of paradoxes in his novels.[193]

He explains in 'Belief and Creativity' how Good and Evil coexist. 'God works in a mysterious way,...and so, it seems, does the devil—or since the word is unfashionable I had better be democratic and call him the leader of the opposition. Sometimes the two seem to work hand in hand.'[194] God set man free and gave him the liberty of choice. Sammy Mountjoy chooses to fall, he ravages Beatrice in his quest for truth and beauty, suffers for his evil through the dark terror of self-knowledge and emerges purified. Golding would agree with Eliot who says in 'Little Gidding:'

'Sin is Behovely, but
All shall be well and
All manner of thing shall be well.'[195]

Man is 'shut in a bone box'[196] as Sammy says, he has to reconcile the duality of his existence, the spirit is to be crucified by the flesh; but recognition of the seething corruption within is vital for the 'scar to become a star.'[197] Self-realisation through pain transforms the guilt of Sammy's scar into a star as he is released from prison.[198]

When the Ancient Mariner blesses the sea-serpents, blue, black and green acknowledging his kinship with the meanest of creation, he makes true reparation for his sin of mindless selfishness in killing the albatross. In this profoundly spiritual experience, his soul is one with Nature and he is liberated into the realm of the Absolute.[199] Man can achieve some measure of freedom and peace only when he has wholly gained mastery over himself, gaining at first knowledge of his most secret, shameful desires and sensations.

Don Crompton observes that Colley's ambivalent act of worship before Billy Rogers is an act of love like his awe of the sea: 'I gazed down into the water, the blue, the green, the purple, the snowy, sliding foam!... I am consumed by a great love of all things,...OUR REDEEMER above all!' Like Mr. Pedigree of *Darkness Visible*, Colley is motivated by a selfless impulse of love for human beauty.[200]

Wilfred Barclay in *The Paper Men* is perpetually evading his corrupt, immoral self by running away physically from Rick. Johnny advises him to shed his exoskeletal carapace, by resorting to the comforts and cure of, sex, adoption of good works' to exorcise the evil within his sick self.[201] The terrifying mystic experience that he has in the ancient cathedral could be explained medically as a stroke, but Wilfred sees in the solid blue steel statue of Christ, Pluto, the pagan God of the Underworld. 'I knew in one destroying instant that all my adult life I had believed in God and this knowledge was a vision of God.'[202] Barclay is a bloated ego, a materially successful novelist spiritually barren, terrified that the nosey, would-be biographer will discover this. He faces Rick with rage across the spilt dustbin. 'Beyond all the contrivances of paper, manipulations of plot, delineation of character, denouements and resolutions, there, in that real world, real dustbin,...' and faces the ugly fact that he has no comfort of morality only immorality.[203] He feels free from fear, not when the priest comes to shrive him, 'mea maxima culpa[204] my greatest fault,' but only when he admits aloud '"Not sin. I. am. sin."'[205]

He tortures Rick in a cruel rite of passage[206] but gains no joy from this revenge. Descending the chthonic paths of madness and delirium, he experiences a pain similar to that of a boil wound he had in the war. Bursting the bonds of his hypocritical self he feels a vulnerable new self, a rebirth of his 'Istigkeit'— awareness of his humanity.[207] The primal Pentecostal joy of resurrection experienced by Sammy, Jocelin and Colley is also experienced by Barclay in Rome where 'All the people were young and like flowers...the heaps of flowers...the radiance. They held hands and moved and the movement was music.

For the singing and the song I have no words at all.'[208] Purged of all hate and evil he feels purified. To link a title of his novel 'All we like Sheep' one nay quote *Isaiah*. 53:6 ... All we like sheep have gone astray; we have turned everyone to his own way; and the LORD hath laid on him the iniquity of us all. These are the corrupt, evil paper men.

Frank Kermode remarks that 'Golding gives full expression to a profound modern need, for reassurance in terms of the primitive, a longing for a possible humanity.'[209] Golding's protagonists often appear absurd, Barclay is the comic clown caught invariably with his pants down, Colley the rustic obsequious parson, Simon the pale intense visionary misunderstood and sacrificed, Jocelin, obsessive maniac priest of Salisbury and Matty, the burnt offering of *Darkness Visible*, ugly, scarred and incomprehensible to others. These people spout an unworldly wisdom, like Nathaniel, Pincher's friend who tries to convince him of the negation of heaven and the technique of dying into it.[210] This is pure folly to Pincher.

Boyd explains that 'the happiness which Christians seek with so many labours is nothing other than a kind of madness and folly. Plato defines philosophy as a preparation for death and the Christians agree that the soul is stifled by the fetters of the body.'[211] Golding echoes the lines of T.S. Eliot,

> 'Do not let me hear
> Of the wisdom of old men, but rather of their folly,
> Their fear of fear and frenzy, their fear of possession,
> Of belonging to another, or to others, or to God
> The only wisdom we can hope to acquire
> Is the wisdom of humility: humility is endless.'[212]

The Bible conveys this clearly, 'Let no man deceive himself. If any man among you seemeth to be wise in this world, let him become a fool, that he may be wise. For the wisdom of this world is foolishness with God: for it is written, He taketh the wise in their own craftiness.... The Lord knoweth the thoughts of the wise, that they are vain.'[213]

The thirst of the many is unconsciously for Love, which, as Pedigree recognises, '"They call it so many things, don't they, sex, money, power, knowledge—and all the time it lies right on their skin! The thing they all want without knowing it—yet that

it should be you, ugly little Matty, who really loved me!...
They've been such people in this neighbourhood, such monsters,
that girl and her men, Stanhope, Good child, Bell and his
ghastly wife—I'm not like them, bad but not as bad, I never
hurt anybody.'"[214] It is the saintly stupid fools like Pedigree
who are redeemed in the refining fire of Love. For 'know ye
not that the friendship of the world is enmity with God?
Whosoever therefore will be a friend of the world is the enemy
of God.'[215] As Dr. Tiger pertinently observes, 'It becomes clear
that central to Golding's vision is an eschatology of the sacrificial
victim, the deity or the saint who performs the necessary
exorcism of fears. The pagan scapegoat, Pangall, is supervened
by the Christian fool, Jocelin.'[216]

One of the ills of modernity is the fallacy that man no
longer needs the scaffolding of theology. Faith cannot be
created by scientific experiments. There is no evolution in the
knowledge of God. Man needs to experience the God-image
within his soul. As Jung observes, 'Christian civilization has
proved hollow to a terrifying degree; it is all veneer, but the
inner man has remained untouched and therefore unchanged.'[217]
Golding feels the 'fabulist's need to devise a religious
mythopoeia suitable to modern man. Contemporary man lacks
vision: he experiences mystery as malignancy, not holiness.'[218]
He experiences his spirituality as darkness.

Golding's powerful use of the symbol of darkness to
represent evil, fear, hate and revenge is part of man's rejection
of the psychic reality of goodness, which is an inherent part of
his spirit. In *Darkness Visible*, Golding essays to reconcile the
antimonies of Good and Evil, having resolved all conflicts of
heaven and hell in his own soul. Colin Wilson states, 'There
are two worlds; or rather, two distinct ways of looking at the
same world, and they can be called, the Inspired and the
Uninspired. It is the task of the artist to connect them.'[219]
Golding allows Sammy to say in *Free Fall* that 'There is no
bridge'[220] between the rational, scientific and the visionary,
religious worlds. But in *Darkness Visible* he builds this bridge
between the two. Matty, Gift of God is born out of a burning
blitz bush like Southwell's Burning Babe who symbollically
stands for indifference to Christian Love:

> 'Alas quoth He, but newly borne, in fiery heates I frye,
> Yet none approach to warm their hartes or feele my fire
> but I.'[221]

'Matty is a proto-Christ, a wounded outcast in the Fourth
Servant Song of Isaiah, who redeems men with his sacrifice.
Sophy is the Great Whore of the Apocalypse (who heralds the
"second death" and "the lake of fire" in *Revelation*: 20). Golding
with all the fury of a lay preacher attacks the total depravity of
the damned.'[222]

The mind boggling pace at which science is spinning our
world, where anti-traditional, rationalist, materialist values
cause the decay of religion is glimpsed in *Darkness Visible*. The
human aspect of religion is distorted and perverted into a
superficial ideology that Sim Goodchild, and the Bells subscribe
to. They approach the Stanhope stable—the Pink Brothel of
Sophy talking about churches and holy wells. Goodchild says,
'"It was holy because men worshipped it. Don't you think that
infinite charity would fix that for us?"' Bell responds mockingly
that infinite charity is choosy, and that he had not struck a
believing streak.[223]

Darkness Visible is heavily allegorical taking its title from
Milton.[224] Matthew, the mutilated Being who carries Salvation
within him is in opposition to Sophy, the mutilator who
epitomises all the self-centredness and evil of the seventies.
Golding uses Jungian symbolism to identify his characters.
Matty is the fire child, the male principle, while Sophy is the
water woman, the female principle of darkness. There are
three essential aspects of the mother in Kali, the mother
archetype in Hindu myth: her cherishing and nourishing
goodness, her orgiastic emotionality and her stygian depths.[225]
Golding focuses Sophy's essence on this last feature. Right
from her childhood, when Sophy stumbles on the sadistic
pleasure of killing the dabchick,[226] she cultivates evil—'a
passionate desire in the darkness to be Weird...Weird and
powerful,'[227] seeking the simplicity of cold stasis by committing
outrages like torture, and kidnapping,[228] her meeting with
Gerry, the hired assassin is a hit '"Two minds without a single
thought."'[229]

Matty personifies Good, but cannot evade the lure of evil
in the form of the temptation of beautiful girls—Miss Aylen at

Frankley's[230] the tragic knowledge of his grotesque inadequacy makes him renounce sex, love, marriage and seek a purpose outside selfhood in life. Perplexed, this prophet throws away his bible, being a literal-minded holy fool.[231] He resembles George Fox, the founder of the Quakers, who advocated discarding of the Bible in favour of direct communication with God.[232] Brave Matty tries to tell the Abo in Australia about Christ and gets virtually crucified by him.[233]

While Sophy the sex ogress, dreams of releasing a black sun with her torture of the kidnapped child,[234] Matty sacrifices his life by saving the child[235]—his end is his beginning. As Lord Northbourne observes 'The world depends on its saints, for it is they who keep in touch with God, independently of whether or not anyone is aware of their presence.'[236] In our twentieth-century Tower of Babel, where religion is mere pretension, unsung saints like Matty who love and radiate love for others are needed. The constant sarcastic use of God's name, a profanity, is the hallmark of a godless age that breathes blasphemy casually—and callously—'"Christ all bleeding mighty. As Bill would say Christ," says Gerry using the holy name as an expletive.'[237] People like Sim Goodchild and Bell do not understand the truth of St. Matthew's 'Judge not, that ye be not judged/For with what judgement ye judge, ye shall be judged and with what measure ye mete, it shall be measured to you again/And why beholdest thou the mote that is in thy brother's eye, but considerest not the beam that is in thine own eye?'[238] After the scandal and enquiry at Greenfields, Sim has to admit '"I am guilty. My fruitless lust clotted the air and muffled the sounds of the real world."'[239] Bell screams at the homosexual Pedigree '"You're a filthy old thing and you ought to be done away with."'[240] It is their intolerance which is the greatest evil. Through the powerful obscurity of various incidents in *Darkness Visible* one great truth emerges, that there is no great victory of Good over Evil. It cannot be destruction of opposition, it is coexistence of Good and Evil—One is One. The bright sun and Dark Cloud, God and Anti-God ('sura' and 'asura') or the tension of opposites that makes the drama of Life. It is easy to say that Darkness is the absence of Light. It needs courage to postulate that darkness may be a pre-condition of light and to believe that good will triumph over evil.

Golding proves conclusively that man evades the reality of the evil of ignorance within himself and suffers for this darkness which impels him to sin. Man either adopts a devil may care attitude towards evil or he launches a frenetic revolt against it. While the former deny the existence of Evil, the latter are irritated by the forces of evil within themselves—A state of wholeness or Vollstandigkeit,[241] to quote Jung, cannot be achieved by man's psyche without his awareness, acceptance and final conquest of the evil forces torturing him.

Golding tries to salvage the light of optimism from the darkness of logical pessimism. 'His novels preach against the sins of the flesh in fleshly colours—sins so strong to his nostrils that there often is a cloacal stench around his most revealing scenes.'[242]

Man cannot escape from evil; he can, however, acquire the power to discriminate between good and evil. This power is vital to cure the religious myopia of our godless and hyper-violent age. Disturbed by the burden of guilt and Original Sin, Golding's sensitive imagination sees man as a profoundly restless creature condemned to shuttle perpetually between dichotomies like a beatific and tragic sense of life, a lapsarian and non-lapsarian view of human nature, between a redemptive and diabolic vision of sexuality. His stern warning seems to be that if we do not learn to live together in peace and love, we shall end by destroying ourselves and the world in which we live.

NOTES

1. Samuel Hynes: 'Novels of a Religious Man,' *The Commonweal*, March 18, 1960, 674-75.
2. Jack Biles: *Talk: Conversations with William Golding*, New York, Harcourt Brace Jovanovich, 1970, 12.
3. W. Golding: A Personal Interview in Cornwall on June 26, 1990.
4. W. Golding: 'Egypt from My Inside,' *The Hot Gates*, 74-75.
5. W. Golding: *An Egyptian Journal*, London, Faber and Faber, 1985, 10.
6. *Ibid.*, 165.
7. Jack Biles: *Op. cit.*, 84-86.
8. W. Golding: 'Utopias and Antiutopias,' *A Moving Target*, 184.
9. W. Golding: *Free Fall*, Ch. 11, 204.
10. Leighton Hodson: *Op. cit.*, 83.

11. W. Golding: *Free Fall*, Ch. 5, 115.

12. *Ibid.*, Ch. 12, 226.

13. *Ibid.*, 226.

14. *Ibid.*, 226.

15. *Ibid.*, 226.
    As Carl Jung rightly points out science can only be science; there are no 'scientific' professions of faith. *Psychology and Alchemy*, trans. R.F.C. Hull, London, Routledge Kegan Paul, 1944, 14.

16. Ambrose Bierce: Quoted from 'The Devil's Dictionary' in *The Great Quotations*, (ed.) George Seldes, New York, Pocket Books, 1966, 814.

17. W. Golding: *Free Fall*, Ch. 2, 56.

18. David Lodge: 'William Golding,' *Spectator*, No. 7085, April 10, 1964, 489.

19. Samuel Hynes: 'William Golding: Moral Models,' *Six Contemporary British Novelists*, (ed.) George Stade, New York, 1976, 165-9.

20. W. Golding: *Darkness Visible*, Ch. 16, 261.

21. Ivy Compton-Burnett on her eightieth birthday in 1964 declared that what she had learnt from life was that people were morally the same but intellectually different.

22. Man's mind cannot accept religion on faith as it attempts to trace causal connections and rationalise what is supra-rational or transcendental.

23. S.J. Boyd: A Personal Interview, University of St. Andrews, June 11, 1990.

24. W. Golding: 'Belief and Creativity,' *A Moving Target*, 201.

25. *Ibid.*, 202.

26. *Ibid.*, 192.

27. W. Golding: *Fire Down Below*, Ch. 17, 219. 'xâpis': Greek word meaning 'thanks,' 'gratitude.'

28. O. Henry describes this selfless love in *The Gift of the Magi* that draws Jim and Della in a close bond of affection. Martin Luther King spoke of this altruistic emotion 'agape'—as love to be shared by all. In Indian philosophy, we rejoice in the recognition of an undying *universal Faith* in an Absolute—the Paramatman or Supreme Soul and the Jeevatman or Life soul.

29. A.L. Tennyson: 'In Memoriam' A.H.H., 11. 16-18, from *Tennyson Selected Poems*, (ed.) M. Millgate, O.U.P., 1963, 163.

30. W. Golding: *Fire Down Below*, Ch. 17, 219.

31. W. Golding: 'Copernicus,' *The Hot Gates*, 38-40.

32. *Encyclopaedia of Religion and Ethics*, Vol. I (ed.) James Hasting, Edinburgh, Morrison & Gibb Limited, 1908, 521.

33. W. Golding: *The Inheritors*, Ch. 2, 35.

Hinduism projects the paradoxical image of the loving and terrible mother archetype in Shanta Durga and Kali—the consort of Shiva. One sees shades of her cherishing goodness, her orgiastic emotionality and her Stygian darkness in Oa the goddess of *The Inheritors*.

34. M. Kinkead-Weekes and I. Gregor: *Op. cit.*, 79.

35. W. Golding: *The Inheritors*, Ch. 5, 105-109.

The Neanderthalers dread the new people's alien, aggressive nature and try desperately to compare them with the terrible torrent, the rotten honey, the famished wolf and the maw of the fire...'fierce, white-red and blinding.' Ch. 9, 171.

36. *Ibid.*, Ch. 9, 184.

37. *Ibid.*, Ch. 10, 194.

38. David Lodge: 'William Golding' in *Spectator*, April 10, 1964, 490.

39. W. Golding: *Darkness Visible*, Ch. 10, 159.

40. Christopher Hadley Martin or Christ bearer is a mere pincher, the personification of the cardinal vice of Greed. Wilfred Barclay means 'resolute peace' for which he craves, and this bar of clay achieves it only in death! Evelyn de Tracy has a trace of Eve in him, while Samuel, in the name Samuel Mountjoy means name of God. Actually he is only a pleasure seeker from Paradise Hill, Rotten Row on the Mount of Venus or Mons Veneris.

41. W. Golding: A Personal Interview in Cornwall on June 26, 1990.

42. Frieda Fordham: *An Introduction to Jung's Psychology*, London, Penguin, 1954, 69-70.

43. W. Golding: *Pincher Martin*, Ch. 6, 88.

44. Janet Burroway: 'Resurrected Metaphor' in *The Inheritors* by William Golding, *Critical Quarterly*, Vol. 23, No. l, Spring, 1981, 63.

45. W. Golding: *The Inheritors*, Ch. 4, 90.

46. *Ibid.*, Ch. 7, 146.

47. *Ibid.*, 145-146.

48. Samuel Hynes: 'William Golding,' *Columbia Essays on Modern Writers*, No. 2, New York, Columbia University Press, 1964, 22.

49. W. Golding: *The Inheritors*, Ch. 12, 233.

50. W. Golding: 'Clonk Clonk,' *The Scorpion God*, 110-114.

51. W. Golding: 'The Scorpion God,' *The Scorpion God*, 52.

52. *Ibid.*, 55.

53. *Ibid.*, 40.

54. *Ibid.*, 55-62.

55. Dr. V. Tiger: *Op. cit.*, 225.

56. W. Golding: 'Digging for Pictures,' *The Hot Gates*, 63.

57. W. Golding: 'Egypt from my Inside,' *The Hot Gates*, 81-82.

58. W. Golding: *Lord of the Flies*, Ch. 9, 168.

59. W. Golding: Quoted in an Interview with John Carey in *William Golding, The Man and his Books*, 173.

60. 'If ye love me, keep my commandments' *John*, 14:15, and The Lord's Prayer 'Thy will be done, on earth as it is in heaven.'

61. *Encyclopaedia of Religion and Ethics*, (ed.) James Hasting, Vol. 3, 581.

62. Gindin qualifies that Golding's novels are orthodox traditional Christian statements about the nature of man. His metaphors underlie man's pride, sin, and guilt.—'Gimmick and Metaphor in the Novels of William Golding,' in *Modern Fiction Studies*, Summer, 1960, 205.

63. Hynes considers *Pincher Martin* a moral document, in which from a right view of the selfless act of dying, right moral principles will follow— 'On Pincher Martin,' *William Golding: Novels, 1954-67*, (ed.) Norman Page, 132-133.

64. M. Kinkead-Weekes speaks of his intensely sceptical and intensely religious vision in 'The Visual and the Visionary in Golding,' in *William Golding: The Man and his Books*, (ed.) John Carey, 65.

65. In Jung's view, Evil which is a debilitating psychic force, does not originate in any ontological duality for it is relative in its origin and ends leading to a greater good.—Raymond Hostie: *Op. cit.*, 188-193.

66. W. Golding: 'The Ladder and the Tree,' *The Hot Gates*, 172-173.

67. The divine element in man is darkened by a perversion of the will, as distortion works havoc in the mind. Satan in Milton's *Paradise Lost* is a good example of 'psychic evil.'

68. W. Golding: *Lord of the Flies*, Ch. 8, 151.

69. *Ibid.*, Ch. 2, 51.

70. *Ibid.*, Ch. 5, 92.

71. W. Golding: *Lord of the Flies*, Ch. 5, 93.

72. *Ibid.*, 97.

73. *Ibid.*, Ch. 6, 113.

74. *Ibid.*, Ch. 5, 103.
    '"If only they could send us something grown up...a sign, or something."' says Ralph.

75. W. Golding: *Lord of the Flies*, Ch. 7, 138.

76. *Ibid.*, Ch. 8, 158.

77. B.S. Oldsey and S. Weintraub: *The Art of William Golding*, New York, Harcourt Brace and World, 1965, 40.

78. W. Golding: *Lord of the Flies*, Ch. 9, 161.

79. *Ibid.*, 168.

80. David Anderson: 'Nostalgia for the Primates,' *The Tragic Protest, Contemporary Literary Criticism*, Vol. II, (ed.) Carollyn Riley, Detroit, Gale Research Company, 1975, 197.

81. W. Golding: 'Fable,' *The Hot Gates*, 97-98.

82. W. Golding: *Lord of the Flies*, Ch. 3, 61.

83. *Matthew*. 18: 3, 5.

84. W. Golding: *Lord of the Flies*, Ch. 12, 223.

85. Samuel Hynes: 'William Golding *Columbia Essays on Modern Writers*, No. 2, New York, Columbia University Press, 1964, 16.

86. Samuel Mathai: *Faith and Morals in the Space Age*, Bombay, Somaiya Publications, 1973, 113.

87. W. Golding: 'An Affection for Cathedrals,' *A Moving Target*, 10.

88. W.S. Bunnell: *Notes on William Golding's 'The Spire,'* London, Methuen Paperback, 1980, 43.

It is lack of self-realisation, of one's fleshly weakness that leads to a distortion of true religion and the stern code of celibacy among the Roman Catholic clergy that ruins Jocelin's peace of mind.

89. W. Golding: *The Spire*, Ch. 3, 65.

90. *Ibid.*, Ch. 5, 97.

Jesus said, 'I am the vine, ye are the branches; He that abideth in me and I in him, the same bringeth forth much fruit; for without me ye can do nothing.'—*John*. 15: 5.

91. *Ibid.*, Ch. 5, 108.

92. *Ibid.*, Ch. 6, 120.

93. *Ibid.*, 121.

94. *Ibid.*, 123.

95. *Ibid.*, Ch. 4, 80.

'Doomsday coming up; or the roof of hell down there. Perhaps the damned stirring...or the living, pagan earth, unbound at last and waking, Dia Mater.' 80.

96. *Ibid.*, Ch. 4, 90.

97. *Ibid.*, Ch. 8, 152.

98. *Ibid.*, Ch. 5, 95.

Pangall's murder can be linked to the Norse myth of Balder being killed by Loki with a mistletoe berry.

99. Jocelin is a pagan in some respects for as Israel Zangwill says 'Scratch the Christian and you will find the pagan-spoiled' 'Children of the Ghetto' quoted from *The Great Quotations*, 158.

100. S.J. Boyd: *Op. cit.*, 95.

101. W. Golding: *The Spire*, Ch. 8, 157.

102. *Ibid.*, Ch. 10, 188.

103. *Ibid.*, Ch. 9, 178.

Huston Smith explains how the doctrine of Atonement, lies in reconciliation, the recovery of at-one-ment. Christ's life had effected an unparalleled rapprochement between God and man—Huston Smith: *The Religions of Man*, New York, Harper and Row, 1958, 328.

104. *Ibid.*, Ch. 12, 220.

105. *Ibid.*, 222.

106. *Ibid.*, Ch. 11, 205.

107. *Ibid.*, 205.

108. Hilda Spear: *William Golding—'The Spire,'* Beirut, Longman York Press, 1985, 34.

109. W. Golding: *The Spire*, Ch. 12, 223.

110. *Ibid.*, 223.

111. The Greek chorus sings that life affords no lasting Elysium of happiness. Only moments of flying rapture lasting no longer than a cloud flight over the sun are felt by man. Galsworthy illustrates it in his short story of a maladjusted civilised man who ill uses and sacrifices a sweet country lass after wooing her under an apple tree. So too Jocelin exploits the innocence of Goody and Pangall. Man's ephemeral flights of joy are but small compared to the eternal loveliness in works of art.—John Galsworthy: 'The Apple Tree,' CARAVAN: *The Assembled Tales of John Galsworthy*, London, William Heinemann, 1933, 333-397.

112. Sigmund Freud: *Civilization and Its Discontents*, trans. Joan Riviere, London, Hogarth Press, 1949, 36-39.

113. 'This is my commandment, that ye love one another, as I have loved you. Greater love hath no man than this, that a man lay down his life for his friends.' *John*. 15: 12, 13.

114. 'The world is too much with us; late and soon,
    Getting and spending, we lay waste our powers:
    Little we see in Nature that is ours;
    We have given our hearts away, a sordid boon!
    ....
    Great God! I'd rather be,
    A pagan suckled in a creed outworn;'
    William Wordsworth: *Op. cit.*, Sonnet, 152.

115. John Ruskin condemns the English of Victorian England as a materialistic nation when he writes, 'Above all, a nation cannot last as a money-making mob: it cannot with impunity, it cannot with existence, go on despising Literature; despising art, despising nature, despising compassion, and concentrating its soul on Pence.' *Sesame and Lilies*, lecture 1, 31, Harvard Classics, New York, P.F. Collier & Sons, 1938.

116. One recollects Schiller's aphorism—'Hunger and love make the world go round.' Quoted in S. Freud's *Civilisation and Its Discontents*. 95.

117. W. Golding: *The Pyramid*, 16.

118. Don Crompton: *Op. cit.*, 68-71.

119. W. Golding: *The Pyramid*, 9

120. *Ibid.*, 91.

121. *Ibid.*, 37.

122. *Ibid.*, 39.

123. *Ibid.*, 39.

124. *Ibid.*, 43.

125. *Ibid.*, 43-44.

126. *Ibid.*, 68.

127. *Ibid.*, 89.

128. *Ibid.*, 109.

129. S.J. Boyd: *Op. cit.*, 122.

130. W. Golding: *The Pyramid*, 113.

131. W. Golding: *Free Fall*, Ch. 7, 151.

132. *Ibid.*, Ch. 9, 184.

133. W. Golding: *Pincher Martin*, Ch. 13, 200.

134. Quoted from William Golding by John Peter in *William Golding's Lord of the Flies*, A Source Book (ed.) William Nelson, New York, 1963, 34.

135. W. Golding: *Pincher Martin*, Ch. 13. 200.
      'The sea stopped moving, became paper...the rock was painted on the same paper.' His illusion is finally shattered, 200.

136. *Ibid.*, 201.

137. Leighton Hodson: *Op. cit.*, 70-71.

138. M. Kinkead-Weekes and I. Gregor: *Op. cit.*, 158-159.

139. In Christian belief, they are: Pride, cupidity or greed, lust, wrath, gluttony, envy and sloth.

140. W. Golding: *Pincher Martin*, Ch. 8, 119.

141. *Ibid.*, Ch. 10, 152.

142. *Ibid.*, 157.

143. *Ibid.*, Ch. 7, 100.
      At the Last Supper Jesus offered the sacrament of Bread and Wine. 'Whoso eateth my flesh and drinketh my blood, hath eternal life; and I will raise him up at the last day.' *John*. 6:54.

144. Quoted from B. Easton's *Basic Christian Beliefs* by B. Oldsey and S. Weintraub: *Op. cit.*, 80.

145. W. Golding: *Pincher Martin*, Ch. 10, 136.

146. *Ibid.*, 136.

147. *Ibid.*, Ch.12, 189.

148. *Ibid.*, Ch. 11, 163.

149. *Ibid.*, Ch. 10, 157.

150.   Samuel Hynes: *Op. cit.*, 29.

151.   W. Golding: *Pincher Martin*, Ch. 1, 14.
       'The mind is its own place, and in itself/Can make a Heaven of Hell
       and a Hell of Heaven.'—John Milton: *Paradise Lost*, Bk I, II, 254-255,
       12.

152.   *Ibid.*, Ch. 5, 70.

153.   *Ibid.*, 71.

154.   W. Golding: Quoted in A.T. Broes: *Lectures on Modern Novelists*, Pittsburg,
       Carnegie Series, No. 7, 1963, 12.

155.   Dr. A. Henry: 'The Pattern of Pincher Martin,' *Southern Review*,
       Vol. 9, No. 1, March 1976, 15.

156.   '"I spit on your compassion!"' Pincher yells as the black lightning
       strikes him—*Pincher Martin*, Ch. 13, 199.

157.   Brian Davies: *An Introduction to the Philosophy of Religion*, Oxford,
       Oxford University Press, 1982, 130.

158.   W. Golding: *Pincher Martin*, Ch. 13, 196.

159.   W. Golding: *Free Fall*, Ch.10, 186-188.

160.   *Ibid.*, 189.
       Samuel acknowledges the irrational, incalculable otherness of the
       universe and its divinity.

161.   C.B. Cox : 'Since 1950: *Lord of the Flies*,' *Critical Quarterly*, 1960, Vol. 1,
       No. 2, 113.

162.   W. Golding: *Free Fall*, Ch.6, 144.

163.   *Ibid.*, Ch. 11, 210.
       Sammy's sense of injustice is strong.

164.   *Ibid.*, Ch. 12, 164.

165.   *Ibid.*, 236.

166.   H.S. Babb: *Op. cit.*, 110-111.

167.   W. Golding: *Free Fall*, Ch. 12, 236.

168.   *Ibid.*, 236.

169.   Dr. A. Henry: 'The Structure of *Free Fall*,' *Southern Review*, Vol. 8,
       No. 2, June 1975, 113.

170.   W. Golding: *Free Fall*, Ch. 3, 74.

171.   Graeco-Roman strains are found in Christianity, especially in the
       Dionysian—Apollonian dichotomy in life. B.F. Dick notes: 'To the
       ancient Greeks, Dionysius was the god of animal potency, the mythol
       ogical incarnation of the life principle; it was he who inspires sacrifices
       while Apollo's civilised world is one of poetry, music and youthful
       wisdom.' E.R. Dodd: *Introduction to Euripides Bacchae* second edition,
       Oxford, 1960, quoted by B.F. Dick in *William Golding*, New York, Twayne
       Publishers, 1967, 29.

172. W. Golding: *Lord of the Flies*, Ch. 8, 151.

173. *Ibid.*, Ch. 9, 168.

174. W. Golding: *Rites of Passage*, 15.

175. *Ibid.*, 198.

176. *Ibid.*, 236.

177. *Ibid.*, 237-239.

178. *Ibid.*, 239.

179. *Ibid.*, 233-234.

      As Jung observes that 'Dark paganism still reigns in the soul of the conventional Christian, a paganism so blatant that it can no longer be denied...swamping the world of Christian culture.' Quoted by Frieda Fordham: *Op. cit.*, 75.

180. *Ibid.*, 21.

      It appears that Cumbershum and the Captain are not aware that a parson has come on board. Cumbershum tells Talbot, '"He was a notable atheist and would as soon have taken the plague into his ship as a parson."' Colley is later assaulted by him.

181. *Ibid.*, 65.

182. *Ibid.*, 68.

183. *Ibid.*, 69.

184. *Ibid.*, 117.

185. W. Golding: *The Spire*, Ch. l, 11.

186. *John*: 15: 11.

      This joy can be shared and understood only by those who can transcend the narrow confines of self and meet others as equal in the eyes of God. Unable to understand the affection in his benediction, Talbot, Brocklebank and Deverel view Colley as bad and mad.

187. W. Golding: *Rites of Passage*, 276.

188. 'Behold, happy is the man whom God correcteth: therefore despise not thou the chastening of the Almighty.' *Job.* 5: 17.

189. *Luke*: 15. 7.

190. *Ibid.*, 15. 24.

      'For this my son was dead, and is alive again; he was lost, and is found.'

191. W. Golding: *Darkness Visible*, Ch. 16, 265.

      We recall Arjuna's vision of Shri Krishna in the *Bhagavad Gita*, his fearful majesty filling Heaven and Earth—'Infinite One source of all: The flames of thy mouths devour all the worlds. Thy glory fills the whole universe. But how terrible thy splendour burns!' *The Bhagavad Gita*, trans. Juan Mascaro, Harmondsworth, Penguin, 1962, 2:11-30, 92

192. Gottfried Leibniz: 'God, Evil and the Best of All Possible Worlds' in *Introduction to Philosophy*, (eds.) J. Perry and M. Bratman, Oxford, O.U.P., 1986, 14.

193. T.S. Eliot in *The Four Quartets* presents Good and Evil as pattern and lack of pattern, the dramatic oppositions between the life of creative organic order and the death of inorganic disorder. Time and change bind man's spirit to the flesh, protecting him from more than mere glimpses of absolute good or evil, ecstasy or agony, which flesh cannot endure. T.S. Eliot: *Four Quartets*, 11. 6-10, 20-21.

194. W. Golding: 'Belief and creativity,' *A Moving Target*, 198.

195. T.S. Eliot: *Four Quartets*, Part III, 11.17-19. 41. Elizabeth Drew explains that these lines are from the writings of the fourteenth century mystic, Dame Julian of Norwich, who also said, 'I am Ground of thy Beseeching,' to mean Love. The 'field of action,' therefore, and the motive force in this spiritual strife is Love.—Elizabeth Drew: *T.S. Eliot, The Design of His Poetry*, London, Eyre & Spottiswoode, 1950, 233.

196. W. Golding: *Free Fall*, Ch. 1, 10.

197. *Ibid.*, 5.

198. *Ibid.*, Ch. 10, 187.

199. 'O happy living things! no tongue
Their beauty might declare
A spring of love gushed from my heart,
And I blessed them unaware.' S.T. Coleridge: 'The Rime of the Ancient Mariner,' Part IV, St. 14, *The Poetical Works of L.S.T. Coleridge*, 13.

Here the evil spell is broken and the mariner can pray. His, sorrow, loneliness and penance are near an end. Coleridge gives the message of universal love in Part VII, St. 22-23 when the mariner tells the wedding guest:
'" ....

He prayeth well, who loveth well
Both man and bird and beast.

He prayeth best, who loveth best
All things both great and small;
For the dear God who loveth us
He made and loveth all."' 26

200. Don Crompton: *Op. cit.*, 155.

201. W. Golding: *The Paper Men*, Ch. 10, 114.

202. *Ibid.*, Ch. 11, 123.

203. *Ibid.*, Ch. 1, 14-15.

204. *Ibid.*, Ch. 11, 124.

205. *Ibid.*, 127.

206. *Ibid.*, Ch. 12, 147.

207. *Ibid.*, Ch. 13, 160-161.

208. *Ibid.*, 161.

209. Frank Kermode: 'On William Golding' in *The English Novel*, Casebook, (ed.) S. Hazell, London, Macmillan, 1978, 153.

210. W. Golding: *Pincher Martin*, Ch. 5, 71.

211. S.J. Boyd: *Op. cit.*, 58.

212. T.S. Eliot: 'East Coker,' *Four Quartets*, Part II, 11. 43-48.

213. 1 *Corinthians*, 3: 18, 20.

214. W. Golding: *Darkness Visible*, Ch. 16, 264-265.

215. *James*: 4: 4.
      Here, obviously friendship of the world refers to the world in the materialistic sense of money, power and success.

216. Dr. V. Tiger: *Op. cit.*, 194-196.

217. Frieda Fordham: *Op. cit.*, 74.

218. Dr. V. Tiger: *Op. cit.*, 15.

219. Colin Wilson: *The Outsider*, London, Pan Books, 1965, 255.

220. W. Golding: *Free Fall*, Ch. 13, 253.

221. R. Southwell: 'The Burning Babe,' *The Penguin Book of English Verse*, (ed.) J. Hayward, Harmondsworth, Penguin, 1956, 30.

222. John Calvin Batchelor: 'Golding Beats the Devil' in *The Village Voice*, New Great Pub. Inc. Vol. 24, No. 45, November 5, 1979, 43-47.

223. W. Golding: *Darkness Visible*, Ch. 13, 222.

224. 'No light, but rather darkness visible
      Serv'd only to discover sights of woe,'—J. Milton: *Paradise Lost*, Bk. I, 11. 63-64, 7.
      Satan, the fallen angel experiences the spiritual darkness of ignorance in hell.

225. C. Jung: *Archetypes and the Collective Unconscious*, 82.

226. W. Golding: *Darkness Visible*, Ch. 8, 109.

227. *Ibid.*, 126.

228. *Ibid.*, Ch. 10, 160.

229. *Ibid.*, Ch. 9, 148.

230. *Ibid.*, Ch. 3, 46.

231. *Ibid.*, Ch. 4, 53.

232. S.J. Boyd: *Op. cit.*, 135.

233. W. Golding: *Darkness Visible*, Ch. 4, 64.

234. *Ibid.*, Ch. 15, 252.

235. *Ibid.*, 248.

236. Lord Northbourne: *Religion in the Modern World*, London, J.M. Dent, 1963, 87.

237. W. Golding: *Darkness Visible*, Ch. 10, 159.

238. *Matthew*: 7: 1-3.
239. W. Golding: *Darkness Visible*, Ch. 16, 257.
240. *Ibid.*, 259.
241. C. Jung: *Psychology and Religion*, 205.
242. B.S. Oldsey and S. Weintraub: *Op. cit.*, 166.

6

CONCLUSIONS

◆

In reviewing Golding's preoccupation with the question of evil, Melville's illuminating observation is befitting: '...all men tragically great are made so through a certain morbidness... all mortal greatness is but disease.'[1] While Golding's rational, scientific self yearns to exorcise the terrors of the dark, his irrational artistic self yearns to preserve the mysteries of the dark. His protagonists woo darkness in quest of themselves, they go beyond the darkness of evil and sin to the greater darkness of God, as T.S. Eliot in *Four Quartets* craves:

'I said to my soul, be still, and let the dark come upon you
Which shall be the darkness of God.'[2]

The study of the problem of evil as created by the major factors in twentieth century civilisation reveals that though controversial and complex, Golding attempts to resolve the riddle of man faced with the contemporary dilemma of reality and the self, Evil and Good. 'What man is, whatever man is under the eye of heaven, that I burn to know....'[3] In lamenting the loss of innocence and goodness of childhood during adolescence and putting on the mantle of knowledge and evil as one grows into an adult, Golding's themes focus on the paradoxical sinfulness and saintliness of man, on pain and suffering, which man cannot evade. He observes that 'the theme of *Lord of the Flies* is grief, sheer grief, grief, grief, grief.'[4] From the bloodthirsty hunter Jack, through Pincher Martin's devouring greed, Samuel's selfishness, to Jocelin's holy lust, a nadir of darkness is reached in Sophy's pitch-black portrait in *Darkness Visible*. Sophy is self-contained in her practice and perception of evil. Her weirdness is a synonym for evil when she is absorbed in killing the vulnerable dabchicks.

The whole vicious circle begins and ends with evil. Evil causes grief which results from human suffering and pain caused by selfish exploitation. Struggle and heroic endurance of pain form the core of Golding's subject. He equates selfishness with Original Sin. As he told John Carey, 'The words could be interchangeable. You can only learn unselfishness by liking and by loving.'[5]

Golding proves conclusively that hate is an evil that is endothermic while the calm of love is exothermic.[6] A sinister pattern of evil emerges in the novels where various kinds of betrayal, spiritual, social and sexual by man lead to guilt, suffering and expiation. The didactic element strikes a grim note of relevance in an age of godless hyperviolence, where palpable forces of evil can be experienced as Darkness Visible. The final tragic vision that emerges is a paradoxical synthesis of Good and Evil in the emergent consciousness of man.

Two interesting points from Christianity, as understood by Ian D. Suttie are also seen in Golding's works under consideration. According to Suttie, 'The Last Supper illustrates a free giving even of the body—it shows that hate and evil have no independent existence but are merely frustrated forms of love, distorted as protest, reproach, and aggression.[7] On reviewing the violent hates of Evie Babbacombe, Sophy, Pincher and Sammy, to cite a few names, it is clear that it is their separation-anxiety, a loss of love, which motivates their negative behaviour. Aggressiveness is a mode or technique of love-seeking. In *Rites of Passage*, Talbot convincingly shows a heartening evolution of character from a selfish, presumptuous, callous Lord to a kind, loving friend. Love is a civilising emotion that brings about a change from egoism to altruism.

Though Golding has been accused of painting only a depressing view of primary evil, of not showing 'if the line of darkness had an ending,'[8] we see 'hope struggling with a natural pessimism'[9] in *Darkness Visible*, where good and evil spirits like Matty and Sophy live. And Sophy's malignancy is mitigated by the Greater good of Matty's selfless altruism.

When Sammy faces the fear of darkness and self-extinction

in the cupboard, he realises his own evil, and discovers like Jocelin that this evil can be conquered by love for others. Thereafter in a fascinating trend, Golding no longer views Good and Evil as irreconcilable Absolutes, but, as essential attributes beneficial to the growth of a human personality. As Golding humbly admits: 'Here is no sage to bring you a distilled wisdom. Here is an aging novelist, floundering in all the complexities of twentieth century living, all the muddle of part beliefs.'[10] Over a period of time Golding's treatment of evil has lost its blackness and his awareness of the mystery of life is mingled with his knowledge of the dichotomy of existence. Golding tries to communicate this vital awareness with a god-like power.

He subjects his protagonists to a 'rite de passage' in which through a cathartic process they achieve a tragic awareness of their own sin and evil. Circumstances, pressures, hate engendered in their spirits reach a point of crisis when by an epiphanic revelation they see the light of truth as Jocelin views the appletree and the upward waterfall on his deathbed, Sim Goodchild views the exquisite beauty of his own palm as Matty shakes his hand—'and then he fell through into an awareness of his own hand that stopped time in its revolution. The palm was exquisitely beautiful, it was made of light. It was precious...Sim...saw that it was holy.'[11] 'That awful Power'[12] as Wordsworth called Imagination can reveal in a flash both darkness and light to man, as shown by Golding too. The crux of Golding's credo then is the necessity of evil, man experiences irrational excess, a 'rite de passage' through evil and darkness towards good.

Golding questions the prevailing religious codes of conduct and presents intensely moving moral crises of man's irrational excesses. The mystery, corruption, death and hypocrisy that envelop the people of Stilbourne in *The Pyramid* are viewed through the emerging consciousness of guilt and evil of young Oliver. Golding felt it was his duty as a writer representative of his age, to show man his image 'sub specie aeternitatis'— in the sight of eternity—and talked of his engagement with 'What is constant in human nature.'[13]

Golding is close to Conrad in his concern for the frailty of man's morals, awareness and control of himself in moments

of peril or joy as Talbot wonders—'Philosophy and religion—
what are they when the wind blows and the water gets up in
lumps?'[14]

The struggle between the powers of darkness and light is
projected in *Darkness Visible*. Golding's most challenging
novel allegorically presents Good and Evil in the persona of
Matty and Sophy—the battle between altruism and entropy. As
Randall Stevenson observes, 'This connection of spiritual
with secular is central to the novel's vision: evil and general
'running down' are a matter 'of course' in contemporary life,
too debased and dispirited to redeem itself, so a revitalising
intrusion from the spirit world Matty seems to inhabit is
essential.'[15]

In Golding's view the greatest evil would be stagnation of
the human spirit as we see it in the wretched decaying humans
of Stilbourne in *The Pyramid*. Change and evolution would
naturally be the 'summum bonum' of human existence. Oliver
and Talbot begin as rather dense, dim-witted characters; they
gradually perceive their own insular perceptions widen as they
understand their own folly and the evils of lust, intolerance
and violence that warp human growth. There is a basic
contradiction in human judgement that blinds people to the
goodness of Matty's spirit, and it is evinced in the other
novels like *The Pyramid*, where Oliver is blind to the selfish
hypocrisy of Imogen Grantley, and Talbot, in *Rites of Passage*,
realises the sterling goodness of Parson Colley only after his
death.

Golding's protagonists are dynamic, at times vibrantly
dark in their evil deeds. They are like Eliot's heroes Guy
Fawkes and Mistah Kurtz, the lost violent souls in *The Hollow
Men*. Here Eliot's philosophy is that it is better to do evil than
to do nothing at all. Better to suffer for sins than to be hollow
men of straw, vacuous, spiritually sterile, a negation of the
living principle of growth. They dread the reality of life as
Golding's Wilfred Barclay flees to escape the grim truth of his
rotten self. As Eliot says in the Chorus from 'The Rock':

'The endless cycle of idea and action,
Endless invention, endless experiment,
Knowledge of speech, but not of silence;
Knowledge of words, and ignorance of the Word:'[16]

Barclay lives his life in a plethora of worthless words and his
symbolic destruction of his papers—'a rite of passage made
out of the detritus...reviews, theses, manuscripts, interlinears,
proofs, the paperweight of a whole life!'[17] liberates him from
sham.

Even the infernal epiphany in the church does not diminish
his amorphous ego. He fancies himself suffering from the
wounds of Christ. His delusions of moral grandeur are dispelled
by the priest, Douglas, who ironically remarks that 'there
were three crosses.'[18] Then the veils of ignorance are ripped
from Barclay's eyes, '...Three crosses—the whole spectrum—
Not for me the responsibility of goodness, the abject terror of
being holy! For me the peace and security of knowing myself
a thief!'[19] Like Pope, Golding asks:

'Presumptuous Man! the reason wouldst thou find,
Why form'd so weak, so little, and so blind?'[20]

Clearly Golding does not favour the Manichaean division of
Good and Evil. Jung had believed that both evil and good
must coexist in God. Golding, like Jung, maintains that evil is
positive and relative, a moral evil that attacks man's psyche
and if he ignores it, it will engulf him like Pincher who is
reduced to a pair of claws. From evil experienced in all its
intensity can come a greater good.

Evil is a debilitating, psychic force, arising from a base
attitude and can be conquered. It does not originate from any
ontological duality for it is relative in origin. In all human
development evil is the way to good. The Christian dogma, by
objectifying evil in Satan causes a myopia by which man
refuses to accept the evil in himself. This is the truth of the
Beast misunderstood by the boys in *Lord of the Flies*. They
succumb to the evil of savagery, violence wrecking their
paradise, and, on the point of annihilation are ironically
SAVED (my capitals) by a Naval officer from a war cruiser
indulging in the same evil, but on a mass scale! The raging
conflict in Jocelin between his spiritual and sensual aspirations
centers on the diagram of prayer, the spire, which is also an
emblem of his phallic lust for Goody Pangall.

To counterbalance the leaden weight of evil, Original Sin,
selfishness, and terror, the artist-philosopher Golding, tips

the scales with joy, unselfishness, goodness and love. Golding is convinced that Hope also lies in art. This spark of creativity in a human being is the nearest to the divine spark—his 'Scintillans Dei'[21] Golding, the artist, tests people on the anvil of life to points of near destruction in the quest for truth. Sammy resembles Golding in one important respect; his art grows out of and is galvanised by a fearless contemplation of the darkness in the human heart, a brave delving into the cesspool of human sin and depravity.

It is in the act of artistic creation that man attains godliness. And Golding, like Coleridge believes that creation is a productive conflict or tension of opposites resulting in a synthesis in which the opposing parts are reconciled into a new whole. The artist's recreation of reality is a spiritualised passion, which he achieves through his secondary imagination,[22] a Being status, a Divine Archetype, purged of all the human dross. But Art cannot be divorced from Nature and the filth of human life—'the fury and the mire of human veins.'[23]

The complex web of the kinship of good and evil, noble and mean, beautiful and ugly, is what Golding projects through the trials of his protagonists. Sammy enjoys the glory of his physical freedom from the dark, and his psychological escape from his guilt-ridden self. His joy is an awareness of kinship, 'Everything is related to everything else and all relationship is either discord or harmony.'[24] When Jocelin realises the human cost of his vision of the spire, one understands the price of art paid in human worth.

Golding tries fervently to salvage the light of optimism from the darkness of logical pessimism. In each of his novels, he does so through the agency of human worth, of the potency of creative genius. He has aroused the conscience in man by his unorthodox and yet traditional approach to twentieth century morals. Mountjoy's dilemma is that of modern man's free fall in space and morality. His interior monologue dramatises the psychological conflicts that torment the psyche of mankind torn between science and spirituality.

Golding is unique in that his study of modern theories in anthropology, psychology, sociology and science is related to a revival of the religious instinct in man. So he puts humanity back into theology while talking of guilt, remorse, and redemption. His faith is based on his own findings of the moral lives of individuals rather than on Christian dogma.

Post-war writers like L.P. Hartley, Lowry, Greene and Orwell are preoccupied with lost innocence, conflicting good and evil, expressed in *The Go-Between* of Living in a 'hideous century...which has denatured humanity and planted death and hate where love and living were.'[25] Golding's art often turns to the grotesque in yoking warring elements to project the state of tension in human nature between the heroic and unheroic qualities of his protagonists. Man's free will allows him to choose between Good and Evil and suffer the consequences.

In Golding we see no withdrawal but the artist's power to celebrate, even in a world full of suffering and evil as our own, the fullness of human life, its splendour and potentiality. He believes in Love as the panacea for human ills. Golding hopes that the spirit of man will respond to the wisdom of the fourteenth century Egyptian sage, PTAH-HOTEP: '"If thou be among people make for thyself love, the beginning and end of the heart."'[26] For those who see only blackness and darkness in Golding's novels in the words of Alexander Pope:

'All Nature is but Art, unknown to thee;
All Chance, Direction, which thou canst not see;
All Discord, Harmony not understood;
All partial Evil, universal Good:'[27]

In the paradox of creation, man is a true child: a vile antithesis, as Golding portrays him.

Man's scientific progress has not precluded evil but contributed to the greater evils of fundamentalism in religion through lack of faith. Savagery and violence have unleashed the demon in man, while the so-called ideals of political systems have only widened the chasm between the classes fostering hate and bitter feuds. Scientific progress and materialism have destroyed the sanctity of sex leading to permissiveness, depravity and the 'Fall of Man' on all counts.

Golding's treatment of the problem of evil in modern life shows his consistent commitment to tell the truth about the world of man today. He is fearless, and willing to take the risk of exposing human depravities that are seldom spoken of.

Three enduring truths emerge. They are: that evil must be faced with courage and mastered; that Love engendered can achieve Good; and finally, that tolerance as found in Matthew: 'Judge not, that ye be not judged,'[28] is a necessity. The gloomy prophet of *Lord of the Flies* having mellowed over the years views the malaise of humanity in the nautical trilogy with a gentler eye, for '"Men, like cables, have each their breaking strain"' as Lieutenant Summers tells Talbot.[29] At the end of the voyage, Lord Talbot gains new insight into the mysteries of human relationship, 'I know fear. I know friendship which would exchange gold armour for bronze. Above all, 1 know love.'[30]

Man's business is not to pry into the nature of God, but to analyse himself. The paradox of his state is that he is placed on this isthmus of 'a middle state' as Pope says:

'Created half to rise, and half to fall;
Great lord of all things, yet a prey to all,
Sole judge of Truth, in endless Error hurl'd,
The glory, jest, and riddle of the world!'[31]

Golding echoes Pope in man's intermediary moral position. His duty is to reason his way through the extremes in himself and Nature, to attain self-knowledge, and thereby come to terms with evil, which is within his own self.

NOTES

1. Herman Melville: *Moby Dick*, New York, Random House, 1926, Ch. 16, 74.

2. T.S. Eliot: 'East Coker', 11, 12-13, *Four Quartets*, 3.

3. W. Golding: *A Moving Target*, 166.
   In Golding we see a mind at once scientific, rational and mystical in outlook.

4. *Ibid.*, 163.

5. Quoted in *William Golding: The Man and His Books*, (ed.) J. Carey, 174.

6. Endothermic process is a chemical process of heating, causing bonds to break, while exothermic process binds together.

7. Ian D. Suttie: *The Origins of Love and Hate*, Pelican Series, Harmondsworth, Penguin Books, 1960, 114.

He posits the view that hate is not a primal independent instinct, but a development or intensification of separation-anxiety, roused by a threat to love.

8.   W. Golding: *The Inheritors*, Ch.12, 233.

9.   W. Golding: *Darkness Visible*, Ch. 1, 24.

10. W. Golding: 'Belief and Creativity,' *A Moving Target*, 192.

11. W. Golding: *Darkness Visible*, Ch. 15, 231.

12. W. Wordsworth: '*The Prelude*,' Bk. VI, 11.399-602, 63-64.

     'I recognise thy glory: in such strength
     Of usurpation, when the light of sense
     Goes out, but with a flash that has revealed
     The invisible world, doth greatness make abode.'

13. W. Golding quoted in Rose Mary Summer's *The Spire*, Hampshire, Macmillan Master Guides, 1986, 35.

14. W. Golding: *Rites of Passage*, 16.

15. Randall Stevenson: *Op. cit.*, 172.

16. T.S. Eliot: Chorus from 'The Rock,' 11, 7-10, *Collected Poems*, Penguin, 1948, 7.

17. W. Golding: *The Paper Men*, Ch. 16, 190.

18. *Ibid.*, Ch.16, 188.

19. *Ibid.*, 188.

20. Alexander Pope: 'Essay on Man,' Epistle I, 11. 35-36, *Collected Poems*, (ed.) Bonamy Dobree, London, Dent, 1975, 183.

21. W. Golding: A Personal Interview in Cornwall on June 26, 1990.

22. S.T. Coleridge: *Biographia Literaria*, (ed.) J. Shawcross, Oxford, Oxford University Press, 1907.

     'The Primary IMAGINATION I hold to be the living Power and prime Agent of all human Perception, and as a repetition in the finite mind of the eternal act of creation in the infinite I AM. The secondary Imagination I consider as an echo of the former. It dissolves, diffuses, dissipates, in order to recreate....' I. 202.

23. W.B. Yeats: 'Byzantium,' St. 1, 11. 6-8, *The Penguin Book of Contemporary Verse*, 45.

24. W. Golding: *Free Fall*, Ch. 10, 186-187.

25. Quoted from L.P. Hartley in Randall Stevenson's *The British Novel since the Thirties*, 116.

26. W. Golding: Epigraph to *The Pyramid*, 9.

27. A. Pope: 'Essay on Man,' Epistle 1, 11. 289-292, *Collected Poems*, 183.

28. *Matthew*. 7: 1.

29. W. Golding: *Close Quarters*, Ch. 17, 269.

30. W. Golding : *Fire Down Below*, Ch. 16, 204.

31. A. Pope: 'Essay on Man,' Epistle II, 11. 15-18, 189-190.

SELECT BIBLIOGRAPHY

◆

PRIMARY SOURCES

William Golding's Novels (in chronological order of publication)

Lord of the Flies, 1954

The Inheritors, 1955

Pincher Martin, 1956

Free Fall, 1959

The Spire, 1964

The Pyramid, 1967

The Scorpion God, 1971

Darkness Visible, 1979

Rites of Passage, 1980

The Paper Men, 1984

Close Quarters, 1987

Fire Down Below, 1989

All the titles mentioned above are published by Faber and Faber, London.

PRIMARY SOURCES (GENERAL)

Bell, Michael: *Primitivism*, Critical Idiom Series, (ed.) J.D. Jump, London, Methuen, 1972.

Blake, William: *The Poetical Works of William Blake*, (ed.) John Sampson, London, Oxford University Press, 1948.

Campbell, Joseph: *Myths to Live By*, London, Paladin Books, Granada, 1985.

Coleridge, S.T.: 'The Rime of the Ancient Mariner,' *The Poetical Works of S.T. Coleridge* Vol. II, London, William Pickering, 1840.

Coleridge, S.T.: *Biographia Literaria*, (ed.) George Watson, London, Every Mans Library, 1967.

Collins, Randall: 'Sociological Insight,' *An Introduction to Nonobvious Sociology*, Oxford, Oxford University Press, 1982.

Conrad, Joseph: *Lord Jim*, New York, Doubleday Page & Company, 1925.

Conrad, Joseph: *Heart of Darkness*, The World's Classics, Oxford, Oxford University Press, 1984.

Darwin, Charles: *The Origin of Species and the Descent of Man*, New York, Random House, 1872.

Eliot, T.S.: *Four Quartets*, London, Faber and Faber, 1955.

Eliot, T.S.: 'Ash Wednesday,' *The Penguin Book of Contemporary Verse*, (ed.) Kenneth Allott, Harmondsworth, Penguin, 1980.

Eliot, T.S.: *The Rock*, New York, Harcourt, Brace & Company, 1934.

Eliot, T.S.: 'The Idea of a Christian Society,' *Selected Prose of T.S. Eliot*, (ed.) F. Kermode, London, Faber and Faber, 1975.

Ellis, Havelock: *Studies, in Psychology of Sex in Relation to Society*, Vol. I, New York, Random House, 1942.

Fielding, Henry: *Joseph Andrews*, New York, Random House, 1950.

Fielding, Henry: *Tom Jones*, Vols. I & II, London, Heron Books, 1962.

Forster, E.M.: 'The Story of a Panic,' *Collected Short Stories*, Harmondsworth, Penguin, 1954.

Freud, Sigmund: *Introductory Lectures on Psychoanalysis*, trans. Joan Riviere, London, George Allen and Unwin, 1949.

Freud, Sigmund: *Civilization and its Discontents*, trans. Joan Riviere, London, The Hogarth Press, 1949.

Freud, Sigmund: *The Interpretation of Dreams*, trans. J. Strachey, Vol. 4, Harmondsworth, Pelican Freud Library, 1976.

Fromm, Eric: *The Crisis of Psychoanalysis*, Harmondsworth, Penguin, 1970.

Gandhi, M.K.: *Non-Violence in Peace and War*, Vols. I & II, Ahmedabad, Navjivan Publishing House, 1948.

Golding, William: *The Hot Gates*, London, Faber and Faber, 1965.

Golding, William: *A Moving Target*, London, Faber and Faber, 1982.

Golding, William: *An Egyptian Journal*, London, Faber and Faber, 1985.

Greene, Graham: *The Heart of the Matter*, London, William Heinemann Ltd., 1948.

Greene, Graham: *The Power and the Glory*, Harmondsworth, Penguin, 1971.

Greene, Graham: *Brighton Rock*, London, William Heinemann & The Bodley Head, 1970.

Greene, Graham: *The Lawless Roads*, London, Penguin, 1938.

Henley, W.E.: 'Invictus,' *The Golden Treasury*, Selected by F.T. Palgrave, London, Oxford University Press, 1943.

Joad, C.E.M.: *The Story of Civilization*, The How and Why Series, London, A & C Black, 1935.

Joad, C.E.M.: *Guide to Modern Thought*, London, Faber and Faber, Pan Books, 1943.

Jung, Carl G.: *Psychology and Religion*, New Haven, Yale University Press, 1938.

Jung, Carl G.: *Two Essays on Analytical Psychology*, Collected Works Vol. 7, (ed.) Constance Long, London, Tindal & Cox, 1953.

Jung, Carl G.: *Archetypes and the Collective Unconscious*, trans. R.F.C. Hull, Routledge & Kegan Paul, 1959.

Jung, Carl G.: *The Integration of the Personality*, trans. S.M. Dell, London, Kegan Paul, 1940.

Kline, Paul: *Psychology Exposed or The Emperor's New Clothes*, London and New York, Routledge, 1988.

Lawrence, D.H.: *Sons and Lovers*, Harmondsworth, Penguin, 1969.

Lawrence, D.H.: *Lady Chatterley's Lover*, Bombay, Jaico, 1961.

Leibniz, Gottfried: 'God, Evil and the Best of All Possible Worlds,' *Introduction to Philosophy*, (eds.) J. Perry and M. Bratman, Oxford, Oxford University Press, 1986.

Mascaro, Juan (trans.): *The Bhagavad Gita*, Harmondsworth, Penguin, 1969.

Mathai, Samuel: *Faith and Morals in the Space Age*, Bombay, Somaiya Publications, 1973.

Maugham, W.S.: *The Summing Up*, London, William Heinemann, 1938.

Maugham, W.S.: *The Razor's Edge*, Pan, London, William Heinemann, 1976.

Melville, Herman: 'Billy Budd,' *Six Great Modern Short Novels*, Bombay, Pearl Publications, 1969.

Melville, Herman: *Moby Dick*, New York, Random House, 1926.

Milton, John: 'Paradise Lost,' *The Poetical Works of John Milton*, Vol. I, (ed.) Helen Darbyshire, Oxford, Clarendon Press, 1978.

Moraes, Dom: *My Son's Father: An Autobiography*, London, Bell Books, 1971.

Morris, Desmond: *The Human Zoo*, London, Jonathan Cape, 1969.

Myers, F.W.H.: *Human Personality*, Vol. II, London, Longmans & Co., 1903.

Northbourne, Lord: *Religion in the Modern World*, London, J.M. Dent, 1963.

Orwell, George: *Animal Farm*, English Language Book Society, London, Penguin, 1971.

Parsons, Talcott: 'The Social System' in *Harmony and Conflict in Modern Society*, (ed.) J. Penn, Translated from the Dutch by Trevor S. Preston, London, New York, McGraw-Hill, 1962.

Pope, Alexander: 'Essay on Man,' *Collected Poems*, (ed.) Bonamy Dobrée, London, Everyman's, J.M. Dent, 1975.

Ruskin, John: *Sesame and Lilies*, Harvard Classics, New York, P.F. Collier & Sons, 1938.

Russell, Bertrand: 'I believe,' *The Gates of Wisdom*, (ed.) V.D. Salgaonkar, Bombay, Macmillan, 1967.

Russell, Bertrand: *New Hopes for a Changing World*, London, George Allen and Unwin, 1951.

Russell, Bertrand: *Why I Am Not a Christian*, London, Oxford Press, 1957.

Shakespeare, William: *The Complete Works*, (ed.) P. Alexander, London, English Language Book Society and Collins, 1964.

Shaw, G.B.: 'Man and Superman,' *The Complete Plays of George Bernard Shaw*, London, Odham's Press, 1934.

Sheen, Fulton J.: *Life of Christ*, New York, Popular Library, 1960.

Shelley, P.B.: 'Ode to the West Wind,' *The Penguin Book of English Verse*, (ed.) J. Hayward, Harmondsworth, Penguin, 1956.

Skinner, B.F.: *Beyond Freedom and Dignity*, Harmondsworth, Penguin, 1943.

Spender, Stephen: *Poems*, London, Faber and Faber, 1933.

Suttie, Ian D.: *The Origins of Love and Hate*, Harmondsworth, Penguin, 1960.

Tagore, Rabindranath: *Gitanjali—Song Offerings*, London, Macmillan, 1989.

Tennyson, A.L.: *Tennyson Selected Poems*, (ed.) Michael Millgate, London, Oxford University Press, 1963.

The Bible: King James Version, London, Collins, 1946.

Vivekananda, Swami: *Hinduism*, Madras, Sri Ramakrishna Math, 1946.

Virgil: *Aeneid*, trans. John Dryden, New York, Airmont, 1968.

Wells, H.G.: *A Short History of the World*, Harmondsworth, Penguin, 1956.

Williams, Tennessee: *Penguin Plays*, Middlesex, Penguin, 1962.

Yeats, W.B.: 'The Second Coming,' *The Faber Book of Modern Verse*, London, Faber and Faber, 1965.

SECONDARY SOURCES

Allen, Walter: *Tradition and Dream*, London, The Hogarth Press, 1986.

Anderson, David: 'Nostalgia for the Primates,' *The Tragic Protest*, Contemporary Literary Criticism, Vol. II, (ed.) Carolyn Riley, Detroit, Gale Research Company, 1975.

Babb, Howard S.: *The Novels of William Golding*, Ohio, Ohio State University Press, 1970.

Baker, James R.: 'The Decline of *Lord of the Flies*,' *South Atlantic Quarterly*, Durham, Duke University Press, Autumn, 5, 1970.

Baker, James R.: 'Golding's Progress' in *Novel*, Fall, 1973.

Batchelor, J.C.: 'Golding Beats the Devil,' in *The Village Voice*, New Great Publications, Vol. 24, No. 45, November 5, 1979.

Bent, C.: 'Brain and Consciousness,' *Bulletin of British Psychological Society*, No. 22, 1969.

Biles, Jack: *Talk: Conversations with William Golding*, New York, Harcourt, Brace, Jovanovich, 1970.

Bowen, John: 'One Man's Meat: The Idea of Individual Responsibility,' in *The Times Literary Supplement*, August 7, 1959.

Bowen, C.M.: *The Romantic Imagination*, London, Oxford University Press, 1957.

Boyd, S.J.: *The Novels of William Golding*, Sussex, The Harvester Press, 1988.

Bradbury, Malcolm: *The Novel Today*, London, Fontana Books, 1977.

Broes, Arthur T.: *Lectures on Modern Novelists*, Pittsburg, Carnegie Series, No. 7, 1963.

Brown, J.A.C.: *Freud and the Post-Freudians*, Harmondsworth, Penguin, 1961.

Bunnell, W. S.: *Notes on William Golding's 'The Spire,'* London, Methuen, 1980.

Burgess, Anthony: *The Novel Now*, London, Faber and Faber, 1967.

Burroway, Janet: 'Resurrected Metaphor in *The Inheritors,'* *Critical Quarterly*, Vol. 23, No. 1, Spring, 1981.

Byatt, Antonia: 'Of Things I Sing,' *New Statesman*, June 2, 1976.

Coleman, John: 'The Facts of Fiction,' *Spectator*, No. 6852, Friday, October 23, 1959.

Cox C.B.: 'Since 1950 *Lord of the Flies*,' *Critical Quarterly*, Summer, 1960, Vol.2, No. 2.

Cox, C.B. and Dyson, A.E. (eds.): *The Twentieth Century Mind—1945-1965*, Vol. III, London, Oxford University Press, 1972.

Crompton, Don: *A View from 'The Spire'—The Later Novels of Golding*, (ed.) Julia Briggs, London, Basil Blackwell, 1985.

Davies, Brian: *An Introduction to the Philosophy of Religion*, Oxford, Oxford University Press, 1982.

Dahrendorf, Ralf: 'Conflict after Class: New Perspectives on the Theory of Social and Political Conflict,' *The Third Noel Buxton Lecture*, University of Essex, March 2, 1967, London, Longmans, 1967.

Dick, Bernard F.: *William Golding*, New York, Twayne Publishers Inc., 1967.

Dickson L.L.: *The Modern Allegories of William Golding*, Tampa, University of Florida Press, 1990.

Drew, Elizabeth: *T.S. Eliot—The Design of His Poetry*, London, Eyre and Spottiswoode, 1950.

Dennis, Donaghue: 'The Ordinary Universe,' *The New York Review of Books*, December 7, 1967.

Eagleton, Mary & Pierce, David: *Attitudes to Class in the English Novel*, London, Thames and Hudson, 1979.

Everett, Barbara: 'Golding's Pity' in *William Golding: The Man and His Books*, (ed.) J. Carey, London, Faber and Faber, 1986.

Fiedler, Leslie A.: 'Class War in British Literature,' in *On Contemporary Literature*, (ed.) Richard Kostelanetz, New York, Avon Books, 1964.

Fordham, Frieda: *An Introduction to Jung's Psychology*, Harmondsworth, Penguin, 1954.

Forster, E.M.: *Aspects of the Novel*, Harmondsworth, Penguin, 1963.

Fraser, G.S.: *The Modern Writer and His World*, Harmondsworth, Penguin, 1970.

Ghose, Sisir Kumar: 'Science without a Soul'—A Review of F. Capra's book in *The Times of India*, September 20, 1987.

Gindin, James: 'Gimmick and Metaphor in the Novels of William Golding' in *Modern Fiction Studies*, Summer, 1960.

Golding, William: 'Pincher Martin,' *Radio Times*, March 21, 1958.

Golding, William: An Interview with John Carey in *William Golding—The Man and His Books, A Tribute on His 75th Birthday*, (ed.) J. Carey, London, Faber and Faber, 1986.

Golding, William: Personal Interviews at his home in Cornwall, June, 1990.

Golding, William: Newspaper Report in *The Times of India* of a Talk at Pune University, March 10,1987.

Golding, William: A Public Lecture at the British Council Division Auditorium, Bombay, March 6, 1987.

Grande, Luke M.: 'The Appeal of Golding' in *Commonweal*, January 25, 1963.

Green, Peter: 'The World of William Golding,' *William Golding— A Casebook*, (ed.) Norman Page, London, Macmillan, 1985.

Halle, Louis J.: 'Small Savages,' in *Saturday Review*, October 15, 1955.

Hasting, James (ed.): *Encyclopedia of Religion and Ethics*, Vols. 1 & 3, Edinburgh, Morrison & Gibb Limited, 1908.

Henry, Dr. Avril: 'William Golding: *The Pyramid*,' in *Southern Review*, Vol. 3, No. l, 1968.

Henry, Dr. Avril: 'The Structure of Golding's *Free Fall*' in *Southern Review*, Vol. 8, No. 2, June 1975.

Henry, Dr. Avril: 'The Pattern of *Pincher Martin*' in *Southern Review*, Vol. 9, No. 1, March 1976.

Hodson, Leighton: *William Golding*, Writers and Critics, Edinburgh, Oliver and Boyd, 1969.

Horton, Paul B. & Chester L. Hunt: *Sociology*, 6th Edition, Singapore, McGraw-Hill, 1984.

Hostie, Raymond: *Religion and the Psychology of Jung*, New Haven, Yale University Press, 1935.

Humphreys, A.R.: *Melville*, Writers and Critics, Edinburgh, Oliver and Boyd, 1962.

Hynes, Samuel: 'Novels of a Religious Man' in *Commonweal*, March 18, 1960.

Johnston, A.: 'Innovation and Rediscovery in Golding's *The Pyramid*' in *Critique Studies in Modern Fiction*, Vol. 14, No. 2, 1972.

Josipovici, Gabriel: *The World and the Book*, London, Macmillan, 1979.

Kandaswami, Dr. S.: 'The Games "Biguns" and "Littleuns" Play in *Lord of the Flies*' in *Aspects of William Golding*, (ed.) S. Kandaswami, Kerala, University of Calicut, 1986.

Kant, Immanuel: *Critique of Pure Reason*, trans. J.M.D Meiklejohn, London, J.M. Dent & Sons, 1950.

Karl, F.R.: 'The Novel as Moral Allegory: The Fiction of William Golding, Iris Murdoch, Rex Warner and P.H. Newby,' *A Reader's Guide to the Contemporary English Novel*, London, Thames and Hudson, 1968.

Karl, F.R.: 'Graham Greene's Demonical Heroes,' *A Reader's Guide to the Contemporary English Novel*, London, Thames and Hudson, 1968.

Kazin, A.: 'Introduction to Moby Dick' in *Melville—A Collection of Critical Essays*, (ed.) R. Chase, New Jersey, Prentice Hall, 1962.

Kermode, Frank: *Puzzles and Epiphanies*, London, Routledge and Kegan Paul, 1962.

Kermode, Frank: 'William Golding,' *On Contemporary Literature*, (ed.) Richard Kostelanetz, New York, Avon Books, 1964.

Kinkead-Weekes, Mark & Gregor, Ian: *William Golding—A Critical Study*, London, Faber and Faber, 1967 and 1984 editions.

Lall, Ramji: *Graham Greene—The Power and the Glory*, New Delhi, Rama Brothers, 1984.

Leavis, F.R.: 'Class War in British Literature,' *On Contemporary Literature*, (ed.) Richard Kostelanetz, New York, Avon Books, 1964.

Lenski, Gerhard E.: 'A Theory of Inequality,' in *Three Sociological Traditions*, (ed.) Randall Collins, Oxford, Oxford University Press, 1985.

Levi-Strauss, Claude: 'Kinship as Sexual Property Exchange,' reviewed in *Three Sociological Traditions* by Randall Collins, Oxford, Oxford University Press, 1985.

Lodge, David: 'William Golding,' in *Spectator*, April 10, 1964.

Mathiessen, F.O.: 'Billy Budd, Foretopman,' *Melville—A Collection of Critical Essays*, (ed.) R. Chase, New Jersey, Prentice-Hall, 1962.

Medcalf, Stephen: 'Bill and Mr. Golding's Daimon' in *William Golding—The Man and His Books*, (ed.) J. Carey, London, Faber and Faber, 1986.

Mennell, Stephen: 'Sociology' in *Twentieth Century Mind*, (ed.) C.B. Cox and A. E. Dyson, Vol.3, 1945-1965, London, Oxford University Press, 1972.

Monod, S.: 'Golding's View of the Human Condition,' *William Golding—Novels 1954-67—A Casebook*, (ed.) Norman Page, London, Macmillan, 1985.

Moody, Philippa: *William Golding's 'Lord of the Flies'—A Critical Commentary*, London, Macmillan, 1966.

Morrison, Blake: 'Men Can Die of Shame,' *New Statesman*, October 17, 1980.

Nossen, Evon: 'The Beast Man Theme in the Work of William Golding,' *FORUM*, 9, Ball State University, Spring, 1968.

O'Hara, J. D.: 'Mute Choir Boys and Angelic Pigs,' in *Texas Studies of English Literature and Language*, University of Texas Press, Vol. 7, No. 4, Winter, 1966.

Oldsey, Bernard S. and Weintraub, S: *The Art of William Golding*, New York, Harcourt, Brace & World, 1965.

Peter, John: 'Fables of W. Golding' in *Kenyon Review*, Fall, 1957.

Pritchard, R.E.: *D.H. Lawrence: Body of Darkness*, London, Hutchinson University Library, 1971.

Pritchett, V.S.: 'Pain and William Golding' in *New Statesman*, August 7, 1958.

Redpath, Philip: *William Golding—A Structural Reading of His Fiction*, New York, Vision Press, 1988.

Ries, Lawrence R.: 'Wolfmasks'—*Violence in Contemporary Poetry*, Kennikat, Kennikat Press, 1977.

Satpathy, C.: 'Cosmic Energy in Pyramids,' *The Illustrated Weekly of India*, February 11, 1990.

Seldes, George: *The Great Quotations*, New York, Pocket Books, 1960.

Sheed, Wilfred: 'William Golding—*The Pyramid*,' in *The Morning After*, Farrar Straus and Giroux Inc., 1971.

Skilton, David: '*The Pyramid* and Comic Social Fiction,' 1978, in *William Golding—Novels 1954-67—A Casebook*, (ed.) Norman Page, London, Macmillan, 1985.

Smith, Huston: *The Religions of Man*, New York, Harper and Row, 1958.

Spear, Hilda: *William Golding's 'The Spire,'* Beirut Longman, York Press, 1985.

Spitz, David: 'Power and Authority,' *The Antioch Review*, A.R. Inc., Vol. 30, No. 1, Spring, 1970.

Stevenson, Baker L.: *The History of The English Novel*, Vol. XI, New York, Barnes and Noble, 1967.

Stevenson, Randall: *The British Novel since the Thirties*, London, B.T. Batsford, 1986.

Storr, Anthony: 'Intimations of Mystery,' in *William Golding—The Man and His Books*, (ed.) John Carey, London, Faber and Faber, 1986.

Stinson, John: 'The Grotesque in the Fiction of William Golding,' *Cithara*, 11, No. 1, 1971.

Sullivan, Walter: 'Long Chronicle of Guilt—William Golding's *The Spire*,' *Hollins Critic*, June, 1964.

Tanner, Tony: *Conrad—Lord Jim*, Studies in English Literature Series, London, Edward Arnold, 1963.

Thomas, C.T.: 'Jocelin's Folly or A Bible in Stone,' *Aspects of William Golding*, (ed.) Dr. S. Kandaswami, Kerala, University of Calicut, 1986.

Thomson, Philip: *The Grotesque*, Critical Idiom Series, (ed.) John D. Jump, London, Methuen, 1972.

Tiger, Dr. Virginia: *The Dark Fields of Discovery*, London, Marion Boyars, 1974.

Trilling, Lionel: 'Manners, Morals and the Novel,' *The English Novel*, Casebook Series, (ed.) Stephen Hazel, London, Macmillan, 1978.

Trilling, Lionel: 'Kurtz: Hero of the Spirit,' *Conrad: Heart of Darkness*, Casebook, (eds.) A.E. Dyson and C.B. Cox, London, Macmillan, 1982.

Vidal, Gore: 'Ladders to Heaven,' *On Contemporary Literature*, (ed.) Richard Kostelanetz, New York, Avon Books, 1964.

Webb, W.L.: 'Golding Goes Down to the Sea Again,' *The Guardian*, October 11, 1980.

Wilson, Colin: *The Outsider*, London, Pan Books, 1978..